Love Meets Wisdom

FAITH MEETS FAITH

An Orbis Series in Interreligious Dialogue

Paul F. Knitter, General Editor

In our contemporary world, the many religions and spiritualities stand in need of greater intercommunication and cooperation. More than ever before, they must speak to, learn from, and work with each other, if they are to maintain their own vitality and contribute to a better world.

FAITH MEETS FAITH seeks to promote interreligious dialogue and cooperation by providing a forum for exchange between followers of different religious paths, making available to both the scholarly community and the general public works that will focus and give direction to this emerging encounter among the religions of the world.

Already published:

Toward a Universal Theology of Religion, Leonard Swidler, Editor
The Myth of Christian Uniqueness, John Hick and Paul F. Knitter, Editors
An Asian Theology of Liberation, Aloysius Pieris, S.J.
The Dialogical Imperative, David Lochhead

FAITH MEETS FAITH SERIES

Love Meets Wisdom

A Christian Experience
of Buddhism

Aloysius Pieris, S.J.

ORBIS BOOKS

Maryknoll, New York 10545

The Catholic Foreign Mission Society of America (Maryknoll) recruits and trains people for over-seas missionary service. Through Orbis Books, Maryknoll aims to foster the international dialogue that is essential to mission. The books published, however, reflect the opinions of their authors and are not meant to represent the official position of the society.

Manuscript editor and indexer: William Jerman

LIBRARY OF CONGRESS
Library of Congress Cataloging-in-Publication Data

Pieris, Aloysius.
    Love meets wisdom : a Christian experience of Buddhism / Aloysius
  Pieris.
      p. cm. — (Faith meets faith series)
    Bibliography: p.
    Includes index.
    ISBN 0-88344-372-4.   ISBN 0-88344-371-6 (pbk.)
    1. Christianity and other religions—Buddhism.   2. Buddhism-
Relations—Christianity.   I. Title.   II. Series: Faith meets
faith.
BR128.B8P54 1988
261.2'43—dc19   88-22536
                                              CIP

Dedicated to

—the Buddhist monks
  the Venerable Dr. Walpola Rahula Thera
        and
  the late Venerable Dr. Kotagama Vacissara Thera

—and to the Christian monks
  Rev. Fr. Jean Leclerq, O.S.B.
        and
  Rev. Br. Bernard de Give, O.C.S.O.

who have all inspired and guided me
  in the Way and the Truth.

Contents

Preface

What is often referred to as "the early Buddhism of the Pali texts" is certainly not what readers will encounter in these pages, for that is not the Buddhism that the average Christian meets in day-to-day life. Yet the academic quest for the original message of the Buddha is as alive in me as in many students of Buddhism, particularly in Sri Lanka. The tradition begun in the nineteenth century by the first European Buddhalogists still continues: that of distilling the true word of the Buddha from the Pali Canon and allowing that authentic word to discern and eventually discard the spurious elements that appear to vitiate contemporary Buddhism. But the average Buddhist in whose company a Christian is engaged in the common struggles of human existence is hardly touched by this praiseworthy, though also exasperating, mission of the enlightened scholar. On the other hand, what right has a Christian to crusade against such alleged deviations of contemporary Buddhism? A Christian should, rather, try to acquire an empathetic perception of Buddhist religiosity within the Buddhist's own self-understanding.

Every practicing Buddhist—robed or not—is an unbreakable link in a chain of individuals who have passed on the tradition as they received and understood it. In their hearts they treasure a collective memory formed by many generations of recluses and exegetes, ascetics and activists, artists and artisans, poets and prophets, and above all, by millions of devotees, male and female, who have, each in a specific way, translated theory into practice and the written text of the scriptures into the living contexts of their social history. The memory of this tradition, sustained to this day by a monastic institution, so pervades and permeates the "Theravada" cultures of Sri Lanka and Southeast Asia as to form what can be vaguely designated as the "Buddhist Ethos"—that is, the religious atmosphere, which Christians in such cultures are invited, in these pages, to breathe freely.

This book, therefore, is clearly marked by a threefold concern: it seeks to construct 1) a *theological framework* enabling Christians to find within Christianity itself a space where 2) an intuitive and emphathetic *grasp of the Buddhist Ethos* can be realized so as to allow 3) a fruitful *dialogue with contemporary Buddhists* that would enrich both partners of the encounter. Though the entire volume is saturated with all three concerns, the ten chapters have been distributed into three parts according to the preponderance of one or other of these three concerns in each chapter. This explains the thematic structure of the book.

To reap the maximum profit, however, from reading this book, one must locate each chapter in the historical context in which it first originated, either as an address or as an article—the nature of the occasion that called for it, the audience or readership it was intended for, and the particular focus that defines the limits within which its theme is developed. This information is furnished at the beginning of each chapter.

Furthermore, these ten chapters are only a fifth of the fifty or more articles from which a selection had to be made. Hence, readers should not expect an exhaustive treatment of the theme here. For instance, my reflections on the Sinhala-Tamil conflict, which has severely affected the Christians' dialogue with Buddhists since 1983, have been excluded from this collection. They need perhaps to be gathered into a separate volume.

There is another drawback that can hardly be avoided in a book of this kind: repetitions. Certain basic ideas and insights recur frequently, and sometimes verbatim. This is inevitable in a series of essays that were originally written not as interconnected chapters of a book but as disparate works intended for different audiences.

Finally, let us remember that all but two of these chapters were written in the period from 1970 to 1980. They register the earlier stages of my pilgrimage toward an ecumenism which has been continuously widening its horizons before me. Hence, no position, theological or otherwise, presented in these pages should be considered conclusive. What this book offers are provisional pointers to an ideal epitomized in its title: the encounter of Christian love with Buddhist wisdom.

This is why, at the time of writing, I had never entertained the faintest hope of seeing these talks and articles reprinted in one single volume. The idea came entirely from my friend Paul Knitter. I endorsed it, not without some initial reluctance. But I found myself overwhelmingly indebted to him as his idea began to take shape. Needless to say, the tedious labor he invested on it found ready support and friendly cooperation from every member of the editorial staff of Orbis Books. To all of them, individually, I owe a great debt of gratitude.

ALOYSIUS PIERIS, S.J.
TULANA RESEARCH CENTRE
GONAWALA—KELANIYA
SRI LANKA

Love Meets Wisdom

PART ONE

Theological Framework

1

Academic Approach to
Interfaith Dialogue:
Its Legitimacy and Limitations

It is common knowledge that the West *studies* all the world religions, whereas the East simply *practices* them. Religion is a department in many a Western university, just as it has become a "department" in life. Among us in the East, however, religion *is* life. The same is true of interreligious dialogue: an academic luxury in the West, and a modus vivendi in the East. The interfaith encounter with all its psycho-sociological tensions constitutes a day-to-day experience in plurireligious societies of the Orient.

Most interreligious seminars organized and financed by Western agencies tend to be overacademic and at times far removed from real life. They may attract criticism of a legitimate nature, such as that of the Anglican monk Yohan Devananda, who expressed the wish that the participants of a certain international conference held in Sri Lanka be put to work in the fields with mammoties (spades). In Asia, where the field and the factory bring religious persons into communities faster than do academic discussions and pompous resolutions made in comfortable circumstances, such criticism needs to be taken seriously.

Yet we know that mammoties cannot solve all problems. One does not use a spade to find the square roots of numbers. There is a certain ideological clarity that must accompany interfaith encounter, and such clarity can come only from academic discipline. We should acknowledge that the academic discipline that characterizes "formal" dialogues conducted in the West has contributed to the clarification of many issues at the core of interreligious tensions, and this needs to be illustrated at length.

Intellectual honesty, essential to academic discussions, imposes on those who

First published in 1974 as the editorial of *Dialogue,* vol. 1, no. 2. It was reprinted seven years later as a guest editorial in *The Month,* May 1981, pp. 147–48, 180.

take part in dialogue the formidable task—at once enchanting and embarrassing—of seeking a doctrinal justification for the phenomenon of religious pluralism, which, in the East, is simply taken for granted. In fact, what is known as "theology of religions" is an attempt on the part of Western Christians to justify, for themselves primarily, that there could be other ways of salvation, even though the theories emerging from such speculations can be as enchantingly persuasive for those who propose them as they can be embarrassingly offensive to those about whom they are proposed. Yet such speculations are an academic necessity.

Let us start with that simple assertion of Marco Polo trying to speak of the Buddha to his medieval Christian contemporaries: "Had he been a Christian, he would have been a great saint of Jesus Christ," he declared. To a Buddhist academician today this may seem a condescending way of appreciating the Buddha. On the other hand, if Marco Polo had placed the Buddha in the highest niche of his theological sanctuary, he would have ceased to be a Christian. It would no more be a specifically Christian appreciation of the Buddha but a Buddhist's taking refuge in the *Buddha-ratana!*

The theology of religions has not moved much further than this casual remark of a medieval Christian. From a church-centered view we have headed on to a Christ-centered theology that sees the Buddha as a precursor of Christ, or Buddhism as a quasi sacrament of salvation, or a good Buddhist as an "anonymous Christian." But in all this, the element of condescension remains unchanged. For it all amounts to saying: You non-Christians are saved because and insofar as you are Christians (like us) in some mysterious way intelligible only to us.

Because commitment to one's own religion is an absolute prerequisite for any formal interfaith encounter, such condescending attitudes are, at least academically speaking, indispensable. But we must be aware that they are a subtle manifestation of an evangelism—that is to say, an academically dignified way of affirming the absolute character of one's own religion vis-à-vis other faiths.

It would be simplistic to suppose that this subtle species of evangelism is peculiar to the biblical religions, influenced as they are by belief in the fact of "chosenness." Rather, it is characteristic of any religion that treats religious pluralism with academic seriousness.

I have often heard well-meaning Buddhists refer to Jesus Christ as a bodhisattva—that is, a potential Buddha. This is the greatest tribute a Buddhist could give the founder of Christianity. But Christians may not be impressed by such a concession, unless they admit that academically nothing more can be expected.

The late Prof. K. N. Jayatilleke, who probed into many contemporary problems from a Buddhological perspective, had addressed himself to this question as well. In a lecture given at the University of Ceylon in 1966 on the Buddhist attitude to other religions, he described this attitude as one of "critical tolerance." In him, too, we see a Buddhist as one ascribing an absolute character to the truth that the Buddha proclaimed, though conceding that this truth could be discovered, fully or partially, by a non-Buddhist. Prof. Jayatilleke's reference to *Pacceka Buddhas*—who discover that same truth and attain salvation (without the explicit knowledge of and guidance from a supreme Buddha)— reminds me of the theory of anonymous Christianity gaining currency in certain theological circles.

The proverbial tolerance of the Hindus deserves a special mention here. Theirs is not a *critical* tolerance but an *absolute* tolerance. Yet it is not totally devoid of that subtle species of evangelism referred to above. By accepting all religions as true and equally valid ways of salvation, the Hindu theology of religions (perhaps the oldest such theology in the history of religious thinking) seems paradoxically intolerant of another religion's particularity in the very act of conceding it a place in the Hindu theological household. The Hindu approach tends to neutralize the other religion by absorbing its individuality into the Hindu theological framework. Was it not perhaps due to such gradual absorption that Buddhism lost its identity in India while receiving the patronizing support of Hindu rulers? Raimundo Panikkar would call it intolerant tolerance.

It may be of interest to record here that during the multilateral interfaith dialogue organized by the World Council of Churches and held in Sri Lanka in April 1980, Prof. K. Sivaraman from McMaster University, Hamilton, Ontario, treated us to a novel presentation of the classic Hindu theory of tolerance developed into a more coherent thesis. Speaking of the Hindu in dialogue with other religionists, Dr. Sivaraman made the following observation:

> It is only when he perceives his own religion as an absolute entity that he can also encounter the absolute claims of other religions; when he can understand his religion as also a faith-experience in terms of its two-way character—the participation of the total man in the experience-situation and the nonavailability of such experience outside the situation, then can he also confront a structure like Islam or Christianity in terms of its incommunicable "otherness."

Dr. Sivaraman then redefined the Hindu view of religions in terms of "alternative absolutes":

> Religions are not equivalent definitions of one absolute, and cannot be reduced to each other. Neither are they all "relative." They are alternative absolutes, excluding each other in any but in a transcendental sense. The sense of oneness is not sacrificed insofar as it is not maintained that the goal defined alternatively has also to be divided against itself. There are, indeed, no *goals* in the plural. Using the metaphor of circle and center (to borrow from my own writing), we may say that there are infinite approaches to the center from the periphery, which may be described as *alternative lines of approach* in the sense that they are *incommensurable*. To each line the center is, surely, "its" center, the terminus of

"its" length. But who can deny that the periphery in its entirety is the periphery of one center?

Here, then, is another instance of an academician attempting to reconcile the *evangelical* need to affirm the absoluteness of his religion with the *dialogical* imperative that demands an honest explanation of religious pluralism. This attempt is symptomatic of a universal concern for interreligious understanding among educated religionists.

Note, however, that the question itself is *not* an academic one. Interreligious confrontations that the modern mass-media system has brought about have now become an occasion for a search of conscience generating a spectrum of reactions ranging from skepticism to syncretism. This, then, is a *religious issue* and constitutes a matter of conscience for those committed to a religion but living in a plurireligious context.

Or, to be more explicit, the "evangelico-dialogical" tension that is now mounting within contemporary religions and even political ideologies is fundamentally a religious issue that we have perceived with academic tools. Not being in itself an academic issue, its resolution at the practical level need not be academic either.

As a matter of fact, a nonacademic solution to this problem was "accidentally" thrust upon us during the multilateral dialogue just referred to. It was a gift we received from three monks with no academic pretensions: Murray Rogers, an Englishman witnessing to the poor Christ in Jerusalem; Thic Nhat Hanh, a Vietnamese Buddhist monk from the Buddhist peace delegation in Paris; and Swami Chidananda, an Indian Sadhu from Rishikesh. Being of diverse religious persuasions and coming from cultural backgrounds separated geographically and historically, they nevertheless fitted together with a spiritual finesse that baffled those of us who observed it.

From us, however, they stood apart, both in attire and behavior. They hardly intervened in the discussions. Or was it that they preferred to speak their own language but feared we academicians would not understand it? Their silence hurt, but healed. Looking back on the intellectual atmosphere we were in, I would say that their speechless participation reaffirmed the religious and transcendent dimension that should never be absent in an interfaith dialogue. Their presence was redeeming.

But they were not passive. They too decided to speak once and once only, and then sink back into silence. The surprise they sprang on us is now known as "the pebble, the flower, and the encounter," a phrase that is bound to evoke a variety of sentiments in those readers who took part in that conference.

One morning, when the seminar was midway in its course, we saw that the tables had been removed from the hall and chairs placed in concentric semicircles. There were puzzled looks everywhere, for we sensed that something not on the agenda was about to happen. As we sat down, the three wise men came up with their gifts: a pebble, some sheets of blank paper, and a basket of temple flowers.

The Buddhist monk held the pebble in his hand and dropped it down (supposedly into the rushing waters of a river, passing through which it would rest on the river bed). He hummed a soul-stirring chant. We, at his invitation, closed our eyes and abandoned ourselves into the stream of becoming until we found rest on the ground of the Ultimate.

Anchored thus on secure ground we were each offered a flower by the Christian monk. After a silent dialogue with the flower, we were asked to write down on a piece of paper any message we might have received from it. Thus, the thoughts that "flowered" in our hearts were gathered by the monks and woven into a garland of poetic insights and offered back to us as a *gift transformed*. Each one of them acquired a new beauty in the context of the ensemble, the All.

Finally, the encounter. The Hindu sage invited us to walk after him, leaving behind us the massive, suffocating walls of the luxury hotel. In a few minutes we were in the Prithipura Home where physically and mentally handicapped children lived on the milk of human love. "If you love," said Brian de Kretser, the head of the institute, "dialogue becomes spontaneous; you don't need seminars!" The encounter was crowned with a meditation led by the swami.

The matter ended there, as far as the three magi were concerned. But the variety of reactions it produced in the participants was a sign that it had had an impact. An entire sitting was needed to analyze and criticize this apparent "drop" from the academic heights. To some this "experiment" was a failure; but, as Prof. Greenberg retorted delicately, it was an experiment *worth failing*.

The academic approach, guided by intellectual honesty, consists in affirming both an evangelical zeal for one's religious commitment and a certain amount of dialogical accommodation to a given pluralism. But there can be a nonacademic approach that transcends this tension, allowing one to meet another in the very depths of the *secular*—which could be a child, or a flower, or even a pebble!

2

East in the West: Resolving a Spiritual Crisis

A WEST WITHOUT AN EAST

The so-called "Oriental religions" dismissed only a century ago as primitive and pagan have registered in recent times a steep ascent to prominence not only in terms of their proven capacity to articulate the cultural ego of some of Asia's decolonized nations, but also as spiritual movements now seeping into Western cultures, threatening to be respectable alternatives to traditional Christianity. Disturbing news of Western youth streaming into Asia like a river flowing backward to its source is given wide coverage in the media.

The average believer views this situation apprehensively as something at least indicative, if not also constitutive, of a crisis of cultural identity in the Euro-American sector of Christianity. It is a decisive moment for the church, an occasion for a "third reformation" as Geoffrey Parrinder suggests on the analogy of the first reformation in the sixteenth century and the second, which came in response to the Enlightenment and the scientific revolution in subsequent centuries.[1]

My contention is that this phenomenon of "new orientalism," to borrow Harvey Cox's phrase,[2] is not really the crisis but its explanation and its eventual resolution. Was not the seed of this crisis sown in the dim past when the light of the East was allowed to set for good in the West? The eclipse of the Absolute from the horizon of human enterprise, the loss of the sense of mystery in human life, the desecration of the sanctuary of human love, the near disappearance of the art of communing with nature—can all be traced back to some such event.

My suspicion, therefore, is that the contemporary West, in allowing itself to be seduced by the mystique of the East, may probably be indulging in a massive sociological ritualization of a deep psychological need to sharpen its Oriental instinct blunted by centuries of disuse. This itself is the third reformation *in germine.*

8

Such indeed is the conclusion that dawns upon us when we turn to that sensitive Christian whose life and works embody the third reformation: Thomas Merton. His much discussed "journey to the East" was itself a symbolic enactment of an undertaking much more profound and prolonged: his life-long search for the Eastern half of his own being. This search culminated in his sudden death in Buddhist Bangkok only a few hours after he had made a passionate plea that Christian monks and nuns recognize their inner affinity with their Eastern counterparts.[3]

The Orient knows another pilgrim from the West: the mystic-scientist Teilhard de Chardin. He traveled eastward in quest of Asia's fossilized past but was, at every turn, confronted by its irresistible present: its religiousness, which was as fascinatingly distant from his thoroughly Western upbringing as it was irritatingly attractive to some underdeveloped part of his being.

His "journey to the East," too, has left an indelible imprint in the spirituality he worked out for the "modern man" (a phrase by which he usually meant the "Western person"). This spirituality turned out to be a symbiosis of what he, like so many before and after him, had inaccurately called "East" and "West," when in reality he was alluding to two modes of mysticism, as Ursula King has noted.[4]

EAST AND WEST: A NEW INTERPRETATION

A new understanding of the words "East" and "West," especially when they are employed to describe and distinguish various spiritual phenomena, is an essential precondition for the third reformation to take place. Even from a geographical viewpoint, East and West are purely correlative terms that can make real sense only if our planet were a flat disc rather than a globe! Conversely, a truly global vision of the earth—"global" in the literal as well as the metaphorical sense—defies this usage, though, paradoxically, the very persons who wished to present a "global" vision of the world's religions and cultures have indulged in this loose terminology; here I refer to the great "generalizers" of this century: Teilhard de Chardin, S. Radhakrishnan, Carl Gustav Jung, and even the otherwise cautious R. C. Zaehner.[5]

My suggestion is that "East" and "West" could retain their conventional meaning when referring respectively to the Asian and the Euro-American areas on the map; but in the case of religious and spiritual phenomena, "east" and "west" should be made to connote, respectively, the *gnostic* and the *agapeic* instincts of the human person regardless of his or her geographical provenance. This interpretation of East and West amounts to more than a mere change of words. It is a change of key—a kind of "paradigm shift" that guarantees a global and comprehensive but unconfusing vision of religion and spirituality.

Gnosis is salvific knowledge and *agape* is redemptive love. They are certainly not soteriological alternatives or optional paths to human liberation. They are two mystical moods that can alternate according to the spiritual fluctuations of individuals, groups, and even of entire cultures, without either of them allowing itself to be totally submerged by the other. Nor can they mix to form a hybrid or a "synthesis," for the "twain shall never meet," as Kipling would insist. They are, in other words, two irreducibly distinct languages of the spirit, each incapable, unless aided and complemented by the other, of mediating and adequately expressing the human encounter with the ultimate. Any valid spirituality, Christian or otherwise, *must* and, as history shows, *does* retain both poles of religious experience. It is the dialectical interplay of wisdom and love that ensures a progressive movement in the realm of the human spirit.

I am aware that the average Western Christian has an acquired distaste for the very word "gnosis." This prejudice is partially responsible for the West's stubborn refusal to revitalize the withered half of its own soul. The infelicitous association of this term with the heretical aberrations of genuine Christian gnosis (heresies such as docetism, Manicheism, Catharism, Albigensianism, Jansenism, illuminism, quietism, etc.) probably hinders one from recognizing its orthodox forms.

The historians of Christian spirituality such as Bouyer declare emphatically that gnosis (which we could provisionally define as the liberating knowledge of the Saving Truth dawning on a person already disposed toward its reception by a process of self-purification or renunciation) constituted a "legitimate" line of thought and practice in the early church thanks especially to the Alexandrian school, whereas the heretical gnoses "were only as it were embroideries along the edge of this continuous line."[6] Regrettably, this gnostic stream of Christian spirituality, which was of Hellenistic provenance, continued to flow almost as a subterranean current for some centuries before it was allowed to dry up altogether.

Because, however, a repressed instinct tends to assert itself through its own deviant forms, it is hardly surprising to meet in the West a dangerous brand of neognosticism. According to Langdon Gilkey, it is the "white-robed clerics" officiating in the Holy of Holies of scientific laboratories who proclaim the neognostic heresy: that the power to liberate humankind resides ultimately in *scientific knowledge* of nature's secrets![7] This, I repeat, is a heretical aberration of genuine gnosticism. Moreover, as Fergus Kerr has convincingly argued, the "gnostic temptation" to regard human reality as disincarnate consciousness, especially in its Cartesian form, has so much pervaded (and even perverted) contemporary Western/Christian culture that not only theologians of the most progressive category but even secular scientists have fallen prey to it.[8] Yet the abuse of a thing does not preclude but demands its good use.

A WESTERN CARICATURE OF THE EAST

The average Western Christian's antignostic bias is manifested in the widespread impression that gnosis is simply a world-denying asceticism. This prejudice is only one step away from that other unexamined assumption—that such world-denying asceticism is a distinctive mark of all "Eastern" religions. This oversimplification "lies" beneath the *Weberian* caricature of Buddhism and Hinduism so much taken for granted among many Western sociologists.

First of all one is astounded by the way the Sino-Indian religions are labeled

"Eastern"; for it implies that the Judeo-Christian heritage with which they are contrasted is Western! In fact there is no surviving major world religion that is not Eastern. The basis on which religions are divided into "Eastern" and "Western" cannot, therefore, be geographical.

Secondly, one should not ignore the Indo-European ancestry of the linguistic and cultural components of such religions as Hinduism, Buddhism, and Jainism; these Indian religions, despite their "Eastern" origin, display a striking affinity with the Greek and Roman thought of the West rather than with the Semitic worldview of the East! In other words, the "Western" content of Christianity (the agapeic idiom, as I prefer to call it) is a direct import from the Semitic culture of the "East," whereas, conversely, Christian gnosis (the so-called Eastern idiom within Christian spirituality) is an immediate product of the "West"—that is, of the Hellenic culture that is one of the foundation stones of European civilization! Is it necessary to labor the point that "East" and "West" are geographical misnomers for two spiritual instincts surging from the deepest zones of any human being, be he or she in the "East" or in the "West"?

Thirdly, the gnostic religions (Sino-Indian or Greco-Roman) hardly ever deny the world but only *relativize* the world in terms of that which is beyond the world. Would this not be a healthy and necessary corrective to our *myopic obsession with the immediate present*—or "consumerism" as it is known in the cultures that have done away with the spirit of gnosis?

My fourth and final observation in this regard is that the religions that are preponderantly gnostic are, however, not unilaterally so; or else they would be extinct by now. The East has developed its own brand of agapeic or affective spirituality *(bhakti-mārga)* as a dialectical counterpart of the path of wisdom or gnosis *(jñāna-mārga)*. In fact bhakti spirituality has inspired many of India's social reform movements since the Middle Ages.[9]

Moreover, Hinduism has also mapped out a third path—namely, the mysticism of action and service, known as the *karma-mārga*. It is a spirituality of self-less involvement in human affairs. In the *Bhagavadgita,* the revealed manual of Hindu spirituality, this path of action (or activism) is invoked by God-Man Krishna himself in order to urge a reluctant Arjuna to take part in a bloody war of liberation! This, of course, is the way the text is interpreted by the Hindus themselves. This spirituality came in handy not long ago when the Hindus of India were agitating for independence from the British Raj.

It must also be recalled that Hinduism developed these three paths of perfection—the contemplative, the affective, and the active—a few centuries before we Christians evolved our own version of the threefold path: the "cherubic," the "seraphic," and the "angelic" (as Joseph de Guibert quaintly refers to them), exemplified respectively in the Thomistic/Dominican emphasis on the (infused) *knowledge* of God, the Franciscan focus on *love,* and the Ignatian charism of *"service* to the divine majesty." They are not mutually exclusive ways, but three accentuations within Christian orthodoxy. The same holds true of the three paths in Hinduism.

Buddhism, too, recognized right from its inception that wisdom without love was inhuman and that love without wisdom was blind. Therefore *prajñā* (Sanskrit for gnosis) and *karuṇā* (the Buddhist approximation to agape) have always been held together as two constitutive dimensions of Buddhahood. For *prajñā* implies a nirvanic disengagement from *saṃsāra* (this "vale of tears")—that is to say, a renunciation of this world of sin and sorrow, whereas *karuṇa* engages the Buddha in a positive and practical program of restructuring the psychosocial texture of human existence here on earth in accordance with the path that leads to nirvanic freedom. By gnosis the Buddha anticipates the beyond in the here and now, but by agape, so to say, he transfigures the here and now in terms of that beyond. The two poles of a genuine spirituality—gnostic disengagement and agapeic involvement—are maintained in their dialectical tension. In fact, this constitutes a basic Buddhological belief that runs down the centuries like a continuous thread binding all schools of Buddhism together.

The conclusion is obvious. East and West have each developed a sapiential as well as an affective/active stream of spirituality, the former accentuated in the gnostic religions (of both East and West) and the latter preponderant in the Semitic or biblical religions. This conclusion should correct once and for all the distorted image of "Eastern" and "Western" religions popularized by contemporary sociologists.

THE EAST THAT THE WEST NEEDS

East, like the Kingdom of God, is within us and among us. So also is the West. Teilhard de Chardin, who was notoriously ignorant of Eastern religions, had nevertheless some grasp of their inner essence by sheer introspection. This was even truer of Merton. It was really not in Asia that Merton discovered the East; there he only recognized and named what he had already sought and found in his own monastic cell. For it is in the monastic tradition of the West that the sap of gnostic spirituality is still circulating beneath a thick encrustation of Occidentalism. The West can recover its *Eastern sense* by dialoguing with its own monks.

But what exactly is this "Eastern sense"? About this too there seems to be a grave misapprehension, which I wish to spell out here in deliberately exaggerated terms in order to make my point effectively clear. I am referring to a popular presupposition that the navel-gazing yogi on the banks of the Ganges, or the philosopher-mystic discoursing on Upanisadic wisdom in the Himalayan hills, or the Zen Buddhist seated still in lotus posture—necessarily, exclusively, or even primarily represents the *Homo religiosus* of Asia. This surely is another caricature of Asian religiousness.

This caricature emanates as the end product of a sequence of reductionist equations. For instance, scholars of the calibre of Radhakrishnan and Zaehner have compressed the whole gamut of Eastern spirituality into what is purely Indian. Many South Asian writers including theologians seem to have extended this reductionist process further by contracting the entire spectrum of Indian religiosity to Hinduism, and the whole range of Hindu experience to its ashramic form, and the ashram tradition to the sole practice of "contemplation" in the formal sense of the word. The sequence of equations is as follows: East = India = Hinduism = ashram = contemplation.

Merton certainly did not indulge in such easy equations. It is the dollar-spinning maharishis roaming in the West who are bent on selling this idea to gullible youth there. According to their diagnosis, the West is ailing from spiritual anaemia and needs a generous transfusion of mediation from the East!

This is decidedly what I am *not* saying here. Contemplation either as a technique or as an institutionalized tradition or as a specialized occupation does not seem to be what the West needs; perhaps it is also not what the West wants. Merton dismissed as "gnosticism" any kind of contemplation that tended to elevate the contemplative above the ordinary Christian. This is not the place to quarrel with him over the pejorative sense implied in his univocal use of the term "gnosticism," but I know his intention was to repudiate a theological mood that lasted at least up to Vatican II, and still continues to dominate a good part of contemporary literature on prayer.

In fact, Merton, according to Bonnie Thurston, clearly distinguished between contemplation in its institutionalized form—with special methods, times, and places (for which he certainly recognized a niche in Christianity)—and contemplation as "a life of focus and quality," which could never be a flight from community, or from politics.[10]

Here Merton might have sensed a striking parallel between the cultural crisis of modern Western believers and that of the fourth-century Christians who took to the desert (to the "East"?) when confronted with the spiritual vacuum of Rome's imperialized Christianity. For Merton interprets this event in a tone that rings with contemporary relevance. Bonnie Thurston sums up Merton's position as follows:

The movement of the desert monks into contemplative life was for a positive goal: to seek *a society where all are equal, where the only authority came from God through wisdom, experience, and love.*[11]

Indeed equality and freedom, the experience of God as wisdom and love—in short, "life of quality and focus"—is precisely what the third reformation is about. The fourth-century Christian's flight to the desert—that is, flight to the "East," indeed a flight to *nature* away from the *culture* of imperial Rome—is an excellent precedent for a disoriented (i.e., un-Oriental) West to follow today in the face of the decadent culture of technocratic imperialism that could have been created only by a West that has done away with the Eastern half of its conscience.

Technocracy as it operates today is a hideous monument to the antignostic bias that official Christianity nurtured for centuries, an insane disorder that, true to its anti-Eastern origins, is now in Asia drying up the very springs of Eastern religiosity there. Its effects spell such disaster in all parts of the world that the responsibility to restore the East-West dialectics in our cultures is at once urgent and universal.

EAST-WEST DIALECTICS IN A TECHNICULTURE

The technocratic worldview is the final evolute of what might have been in its Christian beginnings a simple theory at once subtle and sinister: that all God-made "things" are mere instruments and conversely that all human-made "instruments" are mere things.

What, for instance, would a flute be to the flutist? If our answer implies too neat a distinction between the musician, the mechanical device, and the melody—that is, between the agent, the instrument, and the finished product—then we would be thoroughly at home in a techniculture.

To the musician in many a nontechnocratized culture in the East, the flute is not an instrument as such but one's own extension or "other self." There is, in other words, a creative *companionship* between the player and the flute, the music being the offspring of their communion, a soothing testimony to cultivated harmony between them. In fact, it is a hallowed custom in most of our cultures for the musician to pay homage to the "instrument" as to an intimate "companion *in labor*" by making a gesture of reverence (which varies according to place) before beginning a public performance or even before routine practices. Artisans, too, treat their tools of profession in a similar manner.

This reverential communion with human-made "instruments" is only an extension of a general attitude fostered among these peoples toward all "things" that nature provides: earth, fire, air, and water, plants and beasts, all cosmic forces seen and unseen. Since they are not "things," they are really not "instruments" either. For nature is our own cosmic continuation, our own extended self. To pollute it is to disfigure ourselves.

This belief cannot be dismissed as "animistic" superstition; rather it is really an instance of a "cosmic spirituality" that regards as quasi-living partners what a techniculture treats as mere "things."

This spirituality is not directly derived from the *metacosmic* religions (such as the monastic and mystical forms of Hinduism, Buddhism, Jainism, or Taoism) but a tradition of the *cosmic* religions by which I mean what anthropologists infelicitously call "animism." It is an integral and determinant component of Asian religiosity and is that which makes the Mertonian definition of contemplation—"life of focus and quality"—universally valid in Asian cultures.

COSMIC SPIRITUALITY OF THE EAST

This cosmic spirituality has been preserved almost intact whenever the aforementioned gnostic soteriologies permeate Asian cultures. This is understandable. In the gnostic idiom, the Absolute is, so to say, a "nonpersonal It" to be realized within oneself rather than a "Personal Thou" to be loved and revered; by contrast, therefore, what is *not* the Absolute is accorded a personalist character evoking an I-Thou relationship of reverential communion. Thus when the so-called Asian animists embraced the gnostic religions, the spirit of ecological communion was never renounced but only enhanced as a common patrimony of both the cosmic and metacosmic religions.

This is precisely what did *not* always take place when Christianity made inroads into an Asian culture. Because reverence is an admixture of fear and respect, the missionary zeal to remove the weeds of fear invariably ended up with the uprooting of the wheat of respect. Christianity liberated its converts from the dread of cosmic forces only to deprive them of their age-old practice of communing with nature. It is owing to this species of "desacralization" or "secularization" that the ecological sensitivity so evident in most non-Christian cultures is markedly absent in the Christian communities that form the Asian church; even where this cosmic spirituality is conserved by Asian Christians, one is inclined to repudiate it in toto as "superstition." The Christianity that Asia was made to practice did not seem to have known Francis of Assisi! The Poverello, we are constrained to conclude, was a freak in Christendom, never the norm.

As I suggested in the initial paragraphs of this chapter, I believe that at some point in history the light that rose from the East was allowed to set for good in the West, and with that, the sacramental approach toward cosmic reality began to degenerate into an "instrumental theory of nature." The West turned companions into instruments because it ignored the East, which treats all instruments as companions.

It is difficult to trace the exact steps of this spiritual regression in the West. I suspect that the agapeic idiom of biblical Christianity, which justifiably invests the Absolute with transcendental personhood, has been allowed, by contrast, to diminish the world to a state of nonpersonal cosmic forces meant merely to be mastered and molded by man (often not by woman) to serve him as a series of stepping stones to reach his Maker. The whole creation is reduced to the level of mere "instruments" to be "used" *tantum quantum,* as the familiar phrase goes—that is, "just in so far as" they serve to establish personal communion with God. Communion with nature, pejoratively called "nature mysticism" in many of the older theological manuals, is contrasted too neatly with communion with God, with scant respect for the body of Christ, which the whole cosmos is destined to be through our communion with it.

Moreover, an instrumental theory in Christian spirituality and an instrumental theory in a capitalist technocracy are species of the same genus. In both instances, persons are made to shrink to the size of "thing" "used" as an "instrument" for reaching one's end: God in one case, and mammon in the other! It is not merely a matter of using others as our tools, but even, as Merton once lamented, a case of allowing our own selves to be used as instruments by others, thus forfeiting our innate potency for spiritual creativity.[12]

In a world vitiated by "instrumentalism," neither Christianity in its present form nor technocracy can put us in touch with that cosmic-human-divine continuum that St. Paul called "Christ," the salvific ethos, the *milieu divin* that the *Homo religiosus* instinctively seeks as a plant seeks water and light. Was it not such a Christ that Teilhard de Chardin (a great believer in both Christianity and technology) restored to the Christian West after he had integrated into his own "Occidental" conscience the gnostic perceptiveness of the East?

There is an ancient Christian saying that anticipated, in capsule form, Teilhard's voluminous writings on the cosmic dimension of Christ. It is a soliloquy attributed to God the Creator: *unum locutus sum, haec duo audivi: Christum et mundum*—I [God] made only one utterance in which, however, I heard myself pronounce two words: Christ and cosmos. These two are but one single self-expression of God. Just as "no one can come to the Father except through the Son" (John 14:6; Matt. 11:27), so too there is no way of meeting the Son save by being a conscious part of his cosmic body. This is the sacramental approach to creation, which only a symbiosis of gnosis and agape—"East" and "West"—can restore to the church in the West. It is the "cure" that Merton recommends to an ailing Christianity: "Simple respect for concrete realities of everyday life, for nature, for the body, for one's work, one's friends, one's surroundings."[13]

This is first of all a plea for change: a command to return to Assisi. But it often comes across in the form of a cry of pain in peace marches, antinuclear demonstrations, and ecological movements, which disrupt the mechanized monotony of "advanced" societies. Yet through this *de profundis*, the technocratized humanity of a Christian culture seems to proclaim loud and clear that *reverential intimacy* with nature is the East's way of confessing the *adorable ultimacy* of God, and that it is *the* way to the third reformation.

3

Western Christianity and Asian Buddhism: A Theological Reading of Historical Encounters

MUTUAL JUDGMENT ON RELIGIONS: AN INEVITABILITY

Each religion is a *singular* phenomenon and represents, in a way, a *judgment* passed on every other religion.

In the very process of approving and appropriating the basic insights of *Homo religiosus,* each religion also sets itself apart from all other religions by ordering these insights according to its own cultural pattern, formulating them doctrinally within its own conceptual framework, and crystalizing them into its own hierarchical structure of symbols, so that the resultant synthesis, identified as a psycho-social phenomenon and designated as a concrete "religion," not only corroborates the common contents of all religions but also *judges* every other synthesis as a minor or major deviation from what it regards as Ultimately and Salvifically True.

Phenomenologically, therefore, religions are so many alternative configurations of basic human values. And as such it is in their nature to provoke *comparison* and mutual *criticism, confrontation* and reciprocal *correction,* these being the intermediary stages between mere tolerance, with which dialogue begins, and positive participation, in which dialogue should culminate.[1]

For centuries now it was Christianity, especially Western Christianity, that passed judgment on other religions, generously offering them criticisms and corrections, and indulging in comparisons that were ultimately meant to artic-

Originally given as a lecture for the "German Theology Professors' Seminar," organized by the Protestant Association for World Mission *(Evangelisches Missionwerk),* at Bossey, Switzerland, Sept. 17, 1978. First published in English in *Cistercian Studies,* 15 (1980) 50–66, 150–71.

17

ulate its own uniqueness. Of late, however, the roles seem to have been changed. It is Christianity that is now on the receiving end.[2]

As I proceed with my discussion, I shall clearly state in what way Christianity exercised its legitimate right of passing judgment on other Asian religions and how Christianity came to discover another need—equally legitimate—of exposing itself to the judgment of these same Asian religions.

The West's salutary awareness of this need becomes the basic presupposition of my discussion here. If, therefore, the general thrust of this chapter is judgmental, it is not because I fail to appreciate the immeasurable contribution the West has made to the world. Rather, having received my theological education in Europe and a Buddhist education in Asia, I feel obliged in conscience to exercise a ministry of reconciliation whereby the *implicit judgment of the non-Christian East is brought to the threshold of Western theology.*

In my references to Asian religions I may sound too partial toward Buddhism. There are good reasons for it. The first is that Buddhism is the most Asian among the world religions. It is not only thoroughly Indian, but is equally at home in Chinese, Japanese, Tibetan and other diverse linguistic and racial groups in Asia—something that cannot be said of Hinduism, Taoism, Confucianism, Shintoism, or even Islam. Besides, it originated as a critique of (all) theology, and therefore presents itself as a counter-thesis to traditional Christianity. For this very reason it deserves the church's attention and demands a theological response.

CHRISTIAN JUDGMENT ON OTHER RELIGIONS
IN PHILOSOPHY AND THEOLOGY

During this century the weapon most frequently used in academic circles to defend Christianity's absolute claims was the philosophy of religion. Often the professors who taught this subject and headed the university departments that dealt with it were Christians and, in some cases, members of the clergy. In their writings, even in the most objective and honest studies, these Christian professors did not fully renounce their evangelizing role. It consisted not only in proving rationally the wholeness of Christianity but in neutralizing, by means of subtle philosophical explanations, the challenges that other religions threw at Christian belief—for instance, the religious atheism of the Buddhists.[3] This was because the major part of Western Christianity had not, for centuries, been confronted by the inner dynamism of other religions. Since the christianization of Europe, the West had only one paradigm at its disposal to understand the religious phenomenon: namely, its own Christian experience. Thus "the philosophy of *one* religion" became the "philosophy of religions," as Panikkar has bitingly remarked.[4] This type of extrapolation, valid only within certain limits, could easily lend itself to apologetical abuses when not tested against the self-understanding of other religions.

When, therefore, the philosophy of religion (until recently a mere tool of religion, and particularly of *one* religion) was gradually forced to yield its academic niche to sciences that usurped its role of studying the religious phenomenon—namely, history,[5] sociology,[6] psychology,[7] phenomenology,[8] and the like—Christianity too was removed from its privileged position and treated as one religion among others. At the academic level this was the first exposure of Christianity to other religions in this century, but it only helped sharpen the defensive attitudes of some Christian theologians.

This could be said to have happened in at least three ways. Let me take anthropology as an example. The early studies that tried to understand the origin of religion ended up explaining away, not just Christianity, but religion as such. Hence, two of the earliest Christian reactions to it (in the 1930s) were (1) to campaign against atheism for allegedly utilizing ethnology and the history of religion as a conclusive argument against the validity of all religion (de Lubac, 1937)[9] or (2) to oversimplify the empirical findings of anthropology to prove that there had been a universal consent among peoples of all cultures regarding the existence of God (Rabbeau, 1933, and Chossat, 1939).[10] A third type of apologetics can be seen in the anthropological research of Christians like Wilhelm Schmidt (and Andrew Lang). Their "scientific method"—now in disrepute even among anthropologists[11]—gave birth to the theory of *Urmonotheismus:* a conclusion that was accepted uncritically by some theologians.[12] Similar observations can be made about other sciences, such as psychology, that focused attention on the study of religion.

We are not surprised that, even today, Christian professors of religion who are teaching religion from the standpoint of historical sciences, in place of the earlier standpoint of the philosophy of religion, continue that same apologetical method in their textbooks on comparative religions[13] or the phenomenology of religion[14]—that is, the *Christian* philosophy of religion. Would it not be better to call it by the name it deserves: theology of religions, albeit of a poor kind?

In fact, the emergence of the theology of religions in its contemporary forms in the West—as it appears to me, viewing distantly from Asia—is the fruit of this new apologetics.[15] At least, I am compelled to query whether it is not a legitimate vindication of Christianity's absolute claims in the context of a new awareness of religious pluralism and of the absence of a genuine "philosophy of religion" to complement the "scientific" studies on religion.

The contemporary study of religion within the functional ambit of behavioral sciences needs philosophical analysis as much as philosophy needs to depend on the empirical findings of the former.[16] In the West one hears desperate appeals to revive and renew the philosophy of religions.[17]

Here a lesson from the East may be worth citing. In the Oriental, especially the Indian, systems the concepts of philosophy *(darśana)* and religion *(pratipadā)* are not compartmentalized, as has been done in the West, nor subordinated one to the other. "No Indian philosophical system is merely speculative," explains Murti. "Each is a *darśana,* an insight into the real, which is at once a path of salvation and cessation of pain."[18] In the Buddha's message, the fourfold *truth* and the eightfold *path*—the theory and the praxis—include each other in a mutuality that makes the oft repeated question, "Is Buddhism a philosophy or a religion?," null and void. Could such a mutuality, which respects the identity of each, be possible in the West?

Panikkar's criticism of Western philosophy of religion results in suggesting that the relationship between philosophy and religion be neither *heteronomy* (domination of a religion over philosophy as in Western tradition) nor *autonomy* (independence of the two—being a recent reaction to the earlier heteronomy), but *ontonomy*.[19] It is an orientation that guarantees a philosophical understanding of religion from within every religion.

If there is a valid theology of religions that can understand non-Christian faiths, it should be along these lines suggested by Panikkar. Students of other religions should intuit the self-understanding of the other religions—something quite impossible unless they adopt what I refer to as the "participatory approach" in the latter part of this chapter. True, the West has now agreed that the professor of Hinduism in a theological faculty should be literally a professor—that is, one who *professes that religion*. Oxford University provided an excellent precedent when S. Radhakrishnan was invited to lecture on comparative religions. Though some Christian universities in the U.S.A. have boldly adopted this practice,[20] such is not often the case with theological faculties in Europe. Even this, however, is a far cry from the *participatory* approach, which involves a creative encounter between the untapped gnostic tradition of the West and the renewed forms of monasticism about to emerge in Asia.

What hinders such an openness in our theology, however, is that we have a *philosophical tradition* that resists mutual judgment between religions and that this tradition began very early, with the first reaction of the church to Hellenic thought. Hence my inquiry has to begin with that theological inheritance.

THEOLOGY OF RELIGIONS: ITS INHERITED LIMITATIONS

It has been pointed out that the early Christian reaction to "pagan" thought was threefold, as represented by Tertullian, Justin, and Irenaeus.[21] The first reaction was an extremely intransigent form of *evangelism*. Surprisingly, it came from Tertullian, the very man who passed on the legal idiom of Roman culture to Christian theology. The absolute mystery that God reveals in Christ—Tertullian seems to have held—has to be proclaimed with no concern for the communication system of a given culture, which may have its own religious idiom and symbols. Justin, on the other hand, is alleged to have advocated a *dialogical* approach based on the conviction that the non-Christian religions came within the same providential scheme in which Christianity was the crown and completion. This he does by postulating the activity of *logos spermatikos* in other religions. If it is true that his *Dialogue with Trypho* was addressed to potential converts who were torn between Judaism and Christianity,[22] then it is even more evident that he is applying the Israel-Christ analogy to the other religions. This is the patristic nucleus of the "fulfillment theory," which was restated in 1930 by the Lambeth Conference and (with a certain amount of deceptive clarity) in the 1960s by Vatican II.[23]

Irenaeus combines both these approaches into an "apologetical" synthesis, which was later developed by the great founders of Western theology of religion: Clement of Alexandria, Origen, Athanasius, the Cappadocian fathers, and even the Latin fathers, among whom Augustine is by far the most creative and original.

Here "apologetics" must be understood in its healthy connotation. It is a legitimate exercise by which every religion asserts its uniqueness, and even its "absolute" character. This, as we have shown elsewhere, is an inescapable academic need felt by intellectual adherents of all religions, and is not exclusively a Christian preoccupation.[24] But there were some limitations in the early Christian apologetics and it is these that must be clearly grasped.

First of all, it was mainly Greek *thought* that Irenaeus was busy with, not the religious *practices* that were intimately connected with that thought. There was, probably, a fear of gnosticism eating into Christian behavior. Hence, in the *intellectual* climate of this "apologetics" there developed a tradition of an academic sort, which revolved around the system of *thought* to the exclusion of the *experiential* dimension of concrete symbols and ritual expression. It dialogued with "pagan" *philosophy* rather than with "pagan" *religion,* to use a later terminology; and this uncompromising stand against "pagan" religions went back to a Semitic intransigence that had been continuing up to the early apostolic era.[25]

The second feature is also allied to this. The fathers were interested in non-Christian philosophy insofar as it was apt *intellectual equipment* to grasp revelation conceptually and formulate it in a manner intelligible to the "pagan" culture in which they lived. Thus begins the tradition in which Christian "religion" learned to *instrumentalize* philosophy. In fact, as Pannenberg points out, the later medieval image of philosophy as *ancilla theologiae* was already used by Clement of Alexandria and expressed in its classical form in Peter Damian's allegorical interpretations of Deuteronomy 21:10ff.[26] The "heteronomous" relationship between religion and philosophy, which I have criticized, following Panikkar, had its remote origins here.

This was the *intellectual* position. How much Christian liturgy and Christian mysticism owes to the religious practices of "gentiles," both Western and Eastern, does not need special emphasis here. Such influences began to be noted especially after the "persecutions," when links with Judaism were severed and those with Greco-Roman culture were strengthened.[27] Even then, the non-Christian forms were "utilized" in Christian praxis, without compromising the basic thrust of Western tradition. However, the de facto practice was more accommodative than were the theoretical positions. The first rifts between theory and praxis, between pursuit of knowledge and day-to-day Christian behavior, could already be noticed here.

There is a third element. It entered Christian consciousness in the West and surfaces at certain levels of theological thinking even today. This is the concept of *power.* Could theology ever grow in a socio-political vacuum? Permanent dialogical contact with Greek culture within the first five centuries of Western Christianity coincided with the rise of Christianity as a political *power.* As one gains power, one's need for dialogue diminishes. One exercises what one claims to be one's authority. Thus Christianity, which became Western through dialogue with Greece, now entered the rest of Europe through Rome, the seat of law and government. The spread of Christianity in other European cultures coincided with the extension of Roman authority. The church seems to have lost its incarnational praxis due to its authoritarianism, and was like a huge vine with roots in the center of the Roman empire but branches spreading all over Europe and swallowing the weeds and brambles of primitive cultures—only to discover that after sixteen centuries the old "paganism"—the popular religion of the Christian masses—was there beneath its foliage. As the French historian Delmeau has pointed out, both Reformation and Counter-Reformation ended up being "conversion movements" of the elite against European "paganism," and this in its turn had *negative repercussions in the Asian missions.*[28] The permanent need for dialogue and for continuous incarnation ceased to be felt.

The identification of the church with the kingdom of God, and the ecclesiological appropriation of christological attributes, allowed the medieval church to be conceived as the *societas perfecta* outside of which no power could exist,[29] let alone another religion, or truth. For the only new religion that confronted Christianity in the Middle Ages was Islam and the impact of that encounter was indeed shattering. How could the fulfillment theory of the fathers, as well as the corresponding principle of *preparatio evangelica,* be applied to Islam, a post-Christian religion that made open claims to be the "fulfillment" of all that God had "prepared" from Moses to Christ?[30] Dialogue was not possible. Open conflict and war with Islam reinforced the church's *renunciation of dialogue.* In fact, it is symptomatic that Dante, who exercised a Christian sensitivity toward ancient "pagan" literature, did not hesitate to put Muhammad in hell! The attitude toward early "paganism" of dead literature was less hostile than that toward this new "religion," which had by then become a real threat. Naturally, the Crusades gave added strength to the church's power-consciousness faced with an alien religion.

Thus when the great missionary era began in the sixteenth century and the church met the new Asian religions, it could not adopt an attitude other than what it had acquired in earlier encounters with Islam and its later confrontation with "European paganism." Besides, colonialism was not something limited to Western political power, but was a general ecclesiastical policy of missions in the East, missions that were merely a material protrusion of Europe's local churches into Asia.

It is indeed worth noting here that since the rise of the "power-consciousness," the old fulfillment theory and the patristic theology of *preparatio evangelica* disappear from the official church's theology of religions. It is only in the twentieth century, with the breakdown of this power in the missions and at home, that the "dialogical" approach and fulfillment theory reappear in its theology of religions! But vestiges of "power" are still lurking in this theology as formulated by certain modern thinkers in the West, as will be illustrated in the course of this discussion (see ''Christian Response to Eastern Presence,'' below).

In what immediately follows, therefore, we shall see the interplay of the three elements just described:

1. the ''academic'' and ''philosophical'' approach to religious dialogue;
2. the ''instrumentalization'' or ''apologetical use'' of non-Christian thought, in favor of Christianity;
3. the ''power-consciousness'' of the church.

These three elements in varying degrees of intensity and combination give a very definite character to Western theological discussions on non-Christian religions, whenever such discussions are occasioned by Western Christianity's confrontation with Asian religious thought.

THE EAST COMES WEST: SPIRITUALITY VERSUS THEOLOGY

The nonbiblical religions of Asia, especially Buddhism, have been knocking at the door of the West and even ''trespassing'' there in various ways. The Christian reaction to it, both ancient and modern, provided us with concrete examples of how the above-mentioned theological equipment of the church was used—and even sharpened—in the process of handling these Asian ''encroachments'' since the beginning of Greek Christianity.

There is evidence to show that information about the Indian situation was circulating in Greece both before and after Alexander's invasion (327–325 B.C.).[31] On the Indian side, there are written sources that indicate ongoing Buddhist-Greek dialogue,[32] and the presence of Buddhist missionaries as far West as Greece, Syria, North Africa, and Egypt in the third century B.C.[33] The Indian monastic trends represented by the *samana*s had reached at least as far as Bactria, according to Greek sources.[34] In fact Clement of Alexandria makes an unambiguous mention of the Buddha and the Buddhists of India—namely, that those who followed the Buddha's rules (monks?) regarded him as divine because of his superlative holiness.[35]

I can understand, therefore, the overenthusiasm of certain Western scholars to prove that everything good in early Christianity was of Buddhist origin! Some tried to show Jesus' life and teaching were inspired by Buddhists via the Essenes (Hilgenberg, de Bunsen, Beal) or that Greek gnosticism was purely a Buddhist import (Schmidt, Baur, Bohlem),[36] or that the infancy narratives were borrowed from Buddhists (Edmunds),[37] or even that St. John's Gospel was a piece of Buddhist-Christian literature (Bruns).[38] I wonder whether any scholar of repute would accept these hypotheses. In fact, de Lubac, who has studied all the relevant data with meticulous care, has concluded that in the Western tradition, both pre-Christian and early Christian, there is no significant trace of a Buddhist presence.[39]

This is an important statement. Greek culture was so refined and pervasive that it would not allow itself to be *substantially* affected by an outside religion or philosophy; and if it *did* allow itself to be christianized, it was, at least partially, because Christianity allowed itself to be hellenized. *Hellenism, therefore, remains the door as well as the barrier for any non-Christian religion to make a fresh contribution to Western theology.*

In fact, Clement of Alexandria was so "Greek" in his thought that he would not hesitate to call non-Christians outside Greece "barbarians"—a polite term that Greeks used for non-Greeks. These barbarians, whose philosophy was a "light to the nations" as Clement believed, also included Indian sages. It is in such a context that the Buddha's name too is condescendingly mentioned.[40] This, I presume, is the ancient Western myth of the "noble savage" applied to non-Westerners since the Hellenic age.[41]

If the West wants to meet Asian religions, then at least some Christians must leave the sublime heights of Greek philosophy and go to the desert. It was there that non-Christian and non-Hellenic religious insights percolated into Christian praxis precisely at a time when councils were busy with "theoretical formulations," and the hierarchy with the "expansion of power." The code words are *monasticism* and *mysticism:* we see no other common ground between Western Christianity and Eastern religions.

Here I have in mind someone hardly mentioned at the beginning of this century, but who has attracted the attention of many historians and theologians, at least from about 1923, when he was reintroduced to the West by the German scholar Bousset.[42] He is Evagrius Ponticus, a fourth-century Greek, who seems to have drunk deep from non-Hellenic springs of spirituality. The decisive and lasting influence he exercised in shaping the entire spiritual tradition of both the Latin West and Eastern Christianity, despite the church's ruthless effort to erase his writings and his name from Christian memory, is a fact attested by recent scholarship.[43] His introspective analysis of human consciousness in its deepest layers—which Freud would discover for the West only sixteen centuries later—and also techniques for acquiring mental purity, did not come from biblical sources. Those acquainted with Buddhist *vipassanā-bhāvanā* (insight-meditation) and *abhidhamma* (Buddhist metapsychology) would find themselves at home—as I did—in reading his instructions on prayer. In fact, in H. U. von Balthasar's estimation, Evagrius is more Buddhist than Christian and his basic spiritual experience would be Mahayana idealism! [44]

Evagrius's theological formulations smacked of extreme Origenism, and it was this that brought ecclesiastical censure on him. But this was long before Chalcedon refined and restricted the words and concepts allowed when speaking of the mystery of God. Regrettably, however, the church, which was itself using Greek *philosophy* in its search for a precise formulation of christology, made no effort to go deeper into the *Christic experience* lying behind Evagrian utterances. Once more, the overacademic procedure in scrutinizing Evagrian "philosophy" left the "religious" content of that philosophy unexamined. Thus, von Balthasar, who has always appeared to me as the most formidable apologete for *Western* Christianity, analyzes Evagrius's pre-Chalcedonian experience with post-Chalcedonian concepts and relegates him to a pre-Christian stage of "world-denying" asceticism.[45] However, because Western representatives of the mystico-monastic tradition could empathetically reassess Evagrius's experience and its contribution to Western spirituality, it is hardly surprising that a Benedictine monk, David Griffin, commenting on judgments such as Balthasar's, says:

> The current interpretations of the Trinity are not necessarily and, in fact, were not the same as those in the fourth century. To attempt to categorically define one's experience of the Transcendence of God is impossible. Evagrius was first and foremost a mystic, possessing a mentality that caused him to understand the Trinity in a manner completely different from that of modern Theology.[46]

Let me record here another very significant encounter the church had with Buddhist spirituality—namely, the medieval church's devotion to St. Joasaph, or more precisely, to Sts. Barlaam and Joasaph.

Marco Polo was perhaps the first to bring back the news to Europe that the life of the Buddha, as narrated in Sri Lanka (which he visited in 1293), was very similar in all its details to the story of Joasaph in the *Vitae Patrum;* the Bollandists, the Jesuit historians, have documented the embarrassing fact that St. Joasaph, venerated as a saint in the medieval church, was none other than the Buddha himself.[47] After a brief controversy and a lull in the Roman church, the first avowal of the truth came a few years ago when St. Joasaph (who had appeared in the *Catalagus Sanctorum* of Peter de Natalibus as early as 1370) was silently dropped out of the revised sanctoral calendar!

The story of Baghavan and Bodhisativa, who eventually became Bilauhar and Budasaf in Arabian literature, reached the West through the Georgian church in Crimea where St. Euthymius introduced it to the Greek-speaking world as the story of Iodasaph. The story was so popular in the church that it could be regarded as a best-seller of the time: translations have been found in Syriac, Arabic, Ethiopian, Armenian, and Hebrew editions in the East, and in Greek, Latin, French, Italian, Spanish, Bohemian, and Polish editions in the West. More and more versions are being discovered.[48]

The outstanding feature of St. Joasaph's life leading up to his illumination was one of world renunciation. This "world-denying" asceticism of St. Joasaph seems also to have influenced the Albigensians. In fact, a certain Manichean flavor was quite patent in the moral of the story and thereafter it passed for a Cathar document. Nevertheless, its spiritual influence in the West was so great that, before St. Francis of Assisi acquired popularity in the church, there seems to have been no other saint whose life had such a strong moral hold over saint and sinner. Is there any wonder, then, that some of the episodes of the Buddha story crept into European literature (as, e.g., the story of the three caskets in Shakespeare's *Merchant of Venice*) and that the Jesuits too used them in morality plays?[49]

It is indeed ironical that, at the same time when Franciscan friar William of Rubruck, the first European discoverer of Buddhism, who was in Mongolia on an intelligence mission sent by Louis IX of France in 1253, referred to worshipers of the Buddha as "idolators,"[50] back home his own Christian brethren were venerating the same Buddha as "full of the Holy Spirit." They composed hymns such as the following, in which his "world-rejection" in favor of a superior attainment is praised in no uncertain terms:

> In place of transitory kingship, O Blessed One, you chose the glory which is permanent and unending and you rejoice in unspeakable and eternal happiness.[51]

This indirect canonization of the Buddha as a model Christian, and the liturgical celebration of his religious protest against society as a Christian praxis, demonstrates that the church's *theopraxis* had appropriated what its *theology* repudiated: the gnosis-oriented spirituality of the East. Should not Western theologians' theoretical condemnation of Evagrian spirituality as "pre-Christian" and "Buddhist" deserve a similar confrontation with de facto Christian praxis?

THE EAST AND THE WEST IN CHRISTIAN THEOLOGY: A PARENTHESIS

One may conclude that the East has already been present in the West, of course as a silent but influential guest. On the other hand, dialogue has not reached—and perhaps cannot—an explicitly theological level, due to an antignostic experience of the past and the association of the East with it. Hence a parenthesis at this juncture may be useful to drive away certain emotional overtones from the words "East" and "West," and discover in them a new semantic dimension.

It is a truism that Christianity is as Eastern as is Buddhism. In fact, all surviving world religions rose, like the sun, from the East. The fact that Christianity in its Greco-Roman form spread and conquered Europe, and Europe, in turn, conquered the world, makes the association of Christianity almost exclusively with the West superficially justifiable. Unfortunately this way of opposing "East" and "West" has been canonized by many eminent writers of this century, such as Carl Gustav Jung[52] and Pierre Teilhard de Chardin.[53] They seem to have stereotyped all Eastern religions into a homogeneous block and confronted it with Western culture.

Dr. Radhakrishnan went even further. He could speak, in one breath, of Jesus, Muhammad, Caesar, Napoleon, and Cromwell as representing one pole, pushing India to the other pole, reducing the whole complexity of Asian religiousness to its Indian or, more precisely, to its Hindu expressions.[54] This, of course, is an oversimplification.

However, we may take a clue from a study revealing that, in the ever-changing vocabulary of Teilhard, the words "East" and "West" could only mean two ideal "types" of spirituality or mysticism rather than territorial divisions.[55] And it was these two types that the great mystic-scientist tried to reconcile—in favor, perhaps, of Western Christianity.

But the late R. C. Zaehner, a great comparative religionist who was also critical of the Teilhardian interpretation of Eastern religions, was also led to assert that the principles of *Eastern* and *Western* thought "in practice means *Indian* and *Semitic* thought" (respectively).[56] The fact, however, that Semitic thought, which Zaehner dubs "Western," not only originated in the East, as in the case of Judaism and Christianity, but still holds sway in non-Western continents, as Islam does in Africa and Asia, indicates that, here again, we are busy with "types" rather than exclusively geographical compartments. They seem to refer to two *value systems.* In the happy phraseology of the Vietnamese nun To Thi Anh, they can be circumscribed by saying that the one displays its dynamism *outwardly,* whereas the other unfolds its energy *inwardly:* the West conquers and transforms; the East accepts and endures. Hence Western values are human dignity, reason, freedom, action, organization, science, techniques, wealth, and well-being. Eastern values, on the other hand, are human-heartedness, noninterference, selflessness, enlightenment, compassion, detachment, moderation, patience, and inner peace.[57]

Inasmuch as the source of Western Christian civilization is basically Semitic though shaped by a Greco-Roman culture, whereas Asian values spring from religious insights such as those of Hindu, Buddhist, and Taoist traditions, the ultimate distinction is between the biblical and nonbiblical religions, or to use a more apt nomenclature, which I have introduced in my dialogue with Buddhists, *agapeic* and *gnostic* idioms.[58]

In doing so, I am presenting two religious models that, far from being contradictory, are in fact incomplete each in itself and, therefore, complementary and *mutually corrective.* If this is what "West" and "East" should mean, then we are actually dealing with the *poles of a tension not so much geographical as psychological.* They are *two instincts* emerging dialectically from within the deepest zone of all individuals, be they Christian or not. Our religious encounter with God and humankind would be incomplete without this interaction.

To put it in more precise terms, a genuine Christian experience of God-in-Christ grows by maintaining a dialectical tension between two poles: between action and nonaction, between world and silence, between control of nature and harmony with nature, between self-affirmation and self-negation, between engagement and withdrawal, between love and knowledge, between *karuna* and *prajñā,* between agape and gnosis. Hence the Evagrian mysticism does not become "pre-Christian" because it uses the gnostic idiom, just as bodhisattvas do not become less Buddhistic because their religious experience is one of love! As I have shown elsewhere, Christian agapeic tradition has a gnostic stream and the Buddhist gnostic tradition has an agapeic vein.[59]

Gnosis—the liberating knowledge of the saving truth dawning on a person disposed to its reception by a process of self-purification—constituted the basis of a legitimate line of Christian thought in the early church, thanks especially to the Alexandrian school. "Heretical" gnoses "were only as it were embroideries along the edge of this continuous line."[60]

Abuses of gnostics have created a phobia in the West, which prevents theologians from approaching the question afresh. They forget that the antignostic thrust of the West's involvement with the world has also created abuses, such as the rape of nature. Should the abuse of a good thing deter us from a good use of it? If gnosticism is repressed, it will produce its worst fruits—Manicheism, Encratism, Jansenism. In fact, the modern scientific culture of the West has already produced a very dangerous form of "neognosticism," which, as Gilkey has described for us, equates the *scientific knowledge* of nature's secrets with the *power to liberate* humankind! [61]

Christian theology must revise its philosophical apparatus to accommodate the gnostic idiom of the East already operating in the West. And for that it must, therefore, first dialogue with its own monastic tradition. I believe, as I shall repeat later, that the most creative encounter between East and West could come from the monks whose calling it is to bring about within Western theology a fruitful interaction between Christian *love* and Buddhist *wisdom*.[62]

THE EAST IN THE NINETEENTH-CENTURY WEST: PHILOSOPHY VERSUS THEOLOGY

Having closed the above parenthesis, I now resume my inquiry into the Eastern presence in the Christian West. I have two more instances to comment on: one in nineteenth-century Europe and the other in twentieth-century Europe.

The nineteenth-century episode was one of the most painful and yet the most instructive in the history of the East-West encounter of religions. A Buddhist scholar who made it the theme of a doctoral dissertation at Oxford sees it as the rise of "Protestant Buddhism"—that is, a species of Buddhism that erupted as a "protest" against an openly aggressive Christianity and eventually was exported to Europe under the patronage of anti-Christian movements in the West.[63] As a consequence of this severe breakdown of communication between Buddhism and Christianity, those of us Christians engaged in Buddhist-Christian dialogue have an uphill task even today.

Let me set the background against which this episode must be recounted.[64]

The aggressiveness of the church mentioned above was gathering momentum from medieval times with the mixing up of the things of Caesar with the things of God. But this Christian "power-consciousness" (as I identified it earlier) became a reality in Asia only during the great missionary era of the sixteenth century when the conquest of nations for Christ went hand in hand with the military and mercantile subjugation of lands for Europe. By the seventeenth century the Jesuits De Nobili and Ricci would be battling within the church for a more dialogical approach. They replaced the conquest theory with the adaptation theory, which, according to our hindsight, was not as innovative as it might have seemed then, for it amounted to "using" Eastern *cultures* against Eastern *religions* [65] much as the early fathers "used" pagan "philosophy" against pagan "religion." Even this modest attempt was repressed, and in the eighteenth century the news of Eastern religions traveling westward through missionary accounts suffered from this same missiological bias, quite unlike the accounts of some secular observers.[66]

We have to wait until the nineteenth century to see the beginnings of a "scientific" inquiry into Asian religions, particularly Buddhism. This began with the European discovery of Pali texts and of the doctrines contained therein. By this time, as a fruit of the Enlightenment, *philosophy* had become an autonomous discipline studying *religion* from its own philosophical standpoint. It is natural, therefore, that the "philosophy" revealed in the Buddhist texts redeemed the previous image of Buddhism as an idolatrous "religion." The rationalist quarters of Europe welcomed the new philosophy as a critique of Christian religion.[67]

It is not without reason that Protestant Europe, particularly the German-speaking zone—being the first to respond to the Kantian phase of the Enlightenment—displayed greater enthusiasm than did the Catholic sector with regard to Buddhist philosophy. The very title of George Grimm's pioneering work, *Die Lehre des Buddha, die Religion der Vernunft und der Meditation* (completed in 1915), indicates how Buddhism was received as a rational system minus its religious symbols. Grimm's inspirers, Schopenhauer and Nietzsche, both nineteenth-century thinkers, had already discovered, in this Oriental philosophy, sufficient ammunition to fire at Christianity.[68]

This may explain the excessively apologetical posture that certain Christian Buddhologists such as Barthelemy St. Hilaire of France adopted in their exposition of Buddhism. Not surprisingly, this French scholar expressed the fear that Buddhism and its Western interpretations could challenge the Hellenic and Christian foundations of Western culture.[69] Catholic scholars, such as Bournouf, Levy, and later La Vallée Poussin, probably suffered from the same bias in their interpretation of Buddhist metapsychology. The profound insights into the deepest zones of the mind and its operations, which Buddhism unfolds, did not come within the ambit of Greek philosophy, much less of Cartesianism. The sure method of reaching these insights (in those pre-Freudian days) would have been through the mystical writings of saints, rather than through the philosophical tradition that academicians held fast to.

It is against this European background that one must view the dramatic encounter between Christian missionaries and Buddhist monks in Sri Lanka. While Buddhism, in the form of a respectable *philosophy,* was seeping into the "minds" of certain European elitists, colonial Christianity in Sri Lanka was using all the powers of Caesar to oust the Buddhist *religion* from the "hearts" of the masses. Malalgoda—on whom I depend for the data discussed below [70]—pinpoints the three prongs of missionary aggression: education, the press, and preaching.

The colonial government in power at the time and voluntary organizations in England gave their "aid" to Christian missions to make public education an effective instrument of christianization. Thus a small minority of Christians wielded so much "power" that the non-Christian majority had to depend on them for a job-oriented education. This unfair use of economic aid and political backing from the West to further Christianity is a missionary policy that has not yet been entirely given up.

The press was also a Christian monopoly used not only for the proclamation of the gospel but for an open and persistent attack on the person and the doctrine of the Buddha. The Buddhists were helpless. At that time they had no means of replying to the Christians through the printed word. This way of exploiting technology in favor of Christianity against a non-Christian religion is another policy that continues to this day.

In the matter of preaching, however, the Christian missionaries could not outwit the Buddhist monks! Public debates ended up with Buddhist gains. In this, Christianity did not have an unfair advantage over the Buddhists. In fact it was the news of the famous debate at Panadura in 1873 that brought Colonel Olcott, an American theosophist, to Sri Lanka and it was thanks to his initiative that the Buddhist renewal (already brewing as an internal movement) became an organized force directed against Christianity. Soon Buddhist schools were opened in order to counteract the Christian monopoly in education. A press, too, was acquired from the Buddhist king of Siam, and there was a torrent of abusive and even obscene literature against foreign missions and the foreign religion. It was a century of bitterness.

At this time anti-Christian organizations in England, such as the Nationalist Secular Society, engaged themselves in "comparative study of religion" more to vilify Christianity, now in crisis, than to commend Eastern religions. At the same time, with the empiricism of Berkley, Locke, and Hume, the English intelligentsia was not totally taken unawares by the "no-God and no-soul" philosophy of Buddhism. The anti-Christian arguments used in European rationalist circles began to circulate in Sri Lanka just as Buddhist-Christian polemics there were given publicity in England.

Thus arose "Protestant Buddhism"—the one that reached Europe in the nineteenth century riding on the crest of a wave of anti-Christian polemics. Buddhist missions to the West initiated by Anagarika Dharmapala, himself an offshoot of this movement, also smacked of "Protestant Buddhism." Such a Buddhism, both in Europe and in Asia, preferred to debate rather than dialogue with Christianity, and still does. For even the missionaries like Hardy, who studied Buddhism under the monks, turned the knowledge so acquired against Buddhism itself. Thus, even today, dialogue initiatives of Christians are held in suspicion in Sri Lanka and in the West.[71]

One can, then, speak of a "Western Buddhism," which in fact is a dry, doctrinaire *philosophy* with no *religious* sap to make it live. Essentially a lay movement of a European intelligentsia overconscious of a Christian past, it has no religious institution such as a strong Western *sangha* to nourish and sustain it. It is a system of thought truncated from its religious roots and bandied about as a philosophy of life that can replace Christianity.[72] No wonder "philosophy of religion" became a Christian tool of defense in the wake of this century!

But ironically "Protestant Buddhism," against which this tool was sometimes used, was Christianity's own creation!

THE EAST IN THE TWENTIETH-CENTURY WEST: NEW ORIENTALISM

The middle of the twentieth century saw a different mood dawning in Europe. The East began to present itself to the West as a generator of powerful *religious forces* shaping the destiny of Asian masses, rather than a mere gallery of intellectual luxuries for the gaze of a European elite. I can think of four movements that converged to create this new mood.

The first was the rise of colonized nations against their Western Christian powers. The "Protestant Buddhism" just described had its parallel in Burma and Indochina. The neo-Hindu renewalist currents of India also had their militant streams. Islam in Indonesia, too, acted as a political force. The very association of Western colonial power with Christianity provoked Asians to associate their *religious* beliefs with their *national* consciousness. Therefore, the political conflict between Europe and the Asian nations was registered sociologically as a struggle between Christianity and Asian religions. The outcome of it was that Europe was forced to regard these religions not as mere "philosophies" in the Western sense of the term, but as "philosophies of life" with roots in the life-struggle of the masses. A healthy discovery, indeed!

Secondly, it was a time when the behavioral sciences put philosophy of religion into a crisis, as mentioned earlier. These sciences, too, brought out the living religions of Asia not only in their institutional, cultic, and symbolic richness and exuberance, but also in their political and social dynamism. The reconstruction of an original religion from its texts and the rejection of the religion of the Asian masses as a "corruption" of the pure textual religion was reversed. The living religions of Asia became a locus for textual hermeneutics. Thus many universities became centers of *religious* encounter, not merely institutes for the *philosophical* study of Eastern thought.[73] Thus the academic preoccupation with the definition of religion,[74] which has not yet ended, because no definition has reached unanimous acceptance,[75] has been balanced by phenomenological descriptions of an inductive type.[76] Apparently the academic distance from religious experience is somewhat reduced though not entirely eliminated, for philosophy and religion now stay apart.

The third important feature derives from modern communications media, including opportunities for travel. A live contact is established between the West, which merely *studies* the Asian religions, and the East, which *practices* them. The student accustomed to view religion as a "department in a university" and perhaps a "department of life," is made to realize that in Asia religion is life. Western youth go to the East in search of a "religious view of life."

Finally, there is a new phenomenon that has forced the churches to take Asian religions with greater seriousness. It is the *Eastern religions coming to the West.* Tibetan Lamaism seeking asylum in the West because of the Chinese takeover is one such instance. Today in fact one can see Eastern oases scattered over North Atlantic lands, attracting Western youth to cultic and meditative practices presented in their Oriental cultural garb. The "pagans" whom missionaries went to convert are now at home converting Christian youth, challenging Christianity's exclusivist claims and provoking odious comparisons.

The church obviously views this new mood with mixed feelings and has not yet responded to it creatively. The ambiguity of the situation has led Harvey Cox to write about the "promise" and the "peril" of what he calls "new orientalism."[77] Parrinder calls this the "third Reformation" of the church, counting the Protestant Reformation in the sixteenth century as the first, and the church's reaction to the scientific revolution of the nineteenth century as the second. By "third Reformation," therefore, he means the church's contemporary response to this new orientalism.[78]

The question that arises spontaneously here is whether the Western church is really equipped to handle this situation without consulting and dialoguing with the Asian churches. Is this third Reformation going to be a temporary adjustment or a radical renewal of Western Christianity? If not, why? What, then, could be the contribution of contemporary Asia to Western Christianity?

CHRISTIAN RESPONSE TO EASTERN PRESENCE: MONKS VERSUS THEOLOGIANS

The response to the question posed above is neat and clear. Inasmuch as the West, unlike the East, seems to believe in a "division of labor" between monks who profess their religion and academicians who make theology their profession, the response too is twofold: that of professional recluses and that of professional theologians.

Some monks, quite characteristically, have adopted what I would call a "participatory" approach. They have tried to enter into the Oriental religious experience to sharpen their monastic instinct with Asian sensitivity. This is true not only of some monasteries in the West where the East is not a silent guest but an active collaborator in the Christian search for God,[79] but also of some Christian monasteries in the East where the sap of monachism is sucked up from ancient roots and circulated back to the West, discovering in this process the Asian face of Christ and disclosing it to non-Christian brothers and sisters.[80]

Thanks to Thomas Merton, this venture has assumed international proportions. The Bangkok Conference (1968), at which he died, and the Bangalore Conference (1973), in which his spirit was still alive, brought monks from East and West and of many religions together.[81] The third congress took place in 1980.[82] A series of encounters of the same kind taking place more recently in Europe and America indicate that the "third Reformation" has begun in the cells of monks.[83]

As the background papers of these conferences clearly indicate (see nn. 81 and 82), these monks are quite in touch with the theology of religions elaborated in the West. But the question that poses itself is: Are the theologians equally in touch with the praxis of the monks? Unfortunately, the theology of religions shows a marked distance from this praxis and cannot be traced back beyond the desks of academicians.[84]

Actually, Occidental theology in its approach to other religions has not moved one inch beyond the patristic standpoint described earlier in this chapter. If today's thinking looks revolutionary now, it is because the background against which it is viewed is the medieval ecclesiology that moved far away from the patristic vision. The limitations of the patristic standpoint, which continued to influence the Western theological attitude towards the Eastern religions right through the centuries, have not yet been critically examined.

The conquest theory, which saw Oriental religions as anti-Christian, and the adaptation theory, for which they were merely non-Christian, were both based on a medieval ecclesiology that identified Christ with the church (and the church with the pope), so that salvation impossible outside Christ seemed also impossible outside the church. Therefore, the fulfillment theory, which regards the other religions as pre-Christian, is founded on the recovery of the ancient Christian belief that Christ is a greater reality than the church, not only spatially (the kingdom of God goes beyond the visible limits of the church) but also temporally (salvation history goes beyond what the scriptures and tradition reveal), so that the church and the Bible do not exhaust salvation and revelation, respectively, but are normative guides and sacramental pointers to *God-in-Christ who reveals and saves*.[85]

This theory of fulfillment clearly militates against Catholic triumphalism based on ecclesiolatry (no salvation outside the church) and Protestant fundamentalism based on bibliolatry (no revelation outside the Bible), and all intransigent evangelism that springs from both of them.[86]

But the Western presentation of this theory leaves many loose ends, which its theology has not gathered together. The first question is about the *Israel-church* analogy at the basis of the fulfillment theory. How would one relate the pre-Christian character of Israel and the Old Testament to the pre-Christian character of non-Christian religious traditions? The answer that the former is a supernatural revelation whereas the latter is on the natural plane, is opposed to the belief that there is one order in the world and that is the order of Christ. Anything outside it is sin. If the religions are outside this order, then we are back again with the conquest theory! If they are inside this order, then the distinction is not valid. Nor is Barth's claim[87]— that (non-Christian) religions are humanity's search for God whereas the Christian faith is God's search for humanity—acceptable without returning to the conquest theory. Besides, no human being can seek God unless God seeks that human being. This is the age-old question of grace and nature, divine gratuity and human liberty, reappearing in its insoluble dialectics.

The second question I pose to the Western theologian is about the locus of this fulfillment: Is it the visible church in which other religions find fulfillment? Or is it Christ who fulfills the church and, along with it, all religions? It is here that all the past inhibitions of Western theology surface. For instance, Jean

Daniélou, a great spokesman for the fulfillment theory of the fathers,[88] would take the non-Christian religions as precursors of Christianity. However, he would then speak of "saving" and "baptizing" the pagan soul of Amerindians and Africans in the way the pagan spirit of Semites was saved in Abraham, and in the way the pagan spirit of the West was *baptized* in Plato or Virgil.[89] But he seems never to have asked himself whether it was Christ who baptized the precursor or the precursor Christ![90] Does the fulfillment of all religions imply that the church should "baptize" oriental religions *or* that it should plunge into the Jordan of these religions and come out with the messianic awareness that it must be worthy of being listened to: "Hear ye him"?

The Western church, which still sees "philosophy" where there is "soteriology," is busy talking of instrumentalizing (or more euphemistically, "baptizing") Oriental *thought* and *culture* rather than about the humble need of "being baptized" by the *religious experience* inextricably bound up with that thought and culture. Thills and Rahner and a few others who have, at least theoretically, realized the church's need for a humbler opinion of itself have met with Congar's cautious reservations made from a balanced distance.[91] Also, there is a reluctance to admit that sin and paganism cut across the church as well as other religions, *all* needing redemption. I am happy that this aspect is somewhat emphasized in Rahner's theory of the "anonymous Christian." Though a condescending appellation, the phrase has replaced the "pre-Christian" of the fulfillment theory, and would (in my opinion) refer to Buddhists or Hindus or Muslims who live according to their religious conscience insofar as they are *called to the kingdom of God,* and perhaps not necessarily *to the church,* which is a visible sacrament of that kingdom. Vocation to the church, I believe, is a ministry conferred on a few ("the little flock") to confirm and strengthen in others the universal thrust of the kingdom already operating in them. It is only we who deal with good, practicing Buddhists in our daily life who know how the kingdom preached by Christ has already germinated in them and how our encouragement to make them better Buddhists would imply a true furthering of the kingdom in them and in their environment—except in the case of one who clearly receives the vocation to the church—that is, to be a sacramental expression of the kingdom.

Hence an Asian is rather perplexed to hear Ratzinger's *retorqueo argumentum:* "Why not make a cannibal a 'good cannibal' and the convinced SS-man a thoroughgoing SS-man?"[92] To equate a practicing Buddhist with an SS-man is possible only because of a serious underestimation of Asian religions. But, then, some theologians are not only ignorant of Eastern religions, which of course they handle only with their pens, but are equally unaware of the Christian sinfulness that the East has known too well since the colonial era. Charles Davis, the English theologian, commenting on a similar type of theological judgment, condemns it with these harsh words:

> It is necessary to distinguish faith in Christ as the one Saviour and embodiment of Final Truth, from its parasite: the arrogance of the Christian West.[93]

Hence I make two proposals: The first is that theologians should resume a dialogue with Christian monks who empathetically *participate* in the Eastern ethos. This would help to close the gap between theology and theopraxis, between philosophy and religion, between reflection on contemporary thought and participation in contemporary reality, between monastic theology, which is "God-talk born of God-experience," and scientific theology, which is "God-talk passing judgment on experience," or as Buddhists would say, between the pursuit of the *path* and the pursuit of the *truth*.

The second suggestion is that besides accepting the full theological import of *the Asian presence in the West,* as we have already done, there should also be an effort to make the *Western presence in Asia* the focus of a serious reflection in our theology of religions. This is what I intend doing in the following pages.

WESTERN PRESENCE IN THE EAST: IDEOLOGIES AND THEOLOGIES

What we saw up to now was the way the West treated Eastern religions in their emigrant form. Back home in Asia, the same religions assume quite another guise. How the West meets them in their own Asian context is what needs to be investigated now.

The "Asian context" can be described as a blend of a profound *religiousness* (which could be Asia's greatest wealth) and an overwhelming *poverty* (which makes Asia a Third World continent).

I have chosen these words "poverty" and "religiousness" deliberately: they enucleate the contradictions that characterize the Asian context. For each word contains a *negative* and a *positive* pole, in that it carries with it at once the idea of *bondage* and of *freedom*. Poverty certainly is enslaving and degrading when imposed on some by the hedonism of others. But it is ennobling and liberating when voluntarily embraced as a protest and precaution against imposed poverty. A similar bipolarity can be detected in religion. Religion carries with it an enslaving tendency when it acts as "opium" that deadens the individual conscience so as not to make it perceive the bondage of imposed poverty (this would be the "psychological" dimension) or when it sacralizes an oppressive status quo by building up alliances with the power centers of acquisitive systems that create poverty ("sociological dimension"). But there is also a positive pole: religion (both as an individual psychological experience and as a sociological reality) harbors the seed of an ongoing revolution, indeed a subversive potential. When activated, it can trigger radical changes in socio-political structures. Thus a theology of liberation can now spring from the same religion that had earlier produced a theology of domination!

Note that poverty and religiousness are not only bipolar (each containing a negative and positive pole, as described above) but also bidimensional—that is, each has a *psychological* and a *sociological* aspect. I have already hinted at these two dimensions with regard to religiousness. Let me also give an illustration regarding the positive pole of poverty. In Eastern religions and in Western monastic traditions, voluntary poverty has acted as a "spiritual antidote" against the forces of mammon operating *psychologically* within humankind. But in the lives of leaders, such as Mahatma Gandhi, "opted poverty" served also as a "political strategy" against mammonic powers that subjugated the masses through oppressive systems. This would be a *sociological* dimension.

The point I want to make here is that "poverty" and "religion" are poly-semous terms, each distributing its semantic content in four directions. For each is bipolar and bidimensional. Hence the complexity of the reality they describe! For there is in our cultural ethos a "yet-undiscovered point" at which poverty and religion (each understood in its fourfold sense) seem to coalesce in order to procreate the Asian character of our continent. In fact, history at-tests, as I shall indicate later, that the *theological* attempts to encounter Asian religions with no radical concern for Asia's poor and the *ideological* programs that would eradicate Asia's poverty with naive disregard for its religious di-mension, have both proved to be misdirected zeal. Western theologies and ide-ologies now prevalent in Asia have all to be judged in the light of this discov-ery.

In Asia, there are two "secular" movements committed to the eradication of "poverty" and both of them are Western: namely, *Marxist socialism* and a species of *development ideology* associated with capitalist technocracy. The West is also religiously present through the church, which, for the most part, is an extension of Western Christianity. Thus the church too reflects, in its own *theological* self-understanding, the *ideological* conflicts of the West. An in-quiry into the theological equipment of the church may help us see the wider ideological context in which the West encounters the Asian religions.

The Asian church, for the moment, is caught between two "theologies," both of which are as Western as the secular ideologies just mentioned. The first is the *classic European theology,* which, in its various brands, is officially taught in all major institutions of the Asian church. The second is the *Latin American theology,* which is also making itself felt in certain theological cir-cles. These theologies, of course, are diametrically opposed to each other, as are also the secular ideologies mentioned above.

Classic theology in the West, which was going through the mill of renewal since the nineteenth century, is said to have made a major "breakthrough" in the middle of this century, climaxing in modern theology with its openness to the world. The chief centers of this renewal were the French and German lin-guistic zones, according to Mark Schoof, because, to quote his own words, it was there that "the theologians seem to have the necessary scientific tradition and sufficient creative energy at their disposal." [94] One major source of inspi-ration for Catholic renewal of European theology is traced back to Protestant Germany, according to the same author. [95]

This close-range view of European theology justifies the title of Schoof's work: *Breakthrough.* But an Asian looking from a critical distance sees another picture. The real breakthrough in Western theology seems to have come with the Latin American critique of the same "scientific tradition" that Schoof proudly alludes to. What European theologians achieved up to the 1960s in their dialogue with contemporaneous *philosophies* [96] was only a mild reform compared to what the Latin Americans achieved since the 1960s. They effected a complete reversal of method. They seem to have done to European theology what Feuerbach did to Hegelian dialectics. They put theology back on its feet. They grounded it on theopraxis. What was formerly revolving around a Kantian orbit was made to rotate around a Marxian axis.[97]

For us Asians, liberation theology is thoroughly Western, and yet so radically renewed by the challenge of the Third World that it has a relevance for Asia that the classic theology does not have. The Ecumenical Association of Third World Theologians (EATWOT) was perhaps its first tangible fruit in Asia.[98] In the churches, particularly of eastern and southern Asia, this new method has already begun to compete with the traditional theology. Is this surprising when even First World theologians cannot resist being drawn into dialogue with it? [99]

Features that are peculiarly relevant for our discussion can be gathered from Sobrino's presentation.[100] The first feature is that the Kantian attempt to "liberate reason from authority" paved the way to a theological preoccupation with harmonizing "faith with reason," but the Marxian attempt to "free reality from oppression" did not receive theological attention in Europe until the Latin Americans made an issue of it.[101] Thus the use of "philosophy" to explain away suffering rationally or to define God and the divine nature in such a way as to justify the existence of oppression and injustice was understandable in a European socio-political context, whereas the use of "sociological" analysis to *change* (rather than merely *explain*) the world of injustice became the immediate concern of liberation theology. Such a concern could not come within the scientific purview of European theology, whether Protestant[102] or Catholic.[103]

The second feature, quite important for Asians, is the primacy of praxis over theory. Spirituality, for instance, is not the practical conclusion of a theology but radical involvement with the poor and the oppressed, and is what creates theology. We know Jesus the *truth* by following Jesus the *way*.

Thirdly, this way is the way of the cross, the basis of all knowledge. Thus, the growth of the world into God's kingdom is *not* a "progressive development," but a process punctuated by radical contradictions, violent transformations, and death-resurrection experiences—what Sobrino calls the *ruptura epistemologica,* scripturally founded in the "transcendence of the crucified God."[104]

Fourthly, we see that it is not a "development theology," such as would justify and perpetuate the values of an "acquisitive" culture, but a "liberation theology" demanding an asceticism of renunciation and a voluntary poverty that sneers at acquisitiveness. This "spirituality" is motivated by the desire to bring about the kingdom of God—by battling against mammon in all its guises. Hence it is not just a passive solidarity with the poor in their poverty and oppression, but also a dynamic participation in their struggle to be fully human. Indeed, a dynamic following of Christ![105] I would suggest that in this scheme of thought, voluntary poverty is not merely a spiritual antidote against mammon (as in traditional Christianity and in Asian religions in general) but also a political strategy against the principalities and powers that serve mammon.

Finally, the encounter of God with humankind—that is, the interplay of grace and liberty—is seen as the human obligation to use all *human potentialities* to anticipate the kingdom, which nevertheless remains *God's gratuitous gift*. This explains the liberation theologian's political option for socialism—that is, for a definite social order in which oppressive structures are changed radically, even violently, in order to allow every person to be fully human, the assumption being that no one is liberated unless everyone is. But no liberation theologian is so naive as to identify any political order—even socialist order—with God's gratuitous gift of the kingdom.

This theology, as also its European predecessor, receives its contextual significance in Asia precisely in relationship to the aforesaid Western ideologies with which it is very closely connected. A brief sketch of how these ideologies operate in Asia would immediately situate the two theologies, too, in the context of Eastern *religions*. For both these ideologies are attempts at eliminating Asian *poverty*. Their record in the East is a mirror that reflects the church's own dialogue with the twofold reality of Asia: its poverty and its religiousness.

Marxist socialism, the first ideology I mentioned, has a built-in mechanism to purify Asian religions of their negative aspects in the very process of eliminating poverty. The U.S.S.R., which has two-thirds of its territory in Asia, has had a valuable experience in Mongolia—a Buddhist country where monasteries served as political and economic strongholds until the Marxists took over. The switch-over from a feudalist to a socialist framework (allegedly without going through a capitalist phase) brought about a gradual social transformation in Buddhist monastic establishments.[106] It is on record that Marxists did, in fact, commit reprehensible acts of violence, which, in some instances, delayed expected reforms and even hardened the negative aspects of Asian religiousness. Political expediency then prompted the Kremlin to change its strategy, particularly with regard to Buddhism. It seems to have realized that religion is an inalienable heritage of the Asian masses, and that the reconstruction of society and elimination of social oppresssion can hardly be effected if the masses do not receive a sanction from religion.[107] But it has hardly recognized what I have referred to above as the positive pole of religiousness.

The Chinese, on the other hand, thought religion could be a tool of social change. But they retracted this thesis in the mid-1960s to the extent of unleashing a religious persecution, presumably because collaboration with religious forces, especially Buddhism, in the building up of a new society, contrary to expectation, only strengthened the religious convictions of the people.[108] In either case, the lesson taught—if not learned—is that the *religious* character of Asian peoples cannot be bypassed by those dedicated to Asia's *economic* development.

The other secular force operating in the Asian continent, as already mentioned, is the development ideology of a Western technocratic type. This is the model that some of the so-called free nations of Asia (patterned according to Western democracies and, paradoxically, governed by the privileged) invariably follow.[109] It is the sure, quick method of *economic* development, the same method that precipitated a technocracy in the West. It is a species of modernization that imports all the comforts and all the problems of an industrial society into Asia. In the process what suffers most is rural culture, which preserves Asian religion by being sustained by it.

No religious persecution under a Marxist regime could compare with the subtle undermining of Asian religion that a technocratic development generates in our cultures. In fact, Marxist socialism might at least purify religion of its institutional alliances with powers that create poverty, whereas the development ideology only weakens religion by installing mammon, the anti-God, as the object of worship. Further, Marxism, though a Western secular ideology, has become a religious surrogate in some Asian countries through a process of indigenization, but the technocratic development of Asia as it is taking place now has only continued the early colonialism of the West by furthering the First World's encroachment into the Third. Hence, in my opinion, in Asia there have been several praiseworthy attempts to combine religion with socialism, purifying both, so that the socialist option is given a religious motivation, and religions are given a socialist dimension.[110]

There is no need to stress here that, willy-nilly, the Asian churches are drawn into the whirlwind created by these two contradictory forces. The political conflicts between these two Western ideologies are mirrored in the theological field. In other words, European theology of the official church and the liberation theology of fringe groups are continuing, within the Asian churches, the political battles of Asian nations.

My final query, then, is: How far are these ideological and theological tools of the West effective in penetrating Asian religiousness within its own context of poverty? What would be the Asian churches' contribution in this regard?

THEOLOGY THROUGH PARTICIPATION: THE ASIAN STYLE

It is clear that neither of these theologies is Asian. Nor is Asia independent enough to work out its own theology, because *even in major conferences organized in Asia the theological mood and method remain Western.* The classic European theology, which in its renewed form regards "humanization" as an integral part of "evangelization," does, however, allow its concept of "humanization" to suffer from the strictures imposed by development ideology.

A classic example, which no Asian theologian can forget, is the thesis of Van Leeuwen.[111] The scientific and industrial revolution with its modern and secular culture, according to him, is a product of Western Christianity and is something to be welcomed. Further, this Western product should be carried to the East, so that traditional religious values there, too, could break down! Thus the implication seems to be that Asian poverty and religiousness should both be eradicated by the theology and ideology of the West—a position that Ninian Smart of Lancaster University has aptly described as "Western tribalism."[112] The use of theology to reinforce Western colonialism does not enjoy universal approval. Yet, this extreme case is only an exaggerated form of a missiology still operative in Asia in the form of church-sponsored developmental programs. With massive aid from the West, some Asian churches (being minorities threatened by possible loss of identity) consolidate themselves into Western oases, where a de-asianizing form of "development" is offered to the non-Christian majority, callously regardless of, or positively hostile to, their past religious traditions—the sort of thing that produced a "Protestant Buddhism" in the last century (see above). Development theology today is a continuation of the missiology of conquest and power that dominated the church yesterday.

Liberation theology, on the other hand, springing as it does from Latin American praxis, offers a stopgap alternative to the other brand of theology here in Asia, but lacks a perceptive understanding of the religious ethos of the East.[113] The Marxist embarrassment in the face of persistent religious practice of the Asian masses may reappear in an Asian theopraxis too heavily dependent on the Latin American model. Unfortunately, as I have observed elsewhere, the Christian "ashramic" movement dialoguing with Asian *monastics,* and Christian leftist movements struggling against the creators of *poverty,* have not dialogued among themselves, despite the fact that two non-Christian leaders in Asia, Gandhi and Mao, displayed a superlative sensitivity in combining the social liberation of Asia with the spiritual liberation of the individual.[114] Even the motivation for voluntary poverty and renunciation, which liberation theology has so illuminatingly emphasized in the context of the social option, needs another dimension that the gnostic values of the East seem to demand: compassion, detachment, moderation, and inner peace. "Freedom from poverty" becomes an enslaving pursuit if it is not tempered by the Asian belief in the "freedom that comes from poverty"—that is, freedom from mammon.

A Thai Buddhist scholar, Prof. S. Sivaraksha, after making a scathing criticism of the development ideology and critically sifting certain valuable Marxist insights, has appealed for a *Buddhist approach* (perhaps, more generally, an Asian approach) to development and liberation, based on the religious values mentioned above. The antireligious roots of capitalism and Marxism in the West, he appeals, may hinder the advocates of these ideologies from seeing into the (religious) depths of human nature.[115] Hence one might say that the Asian method of development and liberation must use the tools of *social analysis* in conjunction with the techniques of *psychological introspection* proper to Asian traditions. For the evolution of the *new society* and the emergence of the *new person* constitute one indivisible process: which is to say that Marxist *class analysis* and gnostic *self-analysis* form a pincer movement in the liberation of Asian peoples living in the twofold context of religion and poverty.

A theology that responds to both the monastic and socialist imperatives can be born only of an authentically Asian church—that is, a church fully *baptized* in the waters of Eastern poverty and religion. This praxis, which has already begun on the fringes of the church,[116] will take some time to bring forth fruits. But one can delineate the chief features of this theology in contrast with the Western or the Latin American models:

1. The mutual inclusiveness of the *path* and the *truth* as advocated by Buddhists is almost parallel to the praxis theory circle in liberation theology.

2. There will be the trinitarian experience of the *word* and of *silence* through the experience of the *harmony* that reigns between them. The word-game about nature and person or the mathematics of one and three have only generated centuries of verbosity. It is word-less-ness that gives every word its meaning. This inner *harmony* between *word* and *silence* is the test of Asian authenticity, indeed it is the spirit, the eternal energy, which makes every word spring from silence and lead to silence, every engagement spring from renunciation, every struggle from a profound restfulness, every freedom from stern discipline, every action from stillness, every "development" from detachment, and every acquisition from nonaddiction. But inasmuch as silence is the *word unspoken* and the word is *silence heard,* their "relationship" is not one of temporal priority but of dialectical mutuality. It is the spirit of Buddhist wisdom and Christian love. If there is harmony between our speech and our silence, whether in worship or service or conversation, the Spirit is truly at work.

3. There will be participation through baptism. If the Eastern religions are precursors of Christianity, the paradigm will always be the double baptism of Jesus, first in the Jordan (Mk. 1:9–11) and then on the cross (Mk. 10:35, Lk. 12:50)—that is, a church humble enough to be baptized by its precursors in the Jordan of Asian religion and bold enough to be baptized by oppressive systems on the cross of Asian *poverty.* Does not the fear of losing its identity make it lean on mammon? Does not its refusal to die keep it from living? Hence the call to *participate* in Asians' search for Christ in their struggle for *interior liberation* and for *social emancipation.*[117] The seed that dies will bring abundant fruit: Asian theopraxis is born of a submission to the non-Christian judgment of gnostic soteriologies and revolutionary socialism.

4. Theology will be explicitation rather than excogitation. Theology is an unfolding of a theopraxis. But this is not simply to be equated with the so-called Christian witness among non-Christians; rather, by theopraxis I mean a *God-experience* (which is at once a *human concern*) of God's people living beyond the church, and among whom the church is called to lose itself in baptismal immersion or total participation. It is only in the unfathomable abyss where religion and poverty seem to have a common source—that is, God, who has declared mammon the enemy—that this *God-experience* is disclosed to the church and can be formulated into a *God-talk.* In short, *theology in Asia is the Christian apocalypse of the non-Christian experiences of liberation.*

This *participatory approach* to theology in general, and to theology of religions in particular, has an astounding background that I must disclose before I conclude. Despite the fact that its immediate aim is to sever the economic and theological bonds that enslave the Asian churches to the West, and also to make these churches send their roots deep into the Asian soil, paradoxically, the method has its home in the Christian West! Those who really conserved this theological method for us were the anonymous saints and seers of Western monachism; it is they who indirectly discovered the principle that the door to Asian religiousness is *poverty,* not power; *participation,* not propaganda! There is, however, one proviso.

Their silent dialogue with the East cannot become a valid theological locus for the contemporary church until the spiritual concerns of an Evagrius in the desert expand into the universalism of a Merton in the city. This dialogue should take seriously the conversion that traditional religion and traditional monasticism have undergone in the face of Asian Marxism.[118] For wherever the Asian monastic (let me use Benedictine categories for the sake of easy communication) is compelled to graft the *orare* of monasticism into the *laborare* of Marxism, there indeed the constitutive character of the monastic commitment—Benedict's *conversio morum*—assumes a new significance. Traditional Asian monastics, Buddhist or Christian, are called to turn away from the leisure-class mores of a feudalist or capitalist society and accept an asceticism that demands of them a contemplative but participatory presence in the socialist experiments of Asia's more daring nations. Unless, therefore, the intermonastic encounter between East and West absorbs also this new experience, I suspect that Western Christianity may not soon be allowed to witness the epiphany of a truly Asian church.

PART TWO

Understanding Buddhism

4

Buddhism as Doctrine, Institution, and Experience

It was quite a reduced form of Buddhism that found acceptance in nineteenth-century Europe and continued ever since then to appear in the writings of rationalist interpreters: an arid *doctrine* with no religious sap to make it live.

Thanks to the anthropologists of this century, Western intellectuals are made to appreciate the fact that Buddhism is not simply doctrine, but also an undefinable ethos, a socio-cultural atmosphere permeating vast stretches of Asia and sustained by a firm institutional framework known as the *sasana*.

This again is not all there is to Buddhism. In the ideal environment generated by the religious institution or the *sāsana,* one is bound to come across a number of monks who, in their single-minded pursuit of nirvana, are making the Buddha's own salvific *experience* a living possibility for their contemporaries. Minus this primordial constituent, Buddhism would not pass for a genuine religion.

Thus, a comprehensive study of Buddhism as it presents itself in history involves an inquiry into each of these three facets: the doctrinal, the institutional, and the experiential. In this chapter, therefore, I propose to make a rapid survey of these three areas, forewarning readers, however, that the time and space allotted here will not allow this analysis to be as exhaustive as it will be comprehensive.

THE DOCTRINAL SYSTEM

Phenomenology

Born and nurtured in Indian soil, Buddhism shares with the rest of Indian philosophy the character of being simultaneously a "view" of life *(darśana)* and a "way" of life *(pratipadā),* or more concisely, a way of salvation:

Originally a paper read at the seminar on "Self-Understanding of Religions and Their Approach to Problems of Modern Society," Vatican City, Oct. 3–6, 1972. Later published in *Dialogue,* o.s. 27–28 (1973) 1–22.

No Indian philosophical system is merely speculative. Each is a *darśana,*
an insight into the real, which is at once a path of salvation and cessation
of pain.[1]

An "insight" that is at the same time a "path" of salvation is normally
designated "gnosis" in the West; in Buddhist nomenclature, *paññā, aññā,
abhiññā, ñāṇa,* or *bodhi.* These words express the mutual inclusiveness of the
two dimensions of Buddhism: the view and the way. But for pedagogical reasons, presumably, they are spelled out by the Buddha himself as a fourfold
truth and an eightfold *path.* When doctrinally systematized, this twin aspect of
Buddhism takes the guise of a *phenomenology*[2] interpenetrated with a *soteriology.*

The scriptural text that handles this subject of Buddhist phenomenology is
called the *Abhidhamma-pitaka,* which is the third part of the canon and forms
the basis of later scholasticism. According to *ābhidhārmika* phenomenology,
all that human convention *(sammuti, vohāra)* regards as "beings" are in fact
(param'atthato) no more than a quick succession of "phenomena," or technically, *dhammā*—that is to say, the ultimate and fleeting factors of *existence,*
which are no more, no less, than the ultimate and fleeting factors of *experience.*[3] Hence the term "phenomena."

Though they are discrete data rising into existence and subsiding into nonbe-
ing, they are, nonetheless, interrelated in their fluxional nature and are said to
be *paticcasamuppannā* ("originating interdependently").[4]

Classes of Phenomena

Buddhists have more than one way of classifying these phenomena and these
classifications are an indispensable key to the understanding of Buddhist phenomenology. The most frequently mentioned in the scriptures[5] are the following classifications:

    the five *khandha*s or aggregates
    the twelve *ayatana*s or sense spheres
    the eighteen *dhatu*s or elements.

The first classification sees the human being as composed of a physical constituent called *rūpa* (material form) and four psychic factors grouped as *nāma*
("mind"), all adding up to five components. See Figure 1.

The doctrinal implication of this classification is too obvious to need any
explanation. The world in the ultimate analysis is the human person. All "reality" is conceived exclusively in terms of human beings and their experience.
Even nirvana, the ultimate experience, is "had" within this psycho-physical
sphere called "human person" as the Buddha himself declared.[6] As a matter
of fact, orthodox scholastic tradition admits a contracted list of the aggregates
with nirvana included therein.[7] They are referred to as the four ultimate realities, *param'atthā.* See Figure 2.

Pali scholiasts, therefore, seem to have admitted two types of "ultimate realities": the samsaric ultimates and the nirvanic ultimate. Obviously they belong

Figure 1
The Five Aggregates

NĀMA	1. VEDANĀ 2. SAÑÑĀ 3. SAMKHĀRĀ 4. VIÑÑĀNĀ	= affective functions = cognitive functions = conative functions = consciousness	5 KHANDHAs (aggregates)
RŪPA	5. RŪPA	= material form	

to two orders, the phenomenal and the transphenomenal.

The view of reality implied here comes into clearer focus in the twelvefold series of *ayatanas*. These comprise the six senses, the mind being one of them, and the corresponding sensa. As indicated in Figure 3, they are a more meaningful distribution of the five *khandhas*. Nirvana is included among them.

The series of eighteen elements or *dhatus* need not absorb our attention here, for they coincide with the twelve *ayatanas* except that the sixth base is refracted into sensations:

13. *cakku-viññāna* (visual sensation)
14. *sota-viññāna* (auditory sensation)
15. *ghana-viññāna* (olfactory sensation)
16. *jivha-viññāna* (gustatory sensation)

Figure 2
The Ultimate Realities and the Corresponding Aggregates

The Four Ultimate Realities		The Five Aggregates	
I *citta*, basic consciousness	=	*viññāna*	4
II *cetasika*, functions of *citta*	=	*vedanā* *saññā* *samkhārā*	1 2 3
III *rūpa*, material form	=	*rūpa*	5
IV *nirvāna*, the transphenomenal			

Figure 3
The Twelvefold *Ayatana*s (Senses and Sensa)

(1) eye	= CAKKHU	RUPA	= form, color (7)	
(2) ear	= SOTA	SADDA	= sound (8)	
(3) nose	= GHĀNA	GANDHA	= smell (9)	RŪPA
(4) tongue	= JIVHĀ	RASA	= taste (10)	
(5) body	= KĀYA	PHOṬṬABBA	= tangibility (11)	
(6) mind	= MANO	DHAMMĀ	= mental data (12)	
	= viññāna	vedanā, saññā, samkhārā, NIBBĀNA		NĀMA

17. *kaya-viññāna* (tactile sensation)
18. *mano-viññāna* (mental sensation)

"Phenomenalistic Realism"

The twelvefold *ayatana* series is incontestably the most exhaustive list of realities. It contains all that Buddhist phenomenology regards as ultimately real. As one Theravāda commentator claims, there is no form of existence that is left out of this classification.[8]

Observe, on the other hand, that this matter of distributing the twelve items suggests that Buddhists admit no material existence *(rūpa)* other than the ten sense data (see items 1–5 and 7–11 in Figure 3).[9] These items are "real" *(paramatthā)* only insofar as they are "phenomena" *(dhammā)*.

We are face to face with an unusual combination of "realism" and "phenomenalism," and the various Buddhist schools spread themselves out in a wide spectrum that ranges between two extremes, which they try their best to avoid: absolute phenomenalism and naive realism. Thus even the Sarvastivāda, the school that leans most toward realism, has been called by Stcherbatsky "modified illusionism" and "modified realism."[10]

Scriptural Buddhism can also be described in similar terms. As a recent scholar has cogently demonstrated, the early Buddhist doctrine was also a "form of Realism giving a phenomenalistic interpretation."[11]

Soteriology

The term *"dhammā,"* though it means "phenomenal reality" and describes samsaric factors that are real but relatively so, cannot be univocally predicated of nirvana. Nevertheless nirvana is classed as a *dhamma* or a *dhātu,* or more precisely as a *dhamma-dhātu*—that is, a mental datum belonging to the twelfth *ayatana.*[12] Any more comment on this would plunge us into a question that is very much controverted in the schools. Suffice it to say here that nirvana is also a *dhamma*—that is, a datum of an experience, not, to be sure, of mere sense experience *(viññāna)*, but of a transphenomenal realization *(paññā)*.

Buddhism, moreover, is not a phenomenology pure and simple; it is a theory of phenomena essentially oriented to a realization of that which is transphenomenally real and constitutes the goal of salvation. To be more explicit, the Buddhist analysis of reality so far described is only a means to generate the persuasion that the world we attach so much importance to is in fact a series of phenomena that are transient *anicca* and utterly devoid of any permanent substratum *(an-atta)* and, consequently, hollow and unsatisfying *(dukkha)*.[13]

Spiritually internalized, this conviction leads to the elimination of *taṇhā* or craving for samsaric existence. Once this craving, which is at the root of all ill *(dukkha)*, is done away with, the ultimate condition for the attainment of nirvana is said to have been already achieved.

Thus there are three phenomenologico-soteriological stages culminating in the nirvanic experience:

1. *dhatu-kusalatā:* ability to see samsaric existence as composed of variously classified phenomena *(dhātu)*
2. *manasikāra-kusalatā:* ability to reflect over the nature of phenomena as being *anatta, anicca,* and *dukkha*
3. elimination of all desires
4. nirvana.[14]

The scholiasts down the centuries, especially those of the Pali school, have always held fast to this doctrine, though they prefer to use other names to indicate the three stages,[15] and seem also to weaken the *soteriological* thrust of the doctine by their scholastic preoccupations.

If I too sound rather scholastic in this part of my exposition, it is because I have restricted my inquiry to the phenomenological aspect of Buddhism, intending to complement it later with a direct discussion of Buddhist soteriology.

THE RELIGIOUS INSTITUTION

The Scale of Values

The Buddhist religion or the *sasana* is the institutional formulation of the *Buddhist spirit*. Though difficult to define, it can still be perceived in terms of the *system of values* within which it operates. "Value," I submit, is too abstract. The Buddhist idiom employs the more concrete expression "gem" *(ratana)*—not a value as such, but "that which is valued," the most precious thing in life, a close equivalent of Christianity's "pearl of great price." It is in this extended sense that I shall use the world "value."

The three ultimate values in Buddhism are the Buddha, the *dhamma,* and the sangha (religious community). They are thus called *tri-ratana* or triple gem. One becomes a Buddhist by accepting them as normative in one's life. One does so normally with the ceremonial formula known as *tri-sarana* or triple refuge. This formula is repeated, and the pledge renewed, several times in the lifetime of a Buddhist.

There are other values in Buddhism. The scriptures make frequent mention

Figure 4
Buddhaghosa's Ascending Order of "Gems" *(ratana)*

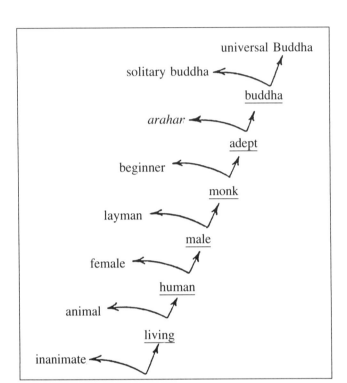

of the seven "gems" or the most valued possessions of a universal king of righteousness (Cakravartin).[16] Men, women, beasts, and inanimate objects are enumerated. They could perhaps be thought of as "secular" values.

But Buddhaghosa, the great fifth-century synthesizer of the exegetical lore of the orthodox school of Buddhism, has placed some of these values in a "religious" perspective. In a passage that has hitherto received scant attention from scholars, he presents what we might call the Buddhist counterpart of the "Porphyrian tree." He lists a series of "gems" graded in an ascending order of value.[17] I have schematized it in Figure 4.

Buddhaghosa maintains that inanimate gems are for the use *(paribhoga)* of living beings, who are superior *(seṭṭha)*. In the domain of the living, the human being prevails over beasts, for they are at human service *(upabhoga)*. Similarly in the human sphere, a woman is called to be of service to the male and cannot outrank him even if she is the consort of a Cakravartin. Up to the level of male and female humans, the superiority of one class of beings over another is associated with "use" and "service." Thence onward, it seems to be assessed in soteriological terms and associated with "obeisance" paid by one class to another.

Thus, among males, a layman—even if he be a Cakravartin—bows in quintuplicate veneration before a novice who may be just a day old in monkhood. Among monks, the beginners in perfection do not enjoy the high status of the adepts (who have realized nirvana). The adepts too are divided into Sāvakas *(arahans)* and Buddhas, there being an infinite gap between these two classes. Also among the Buddhas, the highest category of beings, there are two ranks: that of an individualist Buddha, which is lower and is surpassed by that of an all-knowing Buddha (such as Gautama).

At the crest of the pyramid is the all-knowing or universal Buddha, the like of whom—concludes Buddhaghosa—is not found even in the world of gods. Buddhaghosa is, presumably, giving us a very ancient system of values, a system that does not seem to have changed much since the fifth century.[18] It could, therefore, serve us even today as an ideological background to the study of contemporary Buddhist experience. And I shall use it here as such.

The Institutional Presence of Buddhism (The Role of the Sangha)

Buddhaghosa is not exaggerating when he says that even a king would bend down in veneration before a novice who is hardly a day old in monkhood. This is a normal occurrence in a Buddhist society, though the non-Buddhist Western press thought it sensational that a Sri Lankan prime minister, on a visit to the London Vihāra some years ago, should have crouched in reverence before an Englishman—who was, of course, a monk.[19]

The contrary would be unusual. No monks bow before a secular authority, this being an ancient Buddhist tradition, interrupted, if at all, only by a short-lived and reluctant concession to the emperor cult in China.

The practice goes back to the origins of Buddhism. Recluses who turned their back on the world—and they came mostly from the royal caste—were looked up to by their princely kinfolk. The latter provided them with the basic needs of subsistence and thus maintained them as a "religious value" and an "object of obeisance." This relationship is still preserved in Buddhist cultures. The sangha depends on the laity for material subsistence, and the laity depends on the sangha for spiritual nourishment.

The ability to offer *dhamma,* one of the three preeminent values in Buddhism, gives the monk a superior status over the laity, who can offer only gifts of a material nature. Besides, the renunciation of the world is considered a higher value than a householder's immersion in secular affairs, as Buddhaghosa's scheme suggests.

This creates an understandable tension between the *spiritual* mission of the sangha and the *secular* demands incidental to it.[20] This tension is at its optimum when monastic "participation" in the world is on a *moral* plane; for that would not compromise the integrity of monastic "renunciation" and the dignity that accrues from it. But this is possible only in the ideal Buddhist state, which institutionalizes the mutual dependence that always exists between the sangha and the laity—that is to say, the lay secular authority of the state is legitimized by monastic sanction and, conversely, the moral authority of the monks is legally acknowledged by the state.

Although it is true that this equilibrium was not always maintained (as evidenced by instances of religious persecutions erupting from royal courts and political intrigues hatched within monastic walls), still the ideal Buddhist state is claimed to have appeared more than once since Asoka initiated it, in many a Buddhist country in the world.

It is also on record that whenever a whole nation was converted to Buddhism, it was often a peaceful performance effected under royal patronage.[21] It is equally on record that in many a country so converted to Buddhism, Christian colonizers displaced the monks from a status that tradition had conceded to them. One can therefore understand the Buddhist resurgence that inevitably accompanied decolonization movements, and the participation of the sangha in them.

Thus, since independence, Burmese and Sri Lankan monks have been clamoring for a Buddhist state where they could truly participate in the affairs of the nation while retaining their spiritual status. For many could renounce the world to serve it, if only the world would serve those who renounce it.

The ideal is difficult to achieve and other solutions are seen to have been sought in the history of Buddhism. According to some political historians, the Vietnamese, with their concept of the emperor-monk, have dismissed the antinomy that Chinese Buddhists saw between *nhap the* (participation) and *xuat the* (abstention).[22] But it was left for Tibet to provide history with the most telling example of theocracy. Even there, however, the purely spiritual role of the Panchen Lama, as opposed to the Dalai Lama's double jurisdiction, seems to be a significant concession to the original dialectic.

Formerly, education was the field in which monks found a point of insertion into secular reality. It was the locus of their moral participation in the world. Not now, however. The need to look for other fields of social involvement is felt in many countries. If reports are true, Thai monasticism is about to find another alternative: hundreds of monks are said to have already passed through government-sponsored training courses in community development.[23]

Sri Lanka seems to have found the most ingenious solution. If Gananath Obeysekere's interpretation is right,[24] Sinhala Buddhism has created (or discovered), in the person of the great Buddhist revivalist Anagarika Dharmapala, a new religious symbol. It represents a via media between a lay person's total immersion in mundane affairs and a monk's complete withdrawal. Dharmapala was a celibate apostle. His was a renunciation blended with direct socio-political involvement. Associated with his name, the term *Anagārika*, formerly a synonym for a monk, has now acquired this new connotation. The suggestion to make the Anagārika state a permanent institution has not been wanting since then.[25]

And now, by way of an appendix to the above, I might add here that the Buddhist institution, besides being preponderantly monastic, is also an *all-male* world. Women are mostly at the receiving end. The order of nuns, the *bhik-khuni-sangha,* is now extinct.[26]

On the other hand, the absence of full feminine participation is not peculiar only to contemporary Buddhism. There is scarcely any institutional religion that does not suffer from it. Further, it should be borne in mind that the Buddha was perhaps the first to found a cenobitic institution for women. In all probability he did this against the religious currents of the time, as can be gleaned from the Vinaya text that describes the founding of the *bhikkhuni-sangha.*[27] In instituting the order of nuns, the Buddha is there made to appear as yielding to pressure from Ananda and Maha-pajapati and as regretting the step later. The rules laid down for the nuns (ibid.) reflect the theory of male superiority, a theory that is explicit in Buddhaghosa's scale of values.

Richard Gombrich noted, of Sinhala Buddhism, ''its general lack of feminine elements,'' where doctrinal formulations and religious symbols are concerned.[28] It should not surprise us if this is true also of other Theravada cultures.

The Religious Presence of Buddhism (The Cult of the Buddha)

The temple, the focal point of religious life in a Buddhist village, is oftener than not an architectural embodiment of the three supreme values: the Buddha, the *dhamma,* and the sangha. The suite of buildings that constitute it can, accordingly, be grouped under three heads:

1. First of all, there is a preaching hall where the *dhamma* is proclaimed and the people instructed.

2. Secondly, there is the monastery proper—that is, the residential quarters of the monks, where it is normal for the laity to meet the sangha, pay their respects to them, and offer them *dāna*—that is, gifts of food and other requisites. Certain monasteries have also a chapter room, usually a separate building, reserved for the performance of capitular acts or *vinaya karma.* It is through these communal rites that the Buddhist monastic community expresses and renews its own essential character. But for them, the sangha would not continue to exist as an institutional unit, as the founder himself had warned (D, II, 76f.).

3. Last but not least is the Buddha cultus, focused on three types of objects: (a) *sārīrika-dhātu,* bodily relics of the Buddha, (b) *pāribhogika,* objects used by the Buddha, and (c) *uddesika,* objects that are reminiscent of him.[29] These three kinds of objects are normally made available for veneration.

a. Thus, for instance, most temples have a stūpa believed to contain the bodily relics of the Buddha. This tall white dome, which dominates the landscape, is the most sacred object of worship, for it entails a quasi-physical presence of the Buddha. There are also small reliquaries, which are carried in procession. The more solemn *pirit* ceremonies (see below) are almost always preceded by the installation of the relics in the *pirit* pavilion, which, consequently, acquires a sacral character.

b. Not every temple can claim to possess *paribhogika* relics, such as the bowl or the robes of the Buddha. But there is no temple without a bodhi tree which, if it has sprouted from a sapling of the original tree under which the Buddha attained enlightenment, would be tantamount to a *paribhogika* object. An altar is built before it for devotees to make their offerings.

c. Finally, there is, invariably, a shrine room containing *uddesika* objects, such as statues or painted images of the Buddha, with provision made for the offering of flowers, food, and incense, and for the lighting of lamps.

In the temple, therefore, the cult of Buddha prevails over that of the sangha. Even the monks worship the Buddha under the three forms mentioned above. All worship, in other words, culminates in the worship of the Buddha. The Vesak, the most solemn feast in the Buddhist liturgical calendar,[30] is marked by Buddhocentricity, especially in Sri Lanka. Streets are crowded with gigantic figures of the Buddha, gorgeously illuminated pandals depicting episodes from his life, and improvised pavilions where the Buddha event is dramatized.

The erection of colossal Buddha statues has been another time-honored practice in Buddhist cultures. It seems to reflect the belief that the Buddha's spiritual stature surpasses all human dimensions. Paradoxically, it might have been this same belief that prompted early Buddhists to avoid graven images, and resort instead to symbols like the wheel, the footprint, the stupa, the bodhi tree, and so forth, to represent the Buddha.

The seventh international conference of the World Fellowship of Buddhists held in Sarnath, India, in 1964, declared itself opposed to the irrelevant use of the Buddha image in the mass media. Loud cries of protests were raised against Japan's issuing a Buddha postage stamp. Similar protests by Buddhists stopped India from issuing a postage stamp carrying a Buddha figure.[31] Further, Buddhists in Sri Lanka and Burma abhor the very idea of any human being impersonating the Buddha in a film.

This attitude, too, is rooted in the profound conviction that the founder of Buddhism is over and beyond even the divine spheres of existence. "He finds no equal even in the world of gods," Buddhaghosa has said. In fact, we may safely say that this belief in the supracosmic nature of the Buddha stands out as the common denominator of all Buddhist cultures.

Gautama, let us recall, was born and bred in a culture that accepted the existence of cosmic powers or devas. Far from denying this belief, he made use of it as a cultural idiom to express his doctrine. By placing nirvana above and outside the sphere of gods, he proclaimed its supracosmic transcendence in a language that his contemporaries could not misunderstand. It is this same supracosmic transcendence that the Buddhist masses ascribe to Buddha.

True to the spirit of the Buddha, his missionaries too found themselves at home in cultures that accepted the world of spirits and gods. Folk beliefs were a help rather than a hindrance for the spread of Buddhism. Today, therefore, pre-Buddhist rituals for propitiating gods, exorcising demons, and communing with spirits are found side by side with the authentic Buddhist forms of worship described above. The integration of the two cultic systems is best illustrated by intermediary rituals like the *pirit* ceremony. It is a Buddhist rite of exorcism usually performed by the sangha with the chanting of the Buddha-word. This rite is regarded as the last resort against evil spirits, especially when folk exorcism has failed.

In the view of anthropologists like Ames, the Buddhists themselves do not confuse the two cultic systems; they carefully distinguish between magical practices and Buddhist worship. The former, geared as they are to the acquisition of temporal favors, amount to a profane or a secular system *(laukika),* whereas the latter is oriented toward otherworldly and religious goals *(lok'uttara).*[32] Spiro too sees them as two distinct systems, but he regards them both as religious, with Buddhism, of course, retaining its inalienable primacy.[33]

According to Obeysekere, the two cults have been integrated into one system. The Buddha, in his view, occupies the presidential position in a hierarchically constituted folk pantheon.[34] This interpretation squares with Buddhaghosa's worldview with the Buddha as the peak of the pyramid.

Pursuit of Nirvana

As indicated before, Buddhist phenomenology points to nirvana as the ultimate *goal.* The Buddhist religion discussed above, on the other hand, seems to regard the Buddha as the highest *value.* Which, then, takes pride of place in contemporary Buddhism: the pursuit of nirvana or the cult of Buddha? Is there a conflict between doctrine and practice?

I have anticipated my answer by emphasizing the words "goal" and "value." But before coming to it, we might do well to look for other possible solutions.

We could, for example, take refuge in Gombrich's distinction between the *cognitive* and *affective* levels[35] to explain away this apparent discrepancy. Cognitively, nirvana is taken as the highest reality attained by a purely human Buddha; in the affective plane, however, it yields place to a suprahuman Buddha.

Or we might see them as two stages of development rather than as two levels of belief. Thus, taking Dr. Snellgrove's suggestion, we could say that the ultimacy of nirvana is expressive of a *philosophy,* whereas the Buddha cult (together with the legends about his birth, the conquest of Mara, enlightenment, etc.) points to a *theology* that envisages the Buddha event as a cosmic happening planned eons earlier and fulfilled at a preestablished moment. The shift of accent from the ideal of nirvana to the ideal of Buddhahood would then be the development of a philosophy into a theology.[36]

The medieval scholiast Acariya Dhammapala sees it in a different perspective when he says that "in this phenomenal existence *(sattesu samkhāresu),* the Nirvanic experience *(paññā)* has no equal other than the Buddha himself."[37] The ultimacy of nirvana is implicitly acknowledged here, whereas its attainment *(paññā)* and he who had supremely attained it *(Buddha)* are placed on a par as twin values in this samsaric existence. Nirvana, in other words, is beyond phenomena and beyond the Buddha himself, as Zen masters would also insist today.

Complementary to this is his other observation, that the Buddha is not only an Arahan who has realized nirvana through gnosis *(paññā)* but also the supreme lord of the universe *(Bhagavan)* who lingers in samsara out of *karuṇā,* compassion for the multitudes.[38] These two epithets occur in the oldest and the commonest doxology of Buddhists: *namo tassa Bhagavato Arahato Samma-sambuddhassa.* Their interpretation as given above, however, is a Mahayanic insight, which reconciles the ultimacy of nirvana with the supremacy of the Buddha.

Taking this as a clue, I now propose what I think to be the most plausible answer to the question posed above. I begin with two statements. First, it would be misleading to regard the doctrinal presentation in the first part of this chapter to be "authentic Buddhism" as opposed to the "popular Buddhism" of the second part. The distinction is simply not valid. Secondly, it is attested by history that nirvana and nothing else has always been the ultimate ideal in Buddhism.

What I concede is that this ideal by nature, inconceivable and undefinable, is affirmed and conveyed in history by means of three complementary idioms: the doctrinal, the institutional, and the religious.

It is the *doctrinal presentation,* or *dhamma* pure and simple, that I dealt with first. It is found in texts, and it is taught in monasteries, even today. It is written about also in the West.

The sangha, on the other hand, is the *institutional symbol* of the Arahan ideal. All worship and reverence accorded them and the devotion with which they are maintained are a social acknowledgment of the supremacy of renunciation or the pursuit of nirvana.

Finally, there is the *religious idiom* of the Buddha cult. The transcendent Buddha, the object of this cult, is the symbol most expressive of the supra-cosmic goal of nirvana and, pedagogically, the most effective. In him the ideal of nirvana reveals itself as a realized goal rather than as a receding horizon.

THE SALVIFIC EXPERIENCE

The Historical Setting

If anything is known today of the enlightenment of Gautama and the path that led him to it, it is because a good part of what he did and taught has been woven into a "string of sayings" *(sutta)* and a "formula of life" *(vinaya)* and is conserved by the sangha, which not only shared that same vision but elaborated it into a systematic phenomenology *(abhidhamma)*. It is through these three canonical sources *(vinaya, sutta,* and *abhidhamma),* that one can glimpse into the initial Buddhist experience.

I am not concerned here with the abhidhammic formulation of this experience. What interests me now is the historical mood of the time when this experience was born. As a matter of fact, historians have tried to reclaim it from the data available in the *vinaya* and the *sutta*. The picture they draw of the period in question resembles so much our own times that the modern outburst of interest in the Buddha's message to his contemporaries becomes understandable, and the universality of his insights is brought into sharper focus.[39]

His era, we are told, was one of *violence*. The Magadha feudal kings were waging wars of elimination against neighboring tribes—a *military policy* that continued up to the time of Asoka, who was himself guilty of it. Moreover, the discovery of bronze and iron had already given rise to more sophisticated and more frequent slaughter of humans and beasts. As for animal slaughter, it was in vogue not only among the peasants, but more so in religious circles, which advocated sacrificial rituals as a means of salvation (karma-mārga).

A "protest movement" seems to have sprung up, as could be expected, from among the Ksatriyas—that is, the nobles and in particular the middle-class warriors. This movement took many guises. For instance, there was the *Aranyaka* movement (one would not quite call it "hippy-ism"!). Its protagonists opted for the freedom of the forest *(aranya)* and spurned the fettered security of economic well-being. Discontented also with Brahmanic activisim and liturgism *(karma-mārga),* they craved for a more personal religious experience: the so-called *jñāna mārga,* the way of gnosis.

Besides, there was also an *ahimsā* or peace movement of which Jainism turned out to be the most articulate form. It was a protest against violence indulged in by both the religious and the secular establishments.

Add to this the fact that this kind of contestation against the established norms of religion and state was accompanied by a variety of new theories about the world and its purpose! The Brahmajala Sutta of the Digha Nikaya, describing this *doctrinal confusion,* counts sixty-two such theories or ditthi as they were called. They seem to have represented at least six major trends, all of which the Buddha was to reject, later, as unsatisfactory.

This, then, was the world where the Buddha "woke up," not at once but in stages, as we are just about to see.

The Awakening

Gautama was born and bred in the "ghetto" of the ruling class, cushioned against life's delusions and lulled to security by princely comfort. His first encounter with "reality" was occasioned by the sight of a sick man, an old man, a dead man, and a mendicant—all this while on an excursion. Thus, it was when he *stepped out of his own little world* that he woke up to the true nature of life: sickness, old age, and death; and, shocked into a healthy insecurity, he perceived at once that the mendicant was the symbol of authentic living.

It is not farfetched to think that this was his first glimpse into what he would later formulate as the First Noble Truth, which says that we should not take life for granted but see its true nature as *dukkha* (empty, meaningless, and culminating in death and decay). It was this conviction that spurred him to take the next obvious step: the great renunciation *(mahā-abhinikkhamana)*.

At first he blundered into the beaten track, taking to asceticism like most young men of his day. But it brought no release from *dukkha.* Then he found himself treading the path of gnosis. Given the high degree of moral purity he had acquired by then *(sīla,* in Buddhist terminology), it was not difficult for him to achieve mental one-pointedness *(samādhi),* which eventually resulted in *paññā,* the liberating experience of the truth. This transphenomenal realization is known also as *bodhi.* Hence the epithet "Buddha": he who has been awakened to the ultimate truth.

The next questions was: Was it wise to share this ineffable experience with others? After all, was not the society of his time infested with conflicting theories of salvation? Besides, how many would be ready to take the plunge as he did? The fact, however, is that he opted to preach this ancient path, which after all, he did not invent, but only discovered as the eternal *dharma* (S,I,140).

In the course of his search for the truth and the final discovery of it, he gained many insights, among which was the axiom that true freedom implies absolute nonaddiction *(upekkhā).* Many of his contemporaries ran away from one addiction only to roll into another! For instance, self-torture *(atta-kilamatha)* was as much an egoistic craving as what it reacted against: self-indulgence and torture of others. Religion too could be a selfish obsession, what he called *sīlabbata-parāmāsa*—that is, addiction to rites and rituals.

Intellectualism seemed also an escape from reality. Like the man who is pierced with an arrow but refuses to remove it until he is intellectually satisfied with the information available about the man who shot it (M,II,216), most of his contemporaries were distracted from the existential demands of salvation by theories that were soteriologically inconsequential. The Buddha pointed out how these debates about the world, soul and survival led to endless quarrels and intellectual confusion; he preferred to set them aside altogether (Ud. 66–67; M,I,426). Dogmatism, being itself an addiction, was not conducive to salvation.

Thus the Buddha's path remained one of total nonaddiction. This can be enunciated in a double formula: the cause of *dukkha* is *taṇhā* or *upādāna*—that is, addiction to one of the facets of life (the Second Noble Truth); freedom from every addiction is true freedom from *dukkha* (the Third Noble Truth).

The Middle Course

The Fourth Noble Truth indicates the exact *method* of attaining this freedom from addictions. It is called the middle course *(majjhima-paṭipadā)* precisely because it consists of avoiding extremes in life and maintaining a balanced position in:

1. *views* and *aspirations* (see *samādhi* below)
2. *words, deeds,* and *mode of making a living* (see *sīla* below)
3. *effort, recollection,* and *meditation* (see *paññā* below).

These eight steps can be regrouped to bring out in relief the three moments of the path:

1. *samādhi,* concentration
2. *sīla,* moral behavior
3. *paññā,* gnosis or salvific insight.

Hence it follows that Buddhism is not an extreme form of gnosticism, and also that Buddhist gnosis cannot be reduced to quietism and passivity, for it has a firm ethical basis: *sīla.* The minimum morality required of a Buddhist is expressed negatively in the fivefold ethical practice *(pañca-sīla)*—namely, abstention from harming life, from taking what is not due to one, from the wrong use of the senses, from wrong speech, and from intoxicants that might deaden one's mind. The ethical code of the Eightfold Path, on the other hand, presents a more positive program for those keen on traversing the path up to the heights it promises. For the mastery of the senses implied in *sīla* here, in the context of the path, is an absolute prerequisite for the "gathering of the mind" *(samādhi).*

The mind is gathered when it is focused on a definite point. The Buddhist tradition knows about forty such points of concentration *(kammaṭṭhanas)*. One is advised to select them according to one's temperament. The novice who has a passionate character *(rāga-carita)* would be invited to make his meditation on the ten *asubhas* or revulsive aspects of the human body; a choleric temperament *(dosa-carita)* would profit more from *mettā-bhāvanā* or contemplation of the infinite sphere of altruistic love.[40] And so on, with the other characters.

The danger with *samadhi* is that it can become an end in itself. The trance, vision, levitation, and other psychic powers that may accompany it can be a source of undesirable self-satisfaction and self-aggrandisement. Thus the very purpose of the Middle Course could be defeated. In other words, *samadhi* is not an end, but only a means, which can easily turn into an obstacle. It can enslave rather than liberate the meditator.

The ultimate Buddhist experience, generally referred to as "realization of Nirvana," is *paññā,* which alone releases one from addictions and consequently from *dukkha.* No one has described this experience for us, because it is ineffable. All that we hear is the saint's exclamation that he or she has reached the summit so that there is nothing more to be achieved and that he or she would not any more be entangled in this vale of tears.[41]

The Spirit of Discernment

Nagarjuna, a brilliant exponent of Buddhism who lived toward the beginning of the Christian era, developed the simple mechanics of the middle course into an elaborate system of dialectics—which came to be known as the Madhyamaka philosophy. Every position according to him is an extreme, for it evokes a corresponding opposition, which is no less an extreme. The middle course consists in transcending all such duality. He refused to concede that this was itself a position or a theory.

The truth about the middle course can also be expressed in a much simpler, though not, for that matter, less profound, manner. We have seen the historical context in which it was first formulated. The secular and religious establishments, with their callous disregard for life and disproportionate concern for ritualistic precision, evoked a reaction in which the "protestors" too lost their bearing amid contradictory theories of salvation and unwholesome excesses in the practice of *sīla* and *samādhi*.

The Buddha's advice was that his followers should *discern* for themselves what is right and wrong, rather than allow themselves to be swayed by every theory and tradition in vogue.[42] Thus in the practice of *sīla* and *samādhi* too one was expected to exercise this same *spirit of discernment* so that every form of extravagance, which would be an addiction, might be carefully avoided.

The controversy about asceticism is a case in point. From the point of view of the middle course, the Jains seemed immoderate in their practice of renunciation:

> The Jains, viewing from their standpoint, accused the Buddhists of a luxurious living. That the life of the Buddhist Sangha so appeared in the eyes of the people is attested by a story recorded in the Pali *Vinaya* itself. The parents of a boy named Upali discuss between them as to what vocational course should they choose for their son which would conduce to his future happiness. They think that if he learns writing *(lekhā)* his fingers would be pained, if calculation *(ganana)* his breasts, and in case of money exchange *(rūpa)* his eyes; finally they decide to send him to the Buddhist Order where, it is their impression, the monks live happily and comfortably.[43]

Even today, the relaxed atmosphere that pervades most Buddhist monasteries might scandalize Western observers who expect to see an extraordinary degree of asceticism in them.[44] Asceticism, no doubt, is a source of prestige to the sangha now as it was in the time of the Buddha. This could very well have been one of the motives that drove Devadatta the Schismatic to press for the incorporation of *dhutangas* (certain severe forms of austerity) in the *vinaya*. The Buddha, for his part, did not object to such practices. What he refused to do, even at the risk of schism, was to make them obligatory on the sangha. In other words, he left the whole matter to individual *discernment*.[45]

5

The Spirituality of the Buddhist Monk

MONASTICISM IN A BUDDHIST CONTEXT

In the mainstream of Buddhism, particularly in the orthodox Theravada tradition prevalent in Sri Lanka, a Buddhist society can hardly be conceived to exist without a monastic nucleus to animate and sustain it. *Monastic life constitutes the "institutional center" as well as the "spiritual apex" of a Buddhist community.*

This general observation deserves more comment before I go further. For Sri Lankan monasticism or the spirituality it embodies cannot be discussed unless the whole phenomenon of monastic life is first situated within the general context of Buddhism. Hence, in the following paragraphs of a prefatory nature I shall (1) try to understand monasticism in relation to the origins of Buddhism; then (2) I shall place it within the *religious framework;* and finally (3) I shall study it in terms of *Buddhist soteriology.*

Monastic Origins of Buddhism

If Buddhism is essentially a monastic religion, it is precisely because it had a *monastic origin.* If monasticism is the "seed" from which Buddhism arose, is there any wonder that monasticism is also the "fruit" that Buddhism invariably produces wherever it thrives? The seed of Buddhism was first sown when Gautama, an Indian prince of the sixth century B.C., became a *samana*—that is, a recluse who rejected not only the secular society of his day but also institutional religion, which was infected by Brahmanic clericalism. This "samanic movement" was antiworld and antisacerdotal in character. It was a wild and primitive form of monasticism with all its ambiguities. The authentic religious experience it sought, however, had a distinctly "gnostic" flavor.

Originally written as a study paper in preparation for the Third Asian Monks' Congress, in Kandy, Sri Lanka, 1980. Published in *Inter Fratres* (Fabriano), 27 (1977) 121–32.

Gautama was not the originator of this renewal movement, for it had already gathered momentum when he entered the scene. He was himself shaped by it but was never carried away by its excesses. He domesticated it, corrected it, and remolded it. In fact, he left his own imprint on it when he instituted his own samanic community! It was as a *samana* that he searched for the saving truth *(dhamma)* and was finally "awakened" to it. Hence, the epithet *Buddha,* which means the "awakened one." It was precisely in the context of contemporaneous *samanism*—that is, in a clearly monastic idiom—that he lived this experience personally, formulated it doctrinally, and embodied it institutionally. The samanic groups that rallied around him to share this experience and follow his Eightfold Path gradually evolved into cenobitic communes *(avasas)* governed by a monastic discipline *(vinaya)*. It is these communes that later came to be called a sangha—the technical term for a monastic community even today.

Monasticism within the Religious Framework of Buddhism

This brings me to the second step of my analysis: the monk as a *religious symbol*. In describing the monastic origin of Buddhism, I explained above the three pivotal points of reference in the religious framework of Buddhism: the Buddha, the dhamma, and the sangha. These three, together, are known as the "triple gem" *(tri-ratana),* for they are the three supreme values and ideal norms that guide the religious behavior of Buddhists. In fact, one becomes a Buddhist officially when one accepts them as one's sole "refuge." The ritual formula of the "triple refuge" *(tri-sarana)* runs as follows:

> I take the Buddha as my (sole) refuge.
> I take the dhamma as my (sole) refuge.
> I take the sangha as my (sole) refuge.

They also figure among the accepted themes of meditation. And what is even more significant, they are the three ultimate objects of worship and veneration available to a Buddhist. Thus the monastic institution is one of the three principal elements in the religious framework of Buddhism. Going further into the question, we could ask what place the sangha occupies *within* the trinity of gems.

In the ritual formula given above, the sangha is allotted the third place. This is significant. For the dhamma is the eternal, unchanging truth. It remains, whether a Buddha discovers it or not. But if a Buddha were not to appear on earth and discover it, no sangha would be established. This is the accepted belief. In the order of excellence, therefore, the monastic community has a subordinate place within the trinity.

And yet, from the point of view of the religious system, the sangha remains the most tangible and accessible of the three. After all, the Buddha is reached by the devotee only in the form of relics and material images, for he is believed to have attained a metacosmic dimension *(parinirvana)* utterly incomprehensible to the human mind. The dhamma, too, is something to be grasped through insight *(vipassanā)* and internalized through the spiritual path *(magga)*. Not so the sangha. It is essentially a visible, human institution immediately perceived by human beings and serving them as a quasi-sacramental pointer to a meta-cosmic goal (nirvana) and to a corresponding state of perfection *(arahatta)*, which is the raison d'être of any monastic community.

Moreover, it is the sangha that keeps the knowledge of the dhamma and the memory of the Buddha alive in the hearts of the people. Thus among the three sources of spiritual refuge, the monastic institution acts as the door to the other two. The sangha, in other words, is the most conspicuous and the most reassuring of the three religious symbols engaging the attention of practicing Buddhists.

Monasticism in the Context of Buddhist Soteriology

The third and final consideration I have to make in this introductory part is so vital for the understanding of Buddhist monasticism that I shall have to continue the discussion in the second half of this chapter. The point I have to make here is simply that *the monastic life is an inherent feature of Buddhist soteriology and almost a constitutive dimension of Buddhist spirituality.*

The Buddhist path to perfection is basically gnostic and admits of various degrees of excellence. A clear distinction is made between the noble one *(ariya-puggala)*, who is on the higher rung of the spiritual ladder, and the commoner *(puthujjana)* who has hardly begun the ascent.

But this should not lend support to the popular misconception that the Buddha equated the saint with the monk or the sinner with the lay person. On the contrary, the scriptures *(tri-pitaka)* make clear references to lay men and women who have attained the state of *arahatta*. Similarly, mention is made of monks who were not worthy of their sublime calling. As a matter of fact, more than one eminent scholar has maintained that, at the beginning, the term sangha was used to designate, not just the monastic institution as such, but more generally, the community of noble ones, be they monastics or lay persons. What was meant seems to have been a veritable *communio sanctorum,* implying an invisible bond among the saints *(arahans)*, whoever and wherever they were. Yet the fact remains that it was the monks who publicly professed to traverse the Buddha's path. Thus the "monks of the four quarters"—that is, all the monks wherever they were—were referred to as sangha. It was still later that each *āvāsa* or cenobium came to be recognized by that name. Symbolically, at least, each monastic community appeared to be the ideal society, if not of saints, at least of those striving to be saints by public profession.

It is this society of spiritual elite that is institutionally known as sangha to this day. It is natural, therefore, that the lay man *(upāsaka)* and the lay woman *(upāsikā)* are relegated to a less privileged status. Theoretically they too can reach the highest point of perfection, but in practice the encumbrances of secular life would not allow them to be as free as the monk. It is monastic life that really sets a person free for the pursuit of higher things.

Hence, from the early times, Buddhist spirituality had a *monastic thrust*—a fact I shall proceed to spell out in greater detail in the next section of this chapter.

THE MONASTIC THRUST OF BUDDHIST SPIRITUALITY

Buddhist spirituality consists in realizing the four Noble Truths—namely, that:

1. nothing can satisfy human beings, and therefore everything frustrates them—that is, causes suffering *(dukkha);*
2. the cause of this frustration is innate human thirst *(taṇhā)* or inordinate desire for things that cannot satisfy them;
3. it is by removing this cause of frustration that one can attain nirvana, or interior freedom and peace;
4. the only way to remove *taṇhā* and attain *nirvana* is the Eightfold Path (see below).

What is advocated here is not a theoretical knowledge but a self-transforming internalization of these truths. This spiritual vision is variously called insight *(vipassanā),* wisdom *(paññā),* gnosis *(ñāṇa),* or awakening *(bodhi).* Note that the path is included in the vision, for it is one of the four truths to be realized. On the other hand, the aim of the path precisely is this spiritual vision! Thus the vision and the path are mutually inclusive. They constitute one spiritual event.

The path is called "eightfold" because it demands the proper ordering of one's life in eight areas of human experience. In keeping with the ancient Buddhist tradition, I list these eight areas under three heads: *sīla, samādhi,* and *paññā,* which, in Christian terminology, would connote the moral, ascetical, and mystical dimensions, respectively. Let us take care, however, not to read into these terms any theistic concept such as "grace" or a "personal God," which are both foreign to Buddhist spirituality. With this premise made, the Eightfold Path can be presented schematically as follows:

A. *sīla:* moral purity

    3. *sammā-vāca:* (morally) correct use of speech

    4. *sammā-kammanta:* (morally) correct behavior

    5. *sammā-ājīva:* (morally) correct means of earning a living

B. *samādhi:* ascesis and mental discipline

    6. *sammā-vāyāma:* ascetically conducive use of one's energy

    7. *sammā-sati:* training in mindfulness (introspection)

    8. *sammā-samādhi:* concentration or gathering of the mind

C. *paññā:* gnosis or salvific insight or (nontheistic) mystical knowledge

    1. *sammā-diṭṭhi:* a salvific vision of reality

    2. *sammā-samkappa:* organization of thought conducive to liberation.

This path is open to anyone who dares to traverse it. But the current practice in Sri Lanka seems to indicate that the further one travels along this path, the closer one gets to the *monastic ideal.* Let me illustrate this immediately.

Sīla: *The Moral Dimension of the Path*

The foundation of Buddhist spirituality is moral purity or *sīla* (nos. 3, 4, and 5 of the path). Though it is spelled out in "positive" terms in the Buddha's discourses, its most common formulation is a negative one—namely, *abstention* from the following five evils:

1. harming or killing living creatures
2. stealing
3. lying
4. misuse of the senses, especially sex
5. intoxicating the mind with drinks and drugs.

This is known as the fivefold morality *(pañca-sīla)* and is the *minimum required of a lay person.*

Contrast this with the tenfold morality *(dasa-sīla),* the *minimum required of a monk,* which besides changing the fourth precept into a vow of celibacy, includes five more abstentions—namely:

6. abstention from taking meals after midday
7. shunning all public entertainments
8. avoiding garlands, ornaments, and perfumes
9. refraining from sitting or sleeping in comfortable furniture
10. refusing to accept money.

The practice of this higher morality is not easy for the laity. And yet it is indispensable for one traversing the path. Periodically, therefore, and especially on holy days *(poya),* a lay person would go to the temple dressed in a white garment (a symbol of purity) and spend the day and perhaps the night too in the temple compound, trying to observe the ten precepts at least for that brief period of time. This is only a token effort—a token of a more total renunciation that the person desires but cannot achieve. The fact that the majority of the laity find it easier to spend these holy moments in the meditative atmosphere of the temple rather than at home, shows that every step of the Eightfold Path is a step away from the mundane life of the householder.

This is even more cogently demonstrated by the fact that a *new institution of lay celibates* has appeared in the Buddhist community. The donning of a yellow robe and also, in the case of women, the shaving of the head, have given this new institution an identity of its own. This way, the practice of the ten precepts is made possible for a lay person on a more or less permanent basis. The term *anagārika,* formerly a synonym for a *bhikkhu* (monk), is now exclusively used for a lay man who has opted for this intermediary state. His feminine counterpart is known as *dasa-sil-mav* (the reverend mother of the tenfold morality). Some of these women celibates live in communes *(upasikārāma),* thus filling the vacuum left by the order of nuns *(bhikkuni-sangha)* extinct since the Middle Ages.

This institution leaves the lay person on the threshold of monastic life. To be a monk, one has to go even further. Over and above the ten precepts, the monk agrees to follow the *pātimokkha*, a set of 227 rules that guide him along the path. This is recited in chapter on specific days to enable the monks to recall their rule, acknowledge transgressions, and accept censures. The *pātimokkha* is a negative formulation of a positive and descriptive statement of monastic spirituality, technically called the *vinaya* (monastic discipline).

It is not beside the point to note here that the *vinaya* or monastic rule constitutes the first part of the Buddhist Bible *(tripitaka)*, though the discourses of the Buddha *(sutta)*, which form the second part, originated earlier than the *vinaya*. It was thanks to a disciplined monastic community that the discourses were recited regularly, memorized, and compiled in a definite order for the sake of posterity. The binomial "Bible-church" or "scripture-tradition" in Christianity may serve as a useful analogy to understand the Buddhist parallel dhamma-*vinaya*, often used in sacred literature. For the word of the Buddha was accepted, formulated, and transmitted by the monastic community. The *vinaya* (i.e., the *regula*) was the *praxis* that kept the *theory* (dhamma) alive throughout succeeding generations.

Samādhi: *The Ascetical Dimension of the Path*

Thus the purpose of the *vinaya* is not merely to understand the dhamma but even more especially to practice it. It speaks of the spiritual or ascetical training required of anyone who wants to reach the heights that the path promises—a training that is essentially monastic. For moral purity *(sīla)* must go hand in hand with mental discipline (samādhi), which is the second dimension of the path.

Samādhi, which means "gathering of the mind," also called *samatha* or stilling of the mind, is an ascetical practice that requires the guidance of a master. In most monasteries the abbot who receives the novice *(sāmaṇera)* is also the trainer. It is not infrequent for him to be helped by other senior monks. The task is a delicate one. The master usually must be a shrewd psychologist who can study and understand the character of each novice. Even meditation themes *(kammaṭṭhāna)* have to be allotted to each trainee according to his psychological disposition. This is done in accordance with the characterology that has been developed from ancient times. The traditional method of personal guidance has not been replaced even in modernized seminaries such as the Maharagama Bhikkhu Training Center. *A monk has to be formed by another monk.*

Paññā: *The Mystical Dimension of the Path*

The climactic result of this mental development *(bhāvanā)* is mystical insight *(vipassanā)* or gnosis *(paññā)*, which is accompanied by the final liberation of the mind from "greed, hate, and delusion" *(lobha-dosa-moha)* or the complete elimination of *taṇhā*, which causes suffering. This is what is referred to normally as nirvana. The wholeness and wholesomeness thus realized is what Buddhists call *arahatta*, the state of the perfect human being. This is the aim of the path and is the third and final dimension toward which *sīla* (moral purity) and *samādhi* (mental discipline) are oriented.

It should be evident from the above that, at least in the Theravada tradition of Buddhism, the path of Buddha demands a very high degree of renunciation and that the *vinaya* or monastic code provides the institutional setting within which such a renunciation is possible. The worldly structure that is renounced primarily is family life. Marriage is never a salvific experience according to the orthodox tradition. Celibacy, on the contrary, is the conditio sine qua non for ultimate human emancipation. It is understood, therefore, that it is the monastic institution, and no other, that provides *this* spiritual condition in a supereminent way.

THE MISSIONARY CHARACTER OF BUDDHIST MONASTICISM

What I have described so far may seem, at first sight, to be a self-enclosing spirituality. This is far from the truth. In fact, Buddhist monasticism *(pabbajja)* distinguishes itself from its Hindu equivalent *(saṃnyāsa)* precisely by its missionary orientation. This missionary orientation is traced back to the Buddha himself. The scriptures report that after attaining nirvana, he debated with himself whether he should continue his life of peaceful solitude or go back to the masses to share his discovery. His decision to devote the rest of his life to the preaching of the path of deliverance is believed to be his final decisive victory over *Māra,* the tempter. Thus, the Buddha's six-year search for the saving truth did not end with the acquisition of *paññā* or salvific gnosis, but evolved into forty-five years of *karuṇā* or compassionate involvement with the people. Hence no spiritual treatise dealing with Buddhahood has ever failed to insist on the complementarity of *paññā* and *karuṇā:* "renunciation" of the world in search of an otherwordly *knowledge* and "involvement" with the world through selfless *love* for its people.

The monks who were formed by the Buddha not only participated in the Buddha's missionary efforts during this lifetime, but also accepted their perpetual mission from him when they heard him say sometime before his death: "Monks, go ye . . . and preach this doctrine . . . for the good of the masses." Within the first millennium, the monks traversed the length and breadth of the Asian continent taking the message of the Buddha as far north as Mongolia and to the southern tip of Sri Lanka; as far as Japan to the east and over the western borders of Asia to Alexandria and northern Greece.

To say, therefore, that the religion founded by the Buddha is *essentially monastic* would be incomplete without adding that monasticism as conceived by the Buddha was *essentially missionary.*

This evangelism of the *bhikkhu* is never so clearly marked as in Sri Lankan Buddhism, which has to its credit some of the best known missions in the West. The missionary interest that Sri Lankan monks have taken in Southeast Asian countries goes as far back as the Middle Ages. Already in the fourth century, a group of monks and nuns sailed to China and rectified a discontinuity in the monastic lineage by reordaining Chinese nuns according to the *vinaya.* The very manner in which Buddhism was born and nourished in Sri Lanka seems to have given this evangelistic orientation to a *bhikkhu*'s calling. For the series of events that mark the arrival of Buddhism in this country, its consequent acceptance by the people as their religion and its later development into a stable institution seem to have revolved around the one axis of monasticism.

The first missionaries who brought Buddhism to Sri Lanka in the third century B.C. were all monks. The ancient chronicle *Mahāvaṃsa* makes a significant point where it says that the number of monks who arrived on this occasion was five, which is the minimum required by the *vinaya* for the valid ordination of others into monkhood. What is insinuated here is that when the missionary monks came to preach Buddhism in Sri Lanka, they came prepared to implant the monastic nucleus of Buddhism. Other facts confirm this:

After the king and his subjects became lay subjects *(upasaka, upasika)* by taking the triple refuge *(tri-sarana)* and the *pañca-sīla* or five precepts (see above), the king, accompanied by the monks, immediately set about locating the site for the monastery *(ārāma)* at the Megahavanna Park near the capital city of Anuradhapura. They marked a place each for the chapter room, for the planting of the sacred Bo tree, for the erection of the relic chamber (stūpa), for the refectory and the place for baths. According to the Mahavamsa and the Dipavamsa, which constitute the spiritual diary of our nation recorded for us by the monks themselves, the exact moment when Buddhism was established in the island occurred when the *sīmā* or the ''chapter boundary'' was marked, for the Buddha has clearly said that his monastic institution would not survive if the capitular acts were not regularly performed.

What is suggested there is that *the establishment of Buddhism in a given locality is associated with the establishment of the monastic chapter.* The Pali exegetical tradition, also of monastic origin, makes a further claim that Buddhism is truly implanted in a particular region only with the formation of an *indigenous* sangha. A fifth-century commentary on the *vinaya* expresses this idea through an alleged conversation between the first missionary monk and the newly converted king:

> O Great King, the *sāsana* [religion] is established but its roots are not yet deeply set.
>
> When will the roots be deeply set?
>
> When a child born in Sri Lanka *(Tambapanni-dipa)* of Sri Lankan parents becomes ordained in Sri Lanka, studies the *vinaya* in Sri Lanka, and makes the [capitular] recitation of it in Sri Lanka, then indeed the roots of the Buddhist religion *(sāsana)* are deeply set.

In other words, *Buddhism becomes indigenous only through an indigenous monasticism.* Thus with the subsequent indigenization of the *sangha,* there arose in Anuradhapura what has come to be known in history as "The Great Monastery" or Mahāvihāra. For thirteen centuries it served Sri Lanka and some neighboring lands as a center of learning and a guardian of orthodoxy. From there, Buddhism radiated as a truly *indigenous* religion to other parts of the island. Gradually the whole island of Sri Lanka was clustered with monasteries. Thus even when south Indian invaders forced the monks to abandon Mahavihara, Buddhism continued to be the *focus of (Sinhala) national consciousness,* thanks to the monastic nuclei scattered over the rest of the country.

This is illustrated even more forcefully by the monastic activities of the colonial period, which lasted over four centuries. The spiritual renewal of the eighteenth century, the anti-Christian polemics of the nineteenth century, and finally the twentieth-century agitation for a decolonization of the local culture *all had their inspiration, if not also their origin, in monasteries.* This may surprise a Christian monk. We must concede, however, that the *bhikkhus* were not merely the *missionaries* who brought the dhamma to the island or the pastors who nourish the people with it. They were much more than that. The monks served the ruler and the ruled as their prime *educators* for centuries until Christian missionaries usurped their place after the colonization of the country. They were also the *creators of the Buddhist culture,* which held the people together. Hence they were the *moral guides* of the king and the *prophetic conscience* of the entire Buddhist population. In the light of this self-understanding, the monastic tradition seems to have required of the monk that his "involvement with the people" imply an active spiritual presence in the *politico-social* field. This is what the Venerable Doctor Walpola Rahula has called "the Heritage of the Bhikkhu."

To summarize: Buddhist monasticism has, as its main pastoral concern, the creation of a *socio-cultural milieu* where it can make itself *institutionally available* to those seeking to follow the Buddha's path.

The sheer numerical strength of monks and monasteries in Sri Lanka is a reliable index of the place monasticism occupies in the social and cultural life of the people. The proportion of monks to lay persons is about 1:400 and there seems to be one monastery for every thousand Buddhists. The statistics released by the Department of Cultural Affairs in the sixties show:

> 6,172 temples having 18,670 monks
> 152 hermitages having 548 hermits
> 187 convents with 413 "nuns"

I put the word "nuns" in quotation marks in order to indicate that it is a misnomer for lay women with ten vows *(dasa-sil-mavvaru),* to whom I have referred in the earlier part of this chapter. For, according to one orthodox opinion, there is no validly ordained nun *(bhikkhuni)* surviving today.

Note carefully the distinction made above between "temple" and "hermitage." In the former, the monks are actively involved in the pastoral care of the people. It is there that the laity gathers to worship the Buddha, to hear the dhamma, to make exercises of meditation or observe the five precepts, and so forth. All this is done under the patronage of the sangha, the guardian and transmitter of tradition.

The hermitage, on the other hand, is a place of seclusion where monks withdraw from all pastoral activity and devote their time to meditation. Like the temple monks, they too observe an authentically cenobitic life. For, as in Christian monasticism, the initiators of the samanic movement were solitaries and wanderers but were superseded by organized communities of monks who held in suspicion the wandering loners. There are a few such solitaries in Sri Lanka. But the majority of the hermitages are cenobia run according to the *vinaya*. However, the strict life of meditation does not seal them away from the people who seek their help. Anyone desiring to be guided along the path of spiritual development is welcome and is sometimes given free board and lodging. (Hospitality has ever been an inherent feature of monasticism wherever it is found.) But their involvement is normally restricted to the spiritual guidance of those who wish to enter the higher life.

The distinction between the temple-monk and the hermit has an interesting past. Very early in the history of Sri Lankan monasticism there arose a question that we Christians would formulate in terms of "active" and "contemplative" life. For the Buddhists, the alternatives were *pariyatti* (study) and *paṭipatti* (practice). Which of these needed greater emphasis in the life of the *bhikkhu?* After all, the ancient monastic tradition admitted that a monk could specialize as a *gantha-dhara* (bearer of scriptural knowledge) or as a *vinaya-dhara* (bearer of the monastic discipline). It was now a matter of deciding which of the two needed greater emphasis in Sri Lanka.

The Sri Lankan sangha seemed to have been pastorally inclined. The monks opted for a study-oriented teaching profession. Thus *grāma-vāsa* (living in the village amid the people) became the lifestyle of the majority. The life of meditative seclusion referred to as *vanavāsa* (forest-life) appealed to a small minority. This proportion is maintained even today with the "temples" counting over six thousand as against a mere 152 hermitages! Meditation is not set aside but made to serve a life of pastoral involvement.

WEALTH: CHIEF OBSTACLE TO THE MONASTIC SPIRIT

One final observation. What vitiates the purity of monastic life in Sri Lanka is not the pastoral activism of the monks or even their political options as such. The real threat to monastic integrity comes from wealth and property. The situation in this regard is much more complicated than appears at first sight.

Paradoxically, the monk who renounces all worldly means of livelihood has to depend for his own livelihood on the very persons who use worldly means. The mendicant (for that is what *bhikkhu* literally means) is dependent on the worldling for his daily sustenance. From the beginnings of Indian monachism there was a mutual arrangement between the monk and the laity. The monk's task was to nourish lay persons spiritually while being sustained by them materially. The wealth-acquiring laity form the backdrop for the wealth-renouncing recluses! This makes poverty a difficult virtue, more difficult than celibacy.

The holier the monk appears to be, the more generous is the laity toward him. The poorer he wants to be, the greater are the donations he receives. The more he runs away from riches, the closer he comes to them. The further he removes himself from society, the more crushing becomes the people's devotion to him. Thus, *dependence on the people for material sustenance is at once the most basic condition and the most vulnerable feature of monastic poverty.*

What is true of the individual monk is even more true of the monastery as a whole. Rich benefactors show their appreciation by lavishing land and wealth on monasteries. This practice dates back to the time of the Buddha. He was given two parks as gifts. Thus begins the tradition of monks having common use of land. Daily begging was gradually replaced by daily cooking as the people began to give the monks large quantities of grain instead of giving them a daily meal. Huts and natural caves yielded place to well-constructed cells. When robes too began to be stored up in large quantities for common use, the earlier custom of collecting rags from cemeteries disappeared. As monasticism ceased to be a protest against the civil and religious society and gradually became organized into an institution accepted by society, these changes inevitably crept in. But the Buddha absorbed these changes judiciously into the *vinaya* by introducing constitutional safeguards against abuses.

Were later generations of monks as cautious as he was? It is my contention that the majority of the rural monasteries in Sri Lanka have remained faithful to the original spirit. The same cannot be said of some big monasteries that are today very influential in the politico-social field. They still possess the extensive lands that kings in the past lavished on them. This happened when the mutual arrangement between monk and laity, mentioned above, had been magnified into a church-state dimension. Buddhism in Sri Lanka, used to be the state religion, and the state was feudal. The sangha's moral legitimization of the state was reciprocated by the state's obligation to maintain the sangha.

Today these monasteries have become the focus of much criticism. Certain abuses have crept in and these seriously threaten the very foundation of monastic spirituality. In some cases, monks are permitted to inherit their family bequest while staying monks. The "wealthy monk," according to the average Buddhist, is a contradiction in terms.

Further, according to civil law, the chief monk or the abbot can appoint himself the trustee of temple property. This property, therefore, is only theoretically *sānghika* (belonging to the whole community). The control and ownership of the land, de facto, is in the hands of an abbot. Worse still is the practice by which the abbot ordains a relative in order to pass on the ownership to members of his family. This, needless to say, is a flagrant violation of the *Vinaya*. When successive governments tried to introduce land reforms that affected temple properties, the heads of such monasteries protested against them in the name of religion and tradition. There have been many eminent monks who have disapproved of these monastic abuses openly, but they have been branded "leftists." A residue from the feudal past, this situation appears not only anachronistic but positively harmful in the eyes of rural intellectuals including university-educated monks. Exposed to the winds of socialism blowing here for the last forty years and more, these young critics question what they consider the ''parasitic'' nature of monastic existence.

What would be the alternative? Young monks coming out of the universities seek employment as teachers to earn their living. They refuse to be ''parasites.'' But does the *Vinaya* permit a monk to live by a secular profession? Conservative Buddhists refuse to accept this new trend. Because agriculture, too, is forbidden to the monk, the Western monastic tradition of *orare et laborare* cannot find an exact parallel here. In China, in the ninth century, the Ch'an monks introduced work in the fields as part of the monastic schedule, but in Sri Lanka such work is not regarded proper for a monk. Instead, intellectual labors such as teaching, writing, research, and the like, have become an integral part of the monastic tradition.

To sum up: the *renunciation of wealth and property,* which is the sum and substance of the monastic calling, and also the monk's *relationship to work* are two issues that demand immediate attention from the monks of the Third World. The discussion is very much alive in monastic circles in Sri Lanka.

Before I close, I must state here that, although these issues are discussed by monks themselves within their cells no less than in the political field wherever religion and socialism try to meet, there is still in the vast majority of rural monasteries a genuine spirit of poverty and simplicity, scrupulous fidelity to the ancient injunctions of the Buddha, and very close contact with the poor peasants who are the real citizens of the Third World. Like the leaven in the dough, they are hardly seen by the urbanized bureaucracy that runs the country's administrative apparatus, but their influence is real. When I mentioned at the beginning of this chapter that monasticism is both the institutional center and the spiritual apex of a Buddhist community, it was these monastic communes that I had in mind. Poverty, by which the monks withdraw from the world and its values, is the very foundation of their pastoral involvement with the world and its inhabitants. They are the ones who still conserve the ancient Buddhist tradition combining *monastic renunciation* and *missionary efficacy.*

6

The Buddhist Political Vision

PERSPECTIVES

1. In an inquiry into Buddhism and politics, one would make a false start if one did not preclude from the beginning certain widespread preconceptions about the alleged absence of any historical sense in the Indian religio-cultural systems. It has often been remarked that those who deal with dates and epochs in ancient Indian history realize soon enough that the pegs they plant on the sands of time seem to get somewhat shifted with every wave of new evidence, and that the firm ones are those fixed with the aid of diaries maintained by Chinese visitors to India. Actually, the sense of *chronological time,* which the practical, down-to-earth Chinese are known for, may not be equally evident in ancient Indian literature. This does not mean that Indian culture ignored or glossed over the historical, temporal, and cosmic aspects of human existence. On the contrary.

G.S.P. Misra[1] observes that the volume of historical writings in ancient India available to us is thin, partly because the official royal records of socio-political and cultural achievements were lost in dynastic wars, and because the Indian emphasis was mostly on the preservation of cultural traditions rather than on the activities of the state or on the life and works of "ephemeral individuals." But the myths (even as early as in the Vedic literature) form an important *genre littéraire* that conceals a wealth of historical data. Historical romances too were there, though they were meant more to maintain poetical mannerisms than to record facts. Yet the royal dynastic chronicles and genealogies of sacerdotal clans constituted historical writings of a sort.

The Indian sense of history, notes Misra, was later influenced by three types of philosophies of religion, among them chiefly Buddhism. The theistic school with its *avatāravāda*—that is, the incarnational theory about God entering into

A talk given at the seminar, "A Search for an Alternative Form of Democratic Politics in Asia," sponsored by the Christian Conference of Asia and held in Hong Kong, May 1982. Published in *Dialogue,* 11 (1984) 6–14.

human history "according to the needs of the time" (*yuge yuge:* see *Bhagavad Gida,* IV/7–8), and the *Samkhya/Yoga* school with its own peculiar impact on historiographies of the Puranas and the Epics, constituted the first manner of focusing on historical realities. The other was the *lokāyata* (secularist) approach. Soon to be overshadowed by the overwhelming religiousness of the Indian mind, it had fostered an exclusive emphasis on *artha* and *kāma*—that is, the economic and corporeal aspects of human existence.

The third important influence could be traced back to the so-called "nonorthodox" trends in India—namely, Jainism and more particularly Buddhism. In the latter, the law of karma and rebecoming brought out not only the deterministic nature of human acts (implying that an act necessarily brings about a historical consequence) but also the nondeterministic component in history, in the sense that the future is not left to fate but can be changed through appropriate human actions. Even the cyclic theory of existence, as Misra points out, reflects a social theory. The compassion of the Bodhisattva, who prefers to linger on in *saṃsāra* to serve humankind rather than close himself in his nirvanic bliss, manifests the cosmic and historical substratum of the experience of liberation or nirvana, which however remains metacosmic and metahistorical.

I am concerned here with this third category of "historical sense," especially the one originating in the doctrine and praxis of Gautama the Buddha.

2. The young Gautama, who joined the urbanized youth of his day in their stampede to the forest in search of truth and meaning so deplorably absent in his society, came out of that experience as the fully "enlightened one"—a title that set him apart from every other human or divine being. But he did not, like other sages of his day, stay back to enjoy his solitudinal bliss, but returned to the society he once repudiated and began to preach a dhamma that opened up a new vision and a new path invariably in conflict with the existing order. The new system of social values that the dhamma contained came alive not only in the verbal formulation of the master but also in the *personal style* of his *social involvement.* His preaching, in other words, must be interpreted against the background of his praxis, which, therefore, must engage our attention first.

The real basis of the Buddha's *spiritual* involvement in contemporaneous *secular* realities was his Buddhahood itself: the wisdom and the detached distance that gave him an undisputed freedom to address the world that was falling apart before him. For the Pali scriptures give ample testimony to the unprecedented authority with which he walked the streets and talked with others; his gentle persuasiveness, which converted the harlot and the murderer; the diversity in his pedagogical approach to the rich merchant, to the poor artisan, and to the sectarian philosopher; the sense of social righteousness with which he blazed when he demolished the theological basis of the caste system; the competence with which he proclaimed to politicians the principles of good government; the practical wisdom of the ethical code he bequeathed to the laity to guide social and even economic pursuits; and particularly the all-embracing nature of the *vinaya,* the monastic *regula,* by which the monks could, in their single-minded pursuit of nirvana, serve any given secular society as beacons of light in the manner he himself exemplified.

Though the gnostic idiom in which he couched his message may give the wrong impression that he advocated a world-denying asceticism, his praxis clearly revealed it to be a world-transforming spirituality. This in fact was an important theme of subsequent speculation in Buddhology. An attempt was made to affirm a complementarity between *prajñā* and *karuṇā,* the two constitutive dimensions of Buddhahood. The former denotes "salvific knowledge" implying disengagement from samsara, whereas the latter stands for "redeeming love" that engages the Buddha in a program of restructuring the psycho-social life of human society in tune with the supreme goal of nirvanic freedom. By *gnosis* a Buddha anticipates here and now the beyond; but, by *agape,* so to say, he transfigures the here and now in terms of that beyond. Thus, wisdom *(prajñā)* is thought to have provided him with a vantage-point to serve the world with loving-kindness *(karuṇā).* This then was his twofold posture toward the world: gnostic disengagement and agapeic involvement; wisdom and love: *prajñā* and *karuṇā.*

It is important to note that all branches of Buddhism admitted the mutual inclusiveness of these two basic attitudes to the world, the esoteric schools going to the extremes of employing the sexual idiom, in literature and iconography, to indicate the merging of the two into one, undifferentiated salvific experience. Yet the alternating emphasis given to the one and the other explains the bifurcation of Buddhism into Theravada and Mahayana forms, the former stressing the "gnostic" disengagement proper to the arahant ideal and the latter accentuating the bodhisattva concept with its "agapeic" insertion into cosmic existence. But neither school has ever denied the other aspect. However, even in the Theravadin Lanka, the focus of my study, the tension between these two ideals had, very early in the history of the island, developed into the twofold praxis of the *vana-vāsi* (forest-dwelling) monks retiring into the solitude of the forest in pursuit of interior liberation, and of the greater number of *grāma-vāsi* (village-dwelling) "activists" who live amid the people and exercise a pastoral influence, often even in the socio-political sphere.

There was also the parallel development of the "two wheels"—the socio-spiritual wheel *(dhamma-cakka)* and the socio-political wheel *(ānācakkā).* In this scheme, the Buddha is regarded as the supreme concentration of spiritual authority, and the hypothetical "universal monarch" *(cakravartin)* is his counterpart in the secular sphere. Their mutual relationship becomes the paradigmatic thematization of church-state relationship in later Buddhist theories. Some kings in Sri Lanka (imitating the Indian Emperor Asoka of the third century B.C., who became the closest approximation to the *cakravartin* ideal) wished to acquire Buddhist support by claiming to be, if not actually behaving like, a bodhisattva, while conversely the spiritual lordship of the Buddha is also, to this day, confessed by the common designation "Buddha, the King" *(Budu-rajānanvahansē).* This reciprocal exchange of "titles" between the spiritual and the political symbols of authority indicates a strong bond between the two spheres even in contemporary Sri Lanka. The practice of calling the quondam Prime Minister S.W.R.D. Bandaranayake a bodhisattva, after he was assassinated by a Buddhist monk, and of the rival political party's propaganda posters referring to its dead leader Dudley Senanayaka as one destined to attain *Budubava* (Buddhahood), and of the present president of Sri Lanka repeatedly appealing to his own personal fidelity to the Buddhist ideal, when addressing political meetings, are all indicative of the political effectiveness of this paradigm to this day.

The theory of the two wheels or two authorities is also anticipated in the "messianic myth" to which I shall refer in the second part of this chapter.

3. One more politically significant fact that historians are compelled to note is the governmental form that the Buddhist sangha adopted under the direct inspiration of its founder. The term "sangha" was actually a non-Buddhist technical term for any legitimately constituted society. As the monks grew to be such a society and a monastic constitution had to be formulated, there were two secular models of societies that could have been followed—namely, (what modern writers call) the republican and the monarchical forms of government. The former is perhaps a misnomer for *tribal socialism,* which the Buddha's own Sakyan clan seemed to have exemplified; monarchical was perhaps the fruit of increasing feudalization. What is significant is that the Buddha made a clear option for the former, as is evident from the concept of authority and the mechanism of government envisaged in the *Vinaya.* To call it "republican democracy," as some modern authors do, is to say too little. For the sangha is to be governed as far as possible not by the rule of the majority, but by *consensus* based on the dhamma, for the dhamma ever remains the ultimate norm annulling even a unanimous opinion to the contrary.

The importance of this governmental model is seen in the symbolic fact that the sangha remains the ideal society proffered by Buddhism to the world at large. Hence one can easily see a visible social model that Buddhism has already produced as the concrete illustration of its philosophy of life.

However, in the course of history, the sangha that was also a missionary body had to spread and maintain the dhamma within a feudal setup and under royal patronage. In this way it gradually acquired certain feudal characteristics.

PRINCIPLES

1. Muhammad created a socio-political order and a legal structure in conformity with his spiritual vision. Confucius translated his philosophy of government in and through the state in which he was an active participant. The Buddha did neither of these. The authority he exercised over the sangha was a form of *spiritual leadership.* He did not directly advocate or advertise a particular economic system as opposed to another. And yet his mind is not difficult to interpret when it comes to deciding which type of socio-political order is in consonance and which would be at variance with his spiritual vision. Apart from employing, in a modified form, the tribal-socialist model in the govern-

ment of the sangha, he also gave a large body of direct teachings that throw enough light on the matter. Hence, certain discourses of the Buddha constitute the starting point of much of the Buddhist political visioning in Sri Lanka in recent times.

The Buddha's discourses that have a bearing on the proper ordering of society are many and varied. For my purpose, it will be useful to distinguish between *didactic* and *mythical* discourse. The former deals with practical suggestions of an ethical nature relating to such questions as the proper use of money, equality among human beings, the immorality of a social structure based on castes, the duties of the state, and so on. But in the recent writings of men like the late K. N. Jayatillekes, G. Gunasiri, and Piyasena Dissanayaka, there is a greater appreciation of the mythic discourses that seem to conceal an explosive message on social questions. Obviously, ''myth'' here is not used in its popular or literal sense of untruth or fable, but designates a *genre littéraire*. It is a symbolic device to express a truth that is too profound to be spelled out in prosaic formulas.

There are two myths that are most relevant: the *Aggañña-sutta,* a ''lapsarian'' myth referring to the past, and the *Cakkavatti-sīhanāda-suttanta,* an ''eschatological'' or ''messianic'' myth referring to the future. The one presupposes an ideal from which human society fell and why it fell; the other posits an ideal toward which human society should strive. Yet there is no moralizing of any kind. The style is descriptive, not prescriptive. The moral obligations are only to be inferred from rather than read into the text. Such would be the process of political ''visioning'' of some contemporary Buddhists.[2]

2. The lapsarian myth *(Aggañña-sutta)* begins the story at a point where the cosmic state is one of incipient evolution following a previous devolution. Hence there is no divine creation. The world goes on eternally in alternating stages of evolution and devolution. The beings from whom we derive our existence were self-luminous, formless, sexually undifferentiated, living long before ''time'' came to be, for there was only earth and water, and no sun or moon to mark day and night.

The ''fall'' came through greed for the things of the earth. *Taṇhā okkami:* ''there arose thirst,'' acquisitiveness, avarice; inordinate desire—for this is what *taṇhā* connotes in the Buddhist scheme of things. Once they tasted these earthly things, their radiance was lost; the sun and the moon appeared (to give light) and with it came time. The eating produced solid bodies with beautiful complexion. The earthly things being consumed, more solid food appeared and with it more solid bodies. With the eating of rice came sexual differentiation and indulgence in sexual intercourse. The ordering of family life was made necessary, with a separate house for each unit. Yet they gathered rice from the (commonly owned) fields according to each one's need, without any tendency to accumulate the goods of the earth. Soon it became necessary to store up rice; this invariably led to the dividing of the rice fields. Thus began the institution of private property, giving rise to a whole series of evils such as stealing, quarreling, and dissensions, making it necessary to *elect* a universally accepted ruler who is referred to in the myth by the significant title *Mahāsammata* (the Great Elect). It should be noted that even monarchy is presented here as a human institution arising from a social contract rather than by divine appointment.

Here the myth should be understood against a Brahmanic background. The divine origin theory of human social groups was theologically justified in Brahminism through the myth of the Brahman-body—that is, the divine person. The sacerdotal caste of Brahmins who utter the sacred word represent (originated from) the Brahman's mouth. His hand and shoulders (symbols of government) gave birth to the ruling Ksatriya caste, whereas the stomach (the mainstay of the body) was the source (symbol) of Vaiśyas who sustained the economy of a society through their productive labor. The Sudras (the menial class) were compared to (originated from) the feet of the Brahman.

The social contract theory of the *Aggañña-sutta,* therefore, presents a countermyth by means of a fanciful etymology. Ksatriyas rule because they are "lords of the *ksetra*" (fields), whereas Brahmins are those who renounce *(bāhenti)* the world! Thus Brahman, by implication, should be a saint! The landowners who cultivated the fields are said to be the Vaiśyas. Śūdras were those engaged in hunting and other harsh means of livelihood. No room is left in this myth for a divine legitimization of caste differentiation. Further, proper government is based on human consensus, not on a divine will manifested through a privileged person. This way even monarchy is relativized.

3. The eschatological or messianic myth *(Cakkavatti-sīhanāda-suttanta)* dovetails into the message of the lapsarian myth. It clearly shows that *bad government is the immediate cause of poverty* and that with poverty all hell is let loose. Therefore, in reading this *sutta,* one must recall the thesis set forth in the *Aggaññasutta*—that poverty and wealth result from the institution of private property, which in turn is to be traced back to "innate greed," *taṇhā,* the ultimate cause of all evil.

The messianic myth revolves around the concept of the universal king or the *Cakkavatti* (literally, the wheel-turner). The wheel is the symbol of the universal monarch who rules by the dhamma. His rule extends by righteousness *(dhammavijaya),* not through violent conquests. When the wheel disappears, there is disaster looming large on the horizon. It is a sign of failure. As long as the righteous king feeds those who are accused of stealing (according to the principle that they steal because they are poor) he could survive the crisis. One day, contrary to the principle of righteous government, the king punishes the thieves with death. This brings about a revolt of the poor, who then indulge in mass plunder. With this, all forms of irreligiousness are let loose: the shortening of the life span of humans and their reduction to a near beastly state! Few, very few, will be converted, and will stop misappropriating goods. Then goodness will increase, preparing the way for the birth of Sankha, the universal king, who will once more usher in the *dhammavijaya* (reign of righteousness), and will rule *asatthena adandena dhammena:* with dhamma that does not employ deterrents such as capital punishment to bring order. It is a reign of love characterized by the appearance of the Buddha whose name, significantly, is "friendship" or "love": *Maitreya.* Sankha and Maitreya, the wielders of temporal and spiritual authority, respectively, thus appear together.

The discourse known as the *Kūṭanāda suttanta* quite understandably insists that there is no purpose in punishing evil. The king has to eradicate the cause of evil by providing facilities to the farmers, capital to the traders, proper wages and salaries to the workers, and tax-exemption to the poor.[3]

The principles involved in these myths are quite clear. The ruler is subservient to the will of the people, for he has to be chosen by them. Self-centered acquisitiveness or the accumulative tendency *(taṇhā),* which the Buddha identified as the root of all sorrow (Second Noble Truth), is also the cause of all social sin. Civil disorder is causally connected with the institution of private property, which is the remote result of *taṇhā.* Both poverty and (the accumulation of) wealth are undesirable. Hence it follows logically that the elimination of their polarization is to be sought as a necessary condition for the reign of righteousness *(dhammavijaya).*

Further, the cyclic theory of existence implied here, as shown above, is intimately bound up with the agency of human societies which, through acts posited in history, generate new "times" or eons. The cyclic theory, therefore, is neither asocial nor ahistorical as some biblical theologians would think. At least it is not so in the case of Buddhism.

PART THREE

Dialogue with Buddhism

7

Buddhism as a Challenge
for Christians

BUDDHIST CHALLENGE NEUTRALIZED

Many had hoped with Arnold Toynbee that an in-depth encounter between Buddhism and Christianity would usher in a new era in human history. Like no other two religions of the world, these two are a formidable challenge to each other, and their encounter, one hoped, would result in a *coincidentia oppositorum* that would give birth to a richer and nobler synthesis in each.

Subsequent events, however, have belied these expectations, mainly because these two religions have never really met each other in their *authentic* forms, except perhaps in the hearts of a few individuals. For the most part, the Buddhist-Christian encounter has been a matter of a deformed Christianity colliding with a misapprehended Buddhism. The ideology of "Euro-ecclesiastic expansionism," which masqueraded as the religion of Christ, was not good news but a serious threat to Buddhism. In fact, it was this initial Christian offensive that compelled Buddhists to wear a *defensive mask* when facing Christians. This mask is still on.

A hardening of positions took place in the nineteenth century when a bitter controversy broke out between English Christianity and Sinhalese Buddhism: a Christianity occupying a politically advantageous position in a Buddhist culture in Asia but insecure in Europe in the prevailing climate of scientific rationalism and secular ideologies; and a Buddhism trying to retrieve its rightful place in a colonized nation and vindicate its intellectual respectab'lity in Europe by presenting itself as *a "religion-less" philosophy having a scientific and rationalist basis.*[1]

This was the beginning of what one Buddhist sociologist has described as "Protestant Buddhism"—a Buddhism originating as a protest against an un-

First published in *Christianity among World Religions*. Hans Küng and Jürgen Moltmann (eds.) *(Concilium,* vol. 183), Edinburgh: T. & T. Clark, 1986, pp. 40–44.

christian Christianity aggressive toward and contemptuous of the doctrine and the person of Buddha.[2] This reaction continued up to the middle of our own century in the guise of a "modernist Buddhism" apologetical in style and content. This form of Buddhism did not hesitate to employ such philosophical labels as "rationalism," "empiricism," and even "logical positivism" for the purpose of interpreting the Buddha's spiritual message to the West.[3]

This kind of "export Buddhism" (to borrow a phrase from Edward Conze), though widespread now, failed to be what it was meant to be: a challenge to Christians. Rather, it was just a dry doctrinal system with no religious sap to make it live, with no monastic nucleus to nourish it spiritually and with no Buddha cultus to draw out its essentially soteriological character. This nineteenth-century legacy still continues to hinder Christians from detecting what is truly challenging in Buddhism.

Though the polemical climate has yielded to a friendly atmosphere of dialogue, the nineteenth-century doctrinaire approach to Buddhism still persists in the works of many contemporary theologians. David Snellgrove's sophisticated tract on the "theology of Buddhahood" is an example.[4] John Cobb and George Rupp have been hailed as two Christians who have allowed their theology to be revolutionized by the Buddhist challenge to Christian thought.[5] Though an intellectually fascinating exercise, a confrontation of Whitehead's process philosophy with the subtleties of ancient Buddhist dialecticians like Nagarjuna (Cobb does it brilliantly) is a far cry from an encounter between the gospel and the dharma!

Asian theologians have been even less enterprising. Mahayana Buddhism has received a fair degree of serious attention from Japanese theologians. But the overall impression is that they *neutralize* the Buddhist challenge by filtering it through Western (often German) theological models.

In Asia, it was Lynn de Silva who pushed the doctrinal confrontation to its ultimate limit. His investigation into the Buddhist theory of reincarnation led him to revise his Protestant views on eschatology.[6] But his most daring achievement was the theological appropriation of the Theravada doctrine of *anatta*—the nonexistence of a human or any soul.[7] In the course of a much publicized dialogue between "modernist Buddhists" and Christian theologians on the problem of God, the Buddhist argument, "no soul, therefore no God," made an about-turn in de Silva's theological response: "no soul, therefore God."[8] The Christian concept of *pneuma* was thus elucidated in terms of the Buddhist doctrine of *anatta*.

The Christian use of non-Christian doctrines is an apologetical method begun by the Greek fathers, and is hardly fruitful in the Asia of today, as I have argued elsewhere.[9] Yet in this instance, de Silva freed himself of the nineteenth-century approach by not treating the *anatta* doctrine as a mere philosophical tenet (on a par with, say, that of David Hume who is quoted approvingly in the writings of "modernist" Buddhists). Rather, de Silva saw in it the Buddhist equivalent of the principle and foundation of Christian spirituality: the acknowledgement of one's *creatureliness*. For de Silva always worked within the soteriological parameter of the two religions, though, perhaps he did not give due recognition to the *gnostic idiom* of the Buddhists.

CHALLENGE OF THE GNOSTIC IDIOM

There are two irreducibly distinct languages of the Spirit, each incapable without the other of adequately mediating and expressing one's experience of God and of the world. Gnosis or the *language of liberative knowledge* is one; agape or the *language of redemptive love* is the other.

In Buddhism, *karuṇā* or love is an indispensable prelude to and an inevitable consequence of *prajñā* or wisdom, which alone is considered intrinsically salvific. All affective currents of spirituality must at one point or other flow into the sapiential stream—notwithstanding the pietistic schools of Mahayana Buddhism. The dialectics of wisdom and love—that is, of gnostic detachment and agapeic involvement—constitutes a universally accepted dogma in the mainstream schools of Buddhism. Yet when Buddhism speaks of love, it normally does so in the language of gnosis.

Contemporary Christianity, which is almost exclusively agapeic, has not only lost its earlier familiarity with the gnostic idiom, but has also inherited an antignostic bias, though historians insist that there used to be an orthodox line of Christian gnosis and that the heretical gnoses were only "embroidery" along this legitimate line.[10] A glance at the socio-political history of Buddhist cultures should convince any Christian that gnosticism is not necessarily ahistorical or apolitical. It is the antignostic bias that accounts for the Weberian sociologists' caricature of Buddhism as a "world-*denying* asceticism" when in reality it is only a world-*relativizing* affirmation of the Absolute.

Because language is not just a way of speaking about reality, but a way of seeing and experiencing it, the Buddhist challenge consists primarily in reminding the Christian that there exists *another* legitimate way of seeing and interpreting reality, as the following observations will illustrate. Theresa of Avila, whose *God-experience* is expressed in the idiom of agape, refers to the mystical grace of "suspension" (of senses and understanding) as being such an extraordinary and gratuitous gift of the divine Spirit that it would be presumptuous to make any human effort at acquiring it.[11] But whoever meditates under the guidance of a Theravadan master is soon made to believe that this "suspension" (*nirodha samāpatti* or "cessation trance" as Buddhists call it) is a natural, predictable, and humanly inducible, albeit rarely attained, psychic phenomenon not to be confused with nirvana, which defies human manipulation.

We are dealing here with *two language games,* each having its own set of rules. One game should not be judged/played according to the rules of the other. Thus, the Christian mystic speaks in terms of "sin and grace," but the gnostic vocabulary of the Buddhist arahant knows only of "ignorance and knowledge." The gnostic process of realizing an "Impersonal I" and the agapeic encounter with a "personal Thou" imply two modes of religious discourse, each having its own logic and its own grammar and syntax.

As with God-experience, so also with regard to the *external world,* we can adopt *two postures;* that of the Christian who delights in it and that of the Buddhist who keeps a critical distance from it. Each attitude has its own danger: stark consumerism and stoic indifferentism, respectively. Yet today more than ever, we Christians should be made aware that gnosis and agape are the two eyes of the soul and that our partial one-eyed vision of the world has led us to the brink of cosmic disaster.

Not inclined to *revere or adore the Absolute,* because it is a nonpersonal reality to be realized through gnosis, Buddhists tend, by contrast, to attribute a *quasi-personalist character to all that is not the Absolute.* Hence cosmic forces are personified in the process of being relativized. In other words, the elements of nature evoke a reverential attitude from humans. The cosmos makes *one ecological community* with humanity. Inasmuch as nature is humanity's cosmic extension, it cannot be mishandled without the whole human-cosmic continuum being disrupted. Buddhism knows a way of relativizing the world vis-à-vis the Absolute without in any way "instrumentalizing" it.

Contrast this with *Christian theism.* The Absolute is adored and loved as a person; all else (human persons not excluded) shrinks to the level of an *instrument* to be *used* in the human quest for God. Ignatius of Loyola makes it the foundational principle of Christian asceticism.[12] Cosmic forces are thus regarded as impersonal things to be manipulated in the service of God and humanity rather than as quasi-personal beings to be treated with reverence or as silent companions in our pilgrimage toward the Absolute. It is this "instrumental theory of creatures"—not yet challenged by the gnostic vision of the world—that has paved the way for the current impasse of technocracy, while biospheric pollution grows into an imminent nuclear holocaust.

There was at least one Christian who was endowed with a two-eyed vision: Francis of Assisi. But he seems to have been a freak in Christendom!

CHALLENGE TO CHRISTOLOGY

The Indian sage seated in serene contemplation under the Tree of Knowledge, and the Hebrew prophet hanging painfully on the Tree of Love in a gesture of protest—here are two contrasting images that clearly situate the Buddha (the Enlightened one) and the Christ (the Anointed one) in their respective paradigmatic contexts of gnosis and agape. In no other gnostic religion (Jainism, Taoism, or Vedantic Hinduism) and in no other agapeic religion (Judaism or Islam) is *the person of the Founder* (if there is one) accorded so central a place in his own kerygma as certainly is the case with Buddhism and Christianity.

The parallel processes by which Gautama came to be revered as *the* Buddha and Jesus came to be proclaimed as *the* Christ indicate that any encounter between the dhamma (the message of Buddha) and the gospel has to reckon with an eventual kerygmatic conflict between the two "personality cults."

The nineteenth-century revival of Hinduism in India and of Buddhism in Sri Lanka bear testimony to this fact. The great Hindu reformers, despite their critical stance regarding Christianity, were willing to absorb the figure of the "god-man" Jesus into their soteriological scheme,[13] sometimes giving the impression that they were trying to rescue the founder of Christianity from Christian distortions! Buddhist revivalists, such as Anagarika Dharmapala, on the contrary, were known to have been not only critical of Christianity but also spiteful toward the person of Jesus who, in their writings, contracts into a spiritual dwarf before the gigantic personality of the Buddha.[14]

In this connection we can note that the Pauline missiology of the Letters to Ephesians and Colossians, which installed Jesus Christ as the one cosmic mediator and also as the metacosmic Lord over all visible and invisible forces of the universe, had already been anticipated in Asia by Buddhist missionaries who had enthroned the Buddha over all elements of nature and all gods, spirits, and personified cosmic forces. This makes Buddhism the greatest challenge that the Christian kerygma has ever met in history—and vice versa.

Moreover, both the "ontological" approach of traditional christology and the "soteriological and functional" approach of contemporary theologians find their vague analogies in the history of buddhology.[15] Christians living in a Buddhist culture are therefore challenged to *revise* their *christological formulas*. Perhaps a new "liberational" approach that would complement rather than cancel past achievements might best meet this Buddhist challenge. Because this suggestion has received sustained argumentation and careful formulation elsewhere,[16] I shall content myself here with merely making a few brief statements.

1. The only meeting point of the gnostic and the agapeic models of spirituality is the belief that *voluntary poverty* constitutes a salvific experience. Hence Jesus, as God's own kenosis and as the proof and sign of God's eternal enmity with mammon, is an endorsement of the Buddhist ascesis of renunciation. *The struggle to be poor* is one of the two dimensions of Christian discipleship, and it coincides with the Buddha's path of *interior* liberation—namely, liberation from possessions as well as from greed for possessions.

2. This same Jesus, according to the agapeic formula, is also the new covenant—that is, a defense pact between God and the poor against the prevailing order of mammon. It is precisely when the poor struggle for their freedom and human dignity that God glorifies the Son as God's covenant before the nations, thus breaking through the language barrier between gnosis and agape, turning *human love* into the supreme art of *knowing God* (1 John 4:7–8).

3. Christ, at once human victim and divine judge of *forced poverty,* lives in the oppressed in whom he announces himself to be unmistakably available as the recipient of our ministry (Matt. 25:31–46). *The struggle for the poor* is, therefore, the second constitutive dimension of Christian discipleship and is also the means by which Jesus is proclaimed the Lord of history. All christological speculations that flow from this liberational praxis do not compete with buddhological theories.

4. A rich church that serves Christ who is in the poor now (Matt. 25:31–46), without following Jesus who was poor then (Matt. 19:21), is a neocolo-

nialist threat to Buddhists because it attributes to Christ a false political messianism. Conversely, Christian ashrams that follow *Jesus* by their "struggle to be poor," but do not serve *Christ* through a "struggle for the poor," fail to proclaim Jesus of Nazareth as the Christ and the Lord of history.[17]

8

Monastic Poverty
in the Asian Context

I have been asked to situate and then to evaluate monastic poverty in the context of Asia's socio-economic realities. This is a gigantic task, a part of which lies well beyond my sphere of competence. Hence, I think, I must fix beforehand a modest range for this discussion. Let me do this by means of an elementary observation about which there can hardly be any dispute. The observation is that in Asia there are at least two clearly distinguishable classes of "poor"—namely, the *monks*, who claim to have renounced all possessions, and the *masses*, who have no possessions to renounce!

Hence I shall let this discussion run along two principal themes: the *voluntary poverty* of Asian monks and the *forced poverty* of Asian masses. Inasmuch as the former is a constitutive dimension of Asia's "monastic" religions (Buddhism, Hinduism, and Taoism) and the latter sums up our socio-economic reality, this twofold theme will not allow my discussion to wander beyond the "Asian context"—which I have described earlier (Asian Theological Conference, 1979) as a "coalescence of religiosity and poverty."[1]

Of course, the phrase "voluntary poverty" might not occur in the vocabulary of early Christian monks nor does it find an exact equivalent in non-Christian monastic literature. And yet this is a convenient way of designating a monk's calling; for this word, in its current usage, points to an *interior* attitude of detachment as well as an *exterior* renunciation of material goods. Buddhists, for instance, would employ two sets of terms for them. Interior poverty would correspond, in their vocabulary, to *virāga* (detachment) and *alpicchatā* (desiring only the basic minimum necessary for life). For exterior poverty, they use a series of dynamic expressions such as *pabbaja, abhinikkamana (samnyāsa)*, and others, all of which refer to a "going forth," an abandoning of the security

Address given at the Third Asian Monks' Congress, Kandy, Sri Lanka, August, 1980. First published in *Dialogue*, 7(1980) 104–18.

of home and hearth to embrace the insecurity of a homeless pilgrim in search of truth. These two aspects—interior and exterior poverty—fuse into one, indivisible virtue, as is presupposed in practically every form of monastic tradition.

The Christian understanding of voluntary poverty is based on two radical convictions derived from revelation:

1. the irreconcilable antinomy between *God and mammon,* and
2. the irrevocable covenant between *God and the poor.*

Of these two biblical axioms, the first can find a corresponding doctrine in non-Christian religions. But it is the second that gives a Christian specificity to a monastic vocation and gives also an added relevance to it in Asia. It has no explicit doctrinal parallel in other monastic religions, as far as I know.

Let us begin with the first axiom. God and wealth—for which Jesus preferred two loaded Aramaic words: *Abba* and *mamona*—are two rival masters that claim total allegiance (Matt. 6:24). Devotion to the one involves repudiation of the other. To seek God one must give up all worldly riches. The Buddhists too are emphatic about this. A clear separation from ''the world'' is required for the attainment of nirvana. But note that God's opposite number is money, not necessarily sex. A holy person is primarily a poor person. Celibacy too is something holy only insofar as it is a form of ''poverty.'' Mahatma Gandhi was a father of four children when he was acclaimed a saint by the poor masses! The masses were too illiterate to read Gandhi's confession in the *Harijan:* that he and his wife decided to practice continence in order to serve the people more appropriately. Thus, the only criterion by which the poor could judge his sanctity was his poverty, not his continence, about which they knew nothing at the time. Those who read his confession, of course, did not find it difficult to believe him. For chastity is an invisible virtue that becomes credible *only* through other visible forms of renunciation. Celibacy can never produce its fruits unless cross-fertilized with evangelical poverty. Or else, celibacy would be a misnomer for comfortable bachelorhood and convenient spinsterhood. This, I believe, was also St. Ambrose's argument against vestal virgins.[2] Even in Asia no monk is regarded a man of God if he is also a man of means! This is the verdict of the poor. After all, it is the poor who can really detect a holy person!

However, if the God-mammon antagonism is not put in the context of *God's pact with the poor,* the practice of voluntary poverty remains purely at the *micro-ethical* level. In fact, monastic poverty of the Christian tradition (not to speak of the non-Christian tradition) has suffered too long from this limitation. Their theory of radical detachment is embodied in a kind of individual asceticism. Mammon is seen only as a psychological force operating within the human being in the form of inordinate attachments, acquisitive instincts, and accumulative tendencies. Buddhists describe these innate propensities with very expressive words such as *taṇhā* (insatiable ''thirst'' for more and more), *upādāna* (obsessive ''clinging'' to evanescent phenomena), and *lobha* (greed). It was against these inner compulsions that battles were waged and won within monastery walls. This indeed was the essence of the monastic vocation. And I shall not contest it.

On the other hand, mythology, whether Buddhist or Christian, seems to have visualized these psychological drives as "demons," thus implicitly giving them a cosmic dimension. Mammon is a *cosmic power* that organizes itself into principalities and powers, creating inequalities and injustices among human beings. The battle has to be fought also at the *macro-ethical* level of systems and ideologies in politics and economics. We are dealing here with a human compulsion to institutionalize human greed at the cost of human fellowship. It vitiates even religion—not to mention monkhood, as we shall see.

To raise the practice of voluntary poverty from the micro-ethical level to the macro-ethical level, the monk must take seriously the second datum of revelation: *the covenant relationship between God and the poor*—that is, God's partiality to the poor. If God is mediated by the poor who are God's sacrament, then the struggle against mammon is not merely a struggle for God, but is at the same time a struggle for the poor. Or, to put it within the thematic framework I proposed for this discussion, voluntary poverty must be practiced in direct relationship to the forced poverty of the masses. In other words, *"to be poor for the love of God"* and *"to be poor for the love of the poor"* are two evangelical ideals that merge into one horizon of love, which alone gives voluntary poverty its salvific value. Without ceasing to be an exercise of "individual asceticism," monastic poverty must therefore expand into a "bond of fellowship with the real poor." This is the *second dimension of voluntary poverty* I wish to emphasize here.

In fact, Jesus has left no room for ambiguity in this regard. To the rich man in search of eternal life—that is, in search of God—Jesus recommended that he sell all he had and give (not, certainly, to the temple, but) to the poor (Mark 10:21), implying that the rich should not remain rich, and the poor should not remain poor. For voluntary poverty is an essential prerequisite for a new order of society in which forced poverty has no right to exist either; and such was the kingdom Jesus preached. In fact, the precursor who prepared the people for his coming invited them to accept this new order: whoever had two coats would have to share with one who had none; whoever had food would have to do the same (Luke 3:11). For in his kingdom he would not tolerate a class division between haves and have-nots. If indeed Lazarus remained poor until he died, it was because he was forced to be in that state by the hedonism and indifference of a rich man who refused to share even his excess goods (Luke 16:19–31). Poverty thus forced upon a brother is an evil, the removal of which is a burden laid at the door of the rich. He, the rich man, is called to be poor—so that there would be no poor. In fact, St. Paul could not tolerate some Christians eating sumptuously while others starved; for him it was a *sin against the body of the Lord* (1 Cor. 11:21–27).

Hence voluntary poverty by which forced poverty ceases to exist is an evangelical imperative for all rather than a spiritual luxury of monks. The early

Christians took this seriously. They shared their goods voluntarily with the rest so that "there was not a needy person among them" (Acts 4:34), for these goods were distributed "according to need" (Acts 4:35). By their praxis, they had formulated for the first time the later communist definition of a just society: that in which one gives according to one's ability and receives according to one's need.

Has this experiment failed, as some maintain? Granted that it has, one could still argue that it is the one experiment that is worth failing. The small symbolic beginnings of a just social order must recur in history several times before they can make a permanent dent in human consciousness. There have been at least some monastic communities at all times and in all religions that served human-kind as sacraments of an equitable society. Long before the Christian experiment ever started, the Buddha formulated rules for cenobitic life wherein "even the morsel of food dropped into the begging bowl of a monk had to be shared among the brethren" in order to build unity and solidarity.[3] Some cenobitic communes of early Christian monasticism too were genuine paradigms of an equitable society.

Every such community, wherever it exists, is a city on the mountain and a leaven in the dough. And there will never be too many of them here on earth! Even a monastic community has to contend with principalities and power. When it succumbs to mammon's mighty power, it becomes a part of the wider society, reflecting its false values. The monks may own everything in common, but what is owned in common may be what keeps those around them poor! The lamaseries of Mongolia were fortresses of socio-economic power because of their wealth until the Marxists "forced" them to practice "voluntary poverty" in order that the wealth (land) they owned could be shared with the "real" poor outside the monastery! Tibet tells a similar tale. *Corruptio optimi pessima!* Even today not every Buddhist monastery is a paragon of "voluntary poverty," especially in relation to the forced poverty of the masses. Association with power structures, economic ties with the greedy, political backing from feudal dictators easily turn monasteries from being symbols of a just order to being a religious counterpart of the unjust secular model. Their contemplative life could become a scandalous luxury maintained at the expense of the poor who labor for them.

Could one say that the Asian monastic traditions do not enjoin manual labor on the monks in the way Christians do? True, the Benedictine principle of *orare et laborare* does not find a parallel here, though it has now become an accepted routine in the few monasteries that survive in Marxist states of Asia. This discovery of the value of labor has perhaps one precedent in the pre-Marxist period of Buddhist history. It is said that the Chinese Master Pai Chang, in the ninth century, enjoined on his monks daily work in the fields. Zen monasticism seems to continue this tradition to some extent.

To understand the lack of a strong tradition in this regard we must go to the origins of Indian monachism. First of all the *sramana* movement, from which it arose, was a protest against a Brahmanic society based on the home and

hearth, where "fire" was a medium by which the priest's sacrifice was consumed and by which the family meal was cooked, thus serving as the sacramental focus of priesthood and family life fused together. The *sramana* who
opted out of this structure was regarded as *anagni* ("fire-less") because he
begged for his food, thus "abandoning the fire," the common symbol of both
priesthood and home life. To abandon the hearth *(anagni)* was to abandon the
home *(anagārika).* The monk is a *bhikku*—a mendicant. Thus the ancient tradition that a monk should depend on others to supply him with food is still in
vogue in Asia where, moreover, begging as a means of livelihood is also still
normal. To depend on others for daily sustenance, rather than labor for it, is
the only way out for a specific class of paupers in Asia. It is their lot that the
mendicants share. Their fellowship with the poor prevents them from being a
burden on the poor.

And there is a second reason for this tradition. The caste-ridden society against
which early monasticism protested was based on a division of labor. The recluse who renounced this society automatically opted out of the world of "labor." The world-renouncer *(samāyasin)* in fact lost his place in the world—
namely, his caste. He could not take up any "work" without returning to the
world he renounced; in a way, his "profession" changed from "work" to
"nonwork." Thus a subtle identification of work with the secular world and
nonwork with religious asceticism is noticed from the very inception of Indian
monasticism.

Finally—and this is the third reason—the Buddha prohibited agriculture to
the monks, lest living beings be unintentionally killed (the Jains extended it
even to lay followers), and with it many other professions, such as medicine,
were taboo for various legitimate reasons. A change in this tradition is seen
here and there. Intellectual labor is accepted as proper to monks in Southeast
Asia and there are many university professors and school teachers among them,
though this mode of earning a livelihood may not always seem proper for monks
in the opinion of the laity. Engagement in community development projects is
also gaining currency among Thai and Sri Lankan monks.

Christianity, which was founded by a carpenter born to a peasant woman,
who spent his youth laboring for his daily bread, is bound to have another view
about the place of labor in a monk's life. This is an area for intermonastic
dialogue. Monks must acknowledge that exploitation of labor is one contribu-
tive factor in the genesis of poverty, not only because the capitalist system is
being imposed on Asia, but also because precapitalist feudalism of Asian origin, which still operates here, restricts specialization in religion to the leisure
class that lives on the surplus produced by workers. Hence a new linking of
monastic asceticism with the dignity of labor, now taking place in socialist
countries, would make monastic poverty a more authentic form of renunciation
in today's Asia.

The Christian monk's true partner in dialogue in Asia cannot be found in the
type of monasteries criticized above. He will find his true Asian inspiration in
what I would describe as "religious socialism" practiced in remote areas of

rural Asia where modern technocracy has not yet penetrated. There the monk and the peasant live on the same economic level and with a common philosophy of voluntary sharing. In the clanic societies of Asian villages, the earth, the sky, and all things thereof are everybody's property and nobody's monopoly. If Christian monks need an Asian model, then let them pitch their tent there soon, for Oriental feudalism merging into Western capitalism is eroding into it with incredible speed! To resist this trend and encourage rural socialism may be a new responsibility Asia expects from them.

Perhaps the gravity of this responsibility cannot be adequately gauged unless it is once more placed within a macro-ethical perspective. If Christian monks are aware of the role that governments and private organizations of some Christian nations play in this unfair game against the poor, they would soon recognize the political dynamism of their "voluntary poverty." The Asian masses are not only forced to remain poor but are made to become poorer day by day owing to organized greed—first of all of a few Asians, and then of the circles of greedier persons who use these Asians as pawns in their hands. These circles operate mostly from the Euro-American sector of the world and from certain Westernized and technocratized regions in Asia, manipulating international trade in their own favor, autocratically making decisions and formulating policies that affect the poor nations, exploiting the human and natural resources of Asia to their own advantage, and indulging in cultural aggression by thrusting a dangerous kind of technocracy into the Asian ethos.[4]

Julius Nyerere, a devout Catholic, has repeatedly pointed out this embarrassing fact to his fellow Christians. The great struggle of the poor has begun in the Third World, which is largely non-Christian, especially in Asia, where the demand for a New International Economic Order was strongly articulated. It is a struggle of the poor against the rich. It is God's struggle. Pope Paul VI, representing the Christian conscience to the world, supported this demand of the poor nations with prophetic vigor, especially in his message to the General Assembly of the United Nations on April 9, 1974, and reiterated his solidarity with the poor in later allocutions: This unjust order must change. . . . [Christian] participation in this struggle is imperative.

Note here that it is an ancient monastic insight that is now being blown into planetary proportions. The asceticism of voluntary poverty on the part of the rich few is the only answer to the abolition of forced poverty among the majority. Will this suggestion draw laughter from the secular world? Paradoxically it is from the secular world that we hear this prophetic cry. Albert Trevoedjre, director of the prestigious ILO International Institute of Social Studies in Geneva, in a curiously entitled work, *Poverty, Wealth of Peoples,*[5] advocates this theory with great perspicacity. His definition of poverty—almost coinciding with the Buddhist *alpicchatā* mentioned above—is "the state of someone who has what is necessary and not a surplus." He also demands that this poverty be practiced on a global scale in order to ensure the well-being of the whole of humankind. He is practical enough to realize that this could be a pure dream unless a "solidarity contract" is formed especially in favor of the poorer peoples.

Thus I come to the *third dimension* of voluntary poverty, the *political* dimension. When I referred to God's pact with the poor a while ago, I mentioned only the milder half of the truth—namely, that the "struggle *for* God" coincides with a "struggle *for* the poor." The harsher part of this pact is that the "struggle *of* the poor" becomes "God's own struggle against the principalities and powers that keep them poor." It is a just war; an exercise of divine justice. A holy revolution.

This was also Mahatma Gandhi's political strategy: he derived his prophetic authority from his poverty. Christian monastics, too, have to let their own "voluntary poverty" speak to the rich few, loud and clear, by first of all identifying themselves with the genuinely poor monastics of non-Christian tradition. The credibility gap between Christian and non-Christian monastics is precisely here. An intermonastic dialogue between them will have to face this question, sooner or later. In fact, an Anglican monk—whose life and work was a splendid reflection of this macro-ethical approach to monastic poverty—had long tried to establish a link with the conscientious Buddhist monks who are so involved with the poor as to be drawn into their struggle. But he was the only one of his kind here in Sri Lanka. I must recall here his experience in the course of a "dialogue" meeting we once organized on a university campus in 1974. The prophetic role of the monk in the liberation struggles of the poor was eloquently described in the keynote speech he delivered there. The radical Buddhist monks could not believe that this was a Christian theory! There were loud protests of disbelief from the audience. As the noise subsided, a young monk rose up and summarized the view of his brethren in these words (I repeat them here as recorded in my own report of this meeting published in *Dialogue*, 1/3 [1974], pp. 81–82):

In all revolutionary movements that brought some sort of liberation to the masses (the French Revolution, the October Revolution, etc.), the church clearly failed to take a stand on behalf of the exploited masses but deservedly became—together with the oppressive systems with which it was associated—the target of revolutionary attacks.

In Sri Lanka, too, similar national liberation movements and revolutionary struggles of the masses always included Buddhist sangha among the participants, but never was a Christian priest named among them. The latter remained "unstained" by any such involvement, while it was the Buddhist monks who invariably "sullied their name" for the sake of the masses by being involved in the peoples' struggles. This was quite evident also in the case of the April Revolt.

Further, the evils of capitalism and colonialist exploitation originated in the Christian West and these very Christian countries are continuing to play the same game of manipulation even today.

Therefore, when you Christians speak so enthusiastically in favor of the political liberation of the masses, we cannot help doubting your sincerity. What you say is so different from what you have done! Therefore we even wonder whether this kind of dialogue and this kind of manifesto are another Christian fraud in the series!

Beneath this indignant verdict lies a deeply ingrained Asian conviction that colonialism, Christianity, and the West form an inseparable trio. This is because Asia is not being given a chance to taste the monastic flavor of Western Christianity. For capitalism, which turned money into a god, and colonial Christianity, which made God depend on money, appear as a Western attempt to reconcile what Jesus had declared irreconcilable: God and mammon. Therefore, only a monastic Christianity that, in word and deed, through life and death, proclaims God's pact with the poor, will be the seed of an authentically Asian church. It is this indispensable mission of the Christian monk in Asia that I have tried to present in this short analysis.

9

Doctrinal, Legal, and Cultural Factors in Buddhist-Christian Mixed Marriages

PRELIMINARY CLARIFICATIONS

The term "mixed marriage" is taken here in the generic sense to mean any marriage between two persons of diverse religious persuasions. The terminology of canon law, I grant, does not warrant such a usage.[1] My intention in taking this liberty is to make this discussion intelligible to the average Buddhist and Christian.

This chapter is bound to appear rather theoretical in parts, though it has as its background a twelve-year experience in marriage counseling for nearly fifty mixed couples. In other words, the aim of this paper is practical. Moreover, not being a trained sociologist myself, I have deliberately refrained from making a studied analysis of all the socio-psychological forces at work in such marriages, but have confined myself to the area of my competence. My framework of reference is mainly theological and pastoral, and the suggestions I make here are addressed primarily to the law makers of the Roman Catholic Church, particularly to the leaders of *local churches* in predominantly Buddhist regions of Asia. But thinking aloud as I do, in the hearing of Buddhists, I may have a message for them too.

Reflecting over the cases I have handled so far, I have come to the conclusion that there are *three strands* of conflict arising from Buddhist-Christian mixed marriages and that these are so intricately interwoven as to make it nearly impossible to pick up one without touching also the others. A certain amount of overlapping, therefore, is unavoidable.

Each area of conflict has its own significance. Those that arise from the *legal*

A paper given at a meeting of Buddhists and Christians on mixed marriages at Tulana Research Centre, Gonawala-Kelaniya, Sri Lanka, 1978. Published in *Dialogue,* 5 (1978) 91–107.

ethos of Roman Catholicism are the most irritating to the non-Christian. The most conspicuous, however, are those that can be traced back to the *cultural* ethos that each religion has created in Asia. But it is the *doctrinal* conflicts that seem to be most pervasive, and therefore also the most elusive of the three. But being also the most basic of them all, being at the root of the other two, I make it the main point of reference in this discussion.

THE DOCTRINE OF MARRIAGE: THREE LEVELS OF REFLECTION

When trying to understand the primordial truths as taught in various traditions, one must learn to distinguish between the various founders' *basic intuitions* (which often converge) and their immediate *transmission* within the conceptual frameworks of various cultures wherein different religions originate. These again should be further distinguished from the *doctrinal elaborations* that logically flow from them. Perhaps the doctrine of marriage in Buddhism and Christianity too could be viewed from these three levels of observation.

It is my contention that the *basic intuitions* of Jesus and the Buddha in this matter are not so divergent as to be considered irreconcilable, despite undeniable differences in accentuation. If marriage and celibacy are both seen in an *eschatological perspective,* the New Testament teachings do not seem to collide with those of early Buddhism. Undoubtedly, Jesus upheld the sacrosanct character of marriage in no uncertain terms,[2] but he also clearly oriented it to the reality of the *eschaton,* the perfect end, where, to quote his own words, "there will be neither marriage nor giving away in marriage," because human beings would then be "like the angels in heaven."[3] This statement, which freely uses the conceptual tools of a culture basically Semitic but heavily tinged with Babylonian angelology, is not a far cry from the doctrine of marriage found in most gnostic systems of Asian origin. In the latter, too, marriage is a valid human experience not devoid of a religious content but ever tending soteriologically to the *eschaton,* of which celibacy is an immediate anticipation. This is why the mystico-monastic tradition of Roman Catholicism shows great affinity to the Buddhist religious experience and has become in recent times a fertile soil for fruitful interreligious exchange.

The first real differences begin to emerge only at the second level, where these fundamental insights get formulated and transmitted—each in its own religious idiom. Thus in the "gnostic" perspectives of Buddhism, marriage amounts to a secular *(saṃsārika, laukika)* involvement, whereas disengagement from it, seen as conducive to the salvific experience of gnosis *(bodhi, paññā,* etc.), is symbolized by celibacy. Biblical Christianity, on the other hand, spells out its salvific experience in the language of convenantal love, agape, making marriage and celibacy complementary modes of participating in the *eschaton,* which is the ultimate triumph of love. If these idiomatic differences are kept in mind, it matters little whether marriage in both Buddhism and Christianity is regarded as secular or religious, because the secular reality remains sacramental for the Christian, and what the Buddhist regards as religious is not always soteriological, as will be explained below. What I am at pains to point out is that the differences are to a great extent in the idioms used rather than in the basic insights into the nature of marriage. All that is required, as I have contended on an earlier occasion, is that Buddhists and Christians who live together learn each other's religious idiom, because these idioms are complementary rather than contradictory.[4]

Painful conflicts do arise, however, at the third level, where these idiomatic divergences are pushed to their logical extremes. Christians tend to stretch the sacramentality of marriage to the extent of "mystifying" it beyond recognition. Conversely, Buddhists run the risk of stressing the secularity of marriage so much as to strip marital engagement of all its spiritual enchantment. This creates a wide chasm in the very understanding of marriage to which a Buddhist and a Christian commit themselves for life. The disagreements that result are so profound that in the prenuptial stage one often hears the Christian partner complaining against the "spiritual vacuum" created by the Buddhist partner's attitude to marriage, and the latter is exasperated by the whole complex of *legal precautions* and *canonical inquiries* that are an inevitable concomitant of an overidealized view of marriage.

The complexity of the situation comes out in clearer focus when it is seen against the system of *legal controls* that the Church applies in order to keep marriage within the path that leads to the highly *mystical ideal* it holds up to the couple. In short, the "mystical" aspect goes hand in hand with the "canonical." *Law* is part and parcel of Catholic culture, as much as is *mysticism*. In fact, Catholic culture is intimately bound up with mysticism *and* law. Marriage too contains a mystical and a legal dimension. Because it is in its exaggerated forms that this double aspect of the Catholic position creates unpleasantness to a Buddhist partner, each of them will here be discussed in detail.

OVERMYSTIFICATION OF MARRIAGE: A CHRISTIAN EXAGGERATION

St. Paul, the pastor and theologian of early Christians, has given us a sound theology of marriage, which is at the basis of later exaggerations. Writing to the Ephesians, he stressed quite rightly the mystical dimension of Christian marriage, which he presented as a (sacramental) expression of the love between Christ and the church[5]—that is, the ultimate salvific experience of a Christian with God in Christ. Thus marriage is placed within Christian soteriology.

In doing so Paul was *not* trying to understand the divine/human encounter in terms of human marriage—as if the latter were the paradigm to understand the former. Rather, it is marriage that he tried to understand in the context of the highest Christian experience: human encounter with the saving God. In Paul's theology of marriage, therefore, the point of reference is *mystical*.

The theological consequences of this doctrine are far-reaching. A married Christian's "faith experience" and "marital experience" are placed within the same soteriological perspective. Hence the crucial question: Can a nonbeliever ever be joined in marriage to a believer?

The question seems to have been confused by the historical circumstances in which it was put in its earliest form. First of all, early Christians who were of Jewish origin did not easily shed their ancestral prejudice against gentiles. In fact, the first ecumenical council—that of Jerusalem—was convened precisely to settle this question,[6] but prejudices remained despite Paul's attempts to eliminate them.[7] Let alone marriage, even other forms of human intercourse with gentiles were forbidden. In the second Letter to the Corinthians, Paul cautions against Christians being "yoked together" with nonbelievers. This sounds rude in the Greek version, for the term *heterozygountes* really means yoking together of animals of different species.[8] Even if this passage is a non-Pauline interpolation, as is the opinion of many scholars, the fact that it has found a place in the New Testament illustrates the feeling of superiority Christians had over their gentile neighbors.

In a way this is understandable. Corinth was a cosmopolitan city notorious for its sexual licentiousness and moral corruption. In such a situation encounter with gentiles was not a happy one. It is precisely in Corinth that the question of "mixed marriages" (if we are allowed to use that term retrospectively) was first raised. Evidently, the question was not that of a Christian *marrying* a gentile. The case referred to is that of an already married gentile couple, one partner of whom embraces the Christian faith. The correspondence between faith and marriage, which was deeply ingrained in the Christian conscience, would obviously demand divorce or immediate separation. Would this be the solution?

Paul's answer implies that Christ has left no instructions on the matter and so Paul would of his own authority give a set of pastoral norms to guide them in this ambiguous situation.[9] He would not allow divorce or separation—unless, of course, the faith of the new convert is threatened.[10] This is perfectly consistent with his theology of marriage. He also gives a reason why such a mixed marriage should be allowed to continue—namely, that the nonbeliever be (offered an opportunity to be) saved through association with the baptized partner. Also, contrary to the Jewish idea of ritual impurity of children issuing from a "mixed marriage," Paul insists that even children be regarded "clean" by reason of the believing partner's faith.

Did Paul imply that mixed marriage gave an opportunity for the conversion of the other partner? That seems to be the church's interpretation in the subsequent era.

Note how from the beginning baptism, the sacrament of faith, was linked with marriage. Here again the theological implications are crucial for the understanding of the church's view on mixed marriages. Violation of the baptismal commitment was an infidelity to the covenantal (that is, marital) relationship with God. Apostasy was spiritual adultery. It is this doctrine that is going to assume exaggerated proportions in the centuries to come.

As the church began to grow in "pagan" Rome and began to be romanized by the empire in the very process of trying to christianize it, this doctrine received greater poignancy, especially when couched in the legal idiom of Roman culture—a point I shall discuss later. In fact, one legal code repeats Ambrose's caution that Christians should refrain from any marital contact with Jew, gentile, and heretic, because faith is the first grace of marital chastity *(Prima conjugii fides gratia castitatis est).*[11]

The medieval thinker Prevostin refers to two types of "mixed marriages" (with reference to which, however, he uses the term *dispar cultus*): the "marriage" of a Christian to a non-Christian (Jew or heretic), which is simply not valid; and the Christian marriage in which one partner later abandons the faith. In the latter case, however, the marriage remains valid even after apostasy (by reason of the irrevocability of baptism), but the Christian should not yield marital rights to the apostate partner whose abandonment of faith amounts to spiritual fornication *(Fidelis autem si hoc constet ecclesiae non debet ei reddere debitum spirituali fornicatione impediente).*[12]

This sort of reasoning presupposes a further distinction between the Christian *faith,* on the one hand, and *baptism,* the sacrament of faith, on the other. For the baptized partner remains baptized even after abandoning the faith so that the validity of the marriage persists. If, on the other hand, a person has faith but is not yet baptized, as in the case of a catechumen, a valid marriage cannot take place until that person is baptized! Faith is not sufficient; the sacrament is required. This rather rigid opinion was the most common among the more influential theologians of the Middle Ages: Bonaventure, Albert the Great, and Thomas Aquinas.[13]

This juridical approach to the sacraments of marriage and baptism (bringing down to the earth the mystical idealism that makes marriage something made only in heaven) took definite shape especially in the eleventh and twelfth centuries, and has left its stamp on the canonical understanding of marriage that has continued to our times. Hence the picture of Catholic marriage is not complete without situating its mystical aspect within the *legal culture* of Roman Catholicism. For the evolution of a theory of mixed marriage from a particular situation in Corinth to a universal enforcement is not otherwise understandable.

MIXED MARRIAGE WITHIN THE LEGAL CULTURE
OF ROMAN CATHOLICISM

The cultural trait that distinguished Roman Catholicism from every other religious institution was its remarkable uniformity in a culturally pluralistic world. This uniformity, which was both the strength and the weakness of the Catholic Church, was derived mainly from the *Pax Romana* inherited from Latin culture, the soil in which the church was transplanted in the early centuries of its existence. This culture grew around the *Roman concept* and the *Roman spirit* of *law.* Christianity received a permanent twist from the legal ethos of the Latins. "At the cradle of Latin theology stood a jurist—Tertullian—who exercised an enduring influence," writes Walter Ullmann, who also adds that the church learned to hand out even "religious" principles in the form of "legal" maxims from the time the Christian message came to be framed within the Roman jurisprudential scheme.[14] Even teachings of later councils were in the form of carefully worded formulas followed by "canons."

The romanization of Christianity was immediately followed by a christianization of Europe—and a good part of what was European was non-Christian. By the Middle Ages this development had a lasting influence on the church's attitude to everything non-Christian. In the juridical structure that evolved in the Middle Ages, the church—both as Roman and as European—was the *societas perfecta* that alone could legitimize any other society. The Thomistic thesis that there could be a legitimate society of the natural order outside the supernatural order of the church was vehemently attacked by Rome.[15] It is not only the privileged members of the "perfect society" (who acquired that juridical membership through the sacrament of baptism now reduced to a clerically controlled rite), but even those who were not privileged to have this citizenship in the perfect society called the church, who were under its supreme leader's universal jurisdiction. No one in the world could remain outside the authority of the popes.[16] This was the medieval position.

Now put the Pauline counsels on mixed marriages within this Roman scheme. What was merely a pastoral norm becomes, in the course of centuries, a rigid law. What the church teaches is also legally binding on all, even the non-Christian. If a mixed marriage was not valid, then it was not legal either. The conversion of the non-Christian partner and the baptism of the children—which Paul is interpreted to have regarded as desirable advantages accruing from a mixed marriage—become legal conditions legitimately imposed by the church! Thus the baptism of the non-Christian partner, which also ensures the baptism of all the children that come from that marriage, was not inconsistent with the principles of Roman Catholic culture.

It was already a big concession on the part of the later church to have allowed mixed marriage almost as an exception, a wound in the law, borne with patience but to be cured as soon as possible—namely, by converting it to a Christian marriage. But the legal authority of the church over both partners continued to be exercised by means of a law that required the non-Christian partner to promise that no obstacle would be put in the way of the Christian party to practicing his or her faith. The Roman juridical view of the church was hardly modified when this new concession was made. Nor was the ancient spirit abandoned.

For quite some time, now, the ecclesiology of the Code of Canon Law has been under attack. The juridical view of the church is now counterbalanced by an ecclesiology ("science of the church") that reemphasizes the church as an invisible mystery visibly lived. But canon law has lagged far behind this new theology and consequently the discrepancy between the legal "reforms" coming from above and the theological climate in which the Christian lives today creates tensions that by now are not unknown to the lawmakers.

Even the most recent changes in the law, though a step forward, still lag behind theology. At present the non-Christian is not "bound" to make any promise in writing. The Christian partner, however, is made to do so. He or she promises to be faithful to the faith and to the church's teachings on marriage; and also *promises to make every effort* to bring up the children as Catholics. The non-Christian is *persuaded to acknowledge,* though not necessarily in writing, that he or she is aware of the other's (written) commitments. Also, pressure is applied to have the marriage in the church. Exemption from this form of marriage—*forma canonica*—is now given with less reluctance, but always as a last resort when everything else fails. And even then, it is civil marriage that is permitted, not the religious ceremony of the non-Christian partner! This is where the church stands today.[17]

THE DOCTRINAL AND LEGAL DIMENSIONS OF MIXED MARRIAGES IN A BUDDHIST CULTURE

The clearest line of demarcation between Catholic culture and that of Buddhists consists in what I would call the "correspondence between law and doctrine." Unless a dialogue is initiated in this matter and clarification sought by Buddhists and Christians responsible for the formation of religious consciences, tensions in marital relationships of mixed couples are bound to be perpetuated.

In the Indian heritage, inclusive of Buddhism, there is one comprehensive term for both law and doctrine. It is dharma. In the legal literature such as that of the Dharmaśāstras the law would not imply therefore "an individual obligation system" as in the West but a mere "expression of the natural and moral order."[18] The same is true of doctrine. There is therefore a doctrinal tone in the concept of law but no legal enforcement of doctrine. Here Buddhism stands at the opposite pole of Catholicism.

In the biblical perspective, the closest approximation to the Buddhist notion of dharma is *dabar,* the "word," which could perhaps be regarded as both doctrine and law; it "expresses" the salvific message of God and it also "executes" the salvific program of God. It describes no less than prescribes the divine order. As the church born of a biblical milieu grew into the legal ethos of the Roman world, it drew more and more from the legal books of the Bible[19] and developed the "obligatory" and "prescriptive" aspect to the extent that "law" became the ultimate expression of doctrine, or to borrow a phrase from Ullmann, pure doctrine was transformed into enforceable law.[20] In fact, most medieval universities of Roman Catholicism had only one faculty: that of law and jurisprudence,[21] which included doctrinal matters! The canon law that still governs mixed marriages is a crystalization of this medieval synthesis.

Returning now to the Buddhist position, we see a totally different approach to the whole question of law and doctrine. In conformity with the general Indian tradition, Buddhism regards law as dharma rather than dharma as law. Obviously, the righteous person is *dhārmika,* one living in accordance with dharma. In fact, the word also includes the Western (Christian) concept of conscience—for which there is no other specific term in the whole of Pali Buddhist literature.

An individual obligation system, however, *did* develop in Buddhism—but was restricted to the sangha: the monks. It is none other than the *vinaya,* the monk's *regula,* being only a particular expression of something much more fundamental: the dharma. To be sure, the monastic rule is restricted in scope, whereas dharma embraces also the vast nonmonastic sphere of human life and behavior. Marriage comes under dharma and only the celibate life of cenobites is governed by the monastic *Vinaya*. Hence Buddhism has no legal apparatus to deal with marriage directly as does the Catholic Church.

There is, however, a very specific doctrine of marriage in the teachings of the Buddha. Because this is dealt with quite extensively by my Buddhist colleagues,[22] I wish to confine my observations to the peculiar character of this teaching—namely, that it is one of "moral persuasion" rather than legal enforcement.

However, *legal codes* did arise in Buddhist societies and marriage was extensively treated in them. Inasmuch as some of the Southeast Asian Buddhist countries underwent a process of indianization, the Brahmanic jurisprudence of the Indian *Dharmaśāstra*s happened to be the remote source of their legal literature. Buddhism, even in non-Indian soil, was not averse to the *Dharmaśāstra* tradition: during its early formative centuries, it lived in an Indian society "governed" by that tradition. But unlike the Brahmanic system, where the secular and the religious overlapped, Buddhist society tended to keep the two orders—monastic and lay—interdependently separate. The monastic institution that governed itself through its own internal code, the *Vinaya*, did not formulate civil laws but acted as the *conscience of the secular state*,[23] which followed the guidance of legal literature in formulating civil laws for the masses.

Hence the secular law as found in the *Nīti-niganduva* in Sri Lanka, the *Wagaru* in Burma, or the *Thammasat* (from the Sanskrit *Dharmaśāstra* via Pali *Dhammasattha*) in Thailand was a regionally defined legal system—modeled, of course, on the *Dharmaśāstra*s but adapted to local needs and temperaments under the ethical umbrella of Buddhism. It is not surprising, therefore, that in the early Indian phase of Buddhism the institution of marriage was held up as a high ideal,[24] almost as in the *Dharmaśāstra*s that "governed" Indian society, but in non-Indian Buddhist countries there is greater realism and sobriety, even leniency and humaneness, in the treatment of marriage and its breakdown.[25]

This illustrates the type of "magisterium" the sangha constitutes, especially in a Theravada country such as Sri Lanka. As the conscience of the laity and of the state, it steadfastly preaches the ethical ideal of marriage. But it is the role of the state to enforce the laws formulated in the spirit of the legal tradition that "expresses the dharma: the natural and moral order."

Perhaps the lacuna lamented by Christians, no less than by some concerned Buddhists (names mentioned below), is that in a culture such as that described above, marriage has gradually lost its religious content altogether. This deficiency does not come from the basic insights of the Buddhist religion but from the doctrinal extensions of the gnostic idiom through which the teachings on marriage have necessarily to be communicated. Marriage—as all life of love and sensual pleasures—is a secular involvement and cannot, as such, be "soteriologically meaningful"—or, to use a Christian term, "sacramental." If one were compelled to use the language of sacramentology at all, one would rather have to restrict one's comments to the sangha and its *Vinaya,* which together constitute the visible and juridical embodiment of Buddhist soteriology. The monastic thrust of Theravada Buddhism takes marriage out of the salvific context.

In Buddhism, however, the secular can be religious, though the religious is not necessarily soteriological. There are many religious practices—such as vows to gods—that, in the Buddhist scheme of things, are not salvific. Thus marriage is something deeply religious though not soteriolgoical. This is an important point of difference from Christianity, which regards marriage as soteriological. It is certainly an exaggeration of this position that makes marriage a secular event devoid of any religious significance. This has happened in most Buddhist cultures and is not to be attributed to the basic teachings of the Buddha. The situation, however, needs to be remedied.

In fact, Dr. G. P. Malalasekera, in the interim report of a Buddhist committee of inquiry, complained that weddings and funerals do not reflect a Buddhist culture.[26] Later, making explicit reference to the Christian marriage rite, he confessed that Buddhists have yet to evolve a marriage ceremony that is religiously impressive.[27] Even suitable scriptural texts for use in a marriage ceremony are lamentably lacking, says Ven. Dr. B. Seevali Thera, although for funerals there is no dearth of them.[28]

It is not strange, therefore, that many Buddhists in Japan satisfy their religious needs by marrying in Christian churches or before Shinto priests. Buddhism, as such, has no rite of its own to impress on their minds the seriousness of the commitment and its religious dimension.

On the contrary, Christianity, with its mystico-juridical approach, has so deeply impressed upon its adherents the religious character of marriage that despite the current crisis of secularization and so-called dechristianization in the West, young couples requesting church marriage are on the increase.[29] The very nature of marriage compels them to look for a mode of public consecration, and the West has no cultural model to offer other than the Christian rite of matrimony.[30]

RESOLUTION OF CONFLICTS THROUGH CULTURAL INTEGRATION OF THE CHURCH

I acknowledge that, in the Roman juridical perspective, marriage works best when the tension between theory and praxis is maintained by advocating, on the one hand, a very high "mystical" ideal of marriage in the *doctrine* taught, and on the other, by applying "juridical" controls by means of *law,* which ensures that the praxis is aligned with the theory. This system was born out of the church's praiseworthy and fruitful attempt at inculturation—a process whereby the church christianized a culture by fully allowing itself to be shaped by it. But that culture has now given way to another. Hence the "mystico-juridical" approach of Roman Catholicism too is brought to a crisis point. New patterns in marital behavior in postindustrial society is forcing the church to reconsider the ancient model in terms of Christian values that could be safeguarded in the emergent culture in the West.[31] Inculturation, in other words, has always to continue.

If, therefore, this ancient model is irrelevant in the West, how much more incongruent would it be in Asia, especially in a Buddhist culture that has always inculcated a realistic human approach to the institution of matrimony and in which the dialectic between "doctrine" and "discipline" *(dharma-Vinaya* or *vijjācaraña)* is diametrically different from the "mystico-juridical" approach of Roman Catholicism?

The Roman Catholic Church had an isolated existence for centuries and was not sufficiently exposed to non-Christian cultures. The "pagan" culture of pre-Christian Europe was so easily domesticated by the church that it could not acquire a dialogical approach toward anything non-Christian; it was always in a position of *power*. Add to this the fact that the non-Christian religions that came in its way up to the modern period were Judaism and Islam, against which the church always adopted a defensive posture. Thus, reinforced even when it was exposed to other Asian religions in the East, it reinforced its past attitudes rather than correct them in the face of new exposures. The Jesuit attempts at inculturation in India and China were ruthlessly suppressed.

Looking back, one could not have expected the church to revise its medieval attitudes to mixed marriages—even more so because the doctrine of mixed marriages was spiritually rooted in a rather unhappy experience of "paganism" at Corinth. A fresh look at marriage in a Buddhist culture could remove the superiority complex of Christians.

Hence it is never too late to expose a local church to a Buddhist culture and to the doctrine and discipline it advocates with regard to marital ethics. The church may discover many areas of disagreement, but may also find ethical values that correspond to those of the emergent model in contemporary Christian cultures. A dialogue is imperative.

This cultural integration of the local church is not something preposterous any more! It is a revival of the ancient Christian method that generated a "Roman Catholic Church" in the first three centuries after Christ! Further, the uniform monolithic culture that the Roman church established everywhere is not to be confused with its "catholicity." Pluralism is now acknowledged as the ultimate test of "universality." The local church is responsible for this gigantic task and this essay is an invitation in that direction.

At the same time I feel that without this process of inculturation, the sublime theology of marriage (minus, of course, its later exaggerations) cannot be shared with the Buddhist who may profit by the church's "sacramental" approach to this institution, which the phenomenon of urbanization and modernization is affecting adversely. The Western experience has matured the church and has equipped it to meet a situation that Buddhists are about to face for the first time in Asia.

This presupposes one important attitudinal change in church leadership. The mixed marriage, though a difficult venture in some cases, should not be regarded as a "wound in the law." The freedom to marry is a fundamental human right over which the church has no authority, save that of guiding it. If a Buddhist and a Christian are in love, they have the right to marry each other, and the church has the obligation to help at least the baptized member. After all, we live in a pluralistic society outside the control of the church. Nor should Buddhists feel that they need the church's permission to marry the person they love; they need nobody's permission. This means the church must radically change its discipline regarding:

1. the prenuptial inquiry
2. the *forma canonica* or "church wedding"
3. the religious observances of the couple, and
4. the religious education of the children.

Hence the following concrete proposals are made as items for study by competent authorities of the local church.

CONCRETE SUGGESTIONS FOR REFORM

1. The prenuptial "inquiry" is a healthy practice that need not be given up. It affords a golden opportunity for the priest to explain to couples the religious and sacramental dimension of marriage as viewed by the church. It is a splendid opportunity for an interreligious dialogue—a prelude to marital harmony.

But the imperialistic tones of this inquiry have an irritating effect on Buddhists. After all, their culture does not require that they bring their Catholic partner before a Buddhist monk. Moreover, the authoritarian attitude that a canonically exacting but theologically simple priest adopts during the inquiry is, to say the least, humiliating to a Buddhist.

I have recorded at least three different reactions to this. Some have confessed to me that they have submitted themselves to this ordeal for the sake of peace, for the love of the other partner, out of tolerance—that is, respect for the religious convictions of the other, and so on. This is a typical Buddhist approach.

Others who regard such tolerance a concession to a momentary weakness have reacted violently after the marriage. Some have even gone to the extent of enforcing not only Buddhist practices on their partner, but also a Buddhist eduction on the children. If the Christian party could make similar promises in the presence of the priest, why should not Buddhists execute their duties in a similar manner? Such reactions should open the eyes of church authorities.

In the third category are those who either walk out of the presbytery in rage or just refuse to go there at all. They feel their dignity and religious freedom threatened by the church. They prefer a civil marriage. The religious problems that arise from a mixed marriage are never diminished on that account. But it is *their* way out.

2. The whole question of the *forma canonica* remains to be studied afresh. Were there "church marriages" in the early centuries of Christianity? If, even today, exemption is given from it at times, the implication is that its absolute necessity is not upheld even by the law. Here again the church must educate priests in the "theology of religions" based on *Gaudium et Spes* and *Dignitatis Humanae* of Vatican II. Should the Buddhist be even indirectly pressured to

marry at a church wedding, however impressive it may be? Obviously Buddhists need a religious ceremony and the *poruva* function they are accustomed to is not strictly a Buddhist rite. Therefore, the Christian can easily adopt it for mixed marriages without making it a disguised form of church wedding! In fact, the Christian Workers' Fellowship (C.W.F.) has already made a pioneering attempt in this direction with remarkable results.

According to Christian teaching, the sacrament of marriage is administered not by the priest, but by the baptized partners. Could not the *poruva* rite be prepared in a manner that gives the baptized partner the sacramental or "sanctifying" role as insinuated in the Pauline instructions given in the first Letter to the Corinthians? Could not the *testis qualificatus ecclesiae* be a layperson, an elderly member of the family, as is required by our culture, rather than an ordained minister? Would this not be an opportunity for declericalizing the matrimonial rite without reducing it to a purely civil ceremony?

This way, religious content can be infused into the *poruva* rite of marriage without offending the religious sensibilities of the non-Christian partner. The CWF experiment demonstrates that this rite can be made to express the religious content of marriage to the Buddhist and its sacramental dimension to the Christian.

3. The religious experience of the couple needs even more profound study. Obviously, conversion of one to the other's religion is often desired by Christians and by Buddhists, for this may promote a greater degree of harmony. But, living as we do in a pluralistic society, we must learn to accept the possibility of religious divergence in a successful marriage. St. Ambrose's objection to mixed marriage was that the couple was not united in prayer.[32] Perhaps this is particularly true of a Buddhist-Christian marriage, where prayer and belief in God might not offer any common ground! Here the challenge to the Christian is greater because the opportunity for a deeper spirituality is greater. The whole prayer life of a Christian has to reach the profound level of wordlessness—*silentium tibi laus,* as the fathers of the church used to say. Or, as Swami Abhishiktananda, the wandering Benedictine, would say, every Christian—a fortiori the Christian called to share life with a Buddhist—is "called to plunge into Silence" and be lost there, unable to utter any word, not even a word of adoration or praise.[33]

Would not, then, a mixed marriage be the most coveted locus for an indepth encounter between Christianity, the religion of the Word, and Buddhism's way of silence? It has been a privilege for me to know some couples, very few indeed, who enjoy a brief encounter in silence before they end the day. This, of course, would not dispense them from the other religious practices which each is expected to observe individually.

4. Then comes the religion of children. Obviously, there are two solutions to this problem, besides the one of conversion to one or the other religion. The one I hear often from couples who have found religion a source of division and tension is that the children be allowed to grow up neutral so that when they are old enough, they could choose the religion they prefer. This sounds rather

theoretical. First of all, such a secular humanistic approach is bound to clash with religious practices of the Christian family and the Buddhist family that have come together as a result of this marriage. Besides, our culture emphasizes the religious dimension of education.

Here again, a religious atmosphere has to be created in the home where human values common to both religions are emphasized and a graduated introduction to the deeper form of both religions can be given. Jesus as Son of God, the human expression and readable sign of the ultimate goal of all existence, and the Buddha as the path-pointer to interior liberation, can both have a place in the home of a mixed couple. Because there is no model to go by, this new approach has to be experimented upon and given time to bear fruits. The danger of syncretism has to be averted by a healthy exposure, in later years, to the distinguishing marks and idiomatic accents of each religion. Here Buddhists and Christians have to do more study and experimentation.

In conclusion, I wish to invite Christians to enlarge their notions of baptism, conversion, and paganism in the light of post-Vatican II theology.

Baptism is a universal calling to "live for others to the point of self-immolation," a bodhisattva ideal, symbolized by the cross of Christ. In fact, in Mark 10:35–41 (and parallels), as well as in Luke 12:50, Christ refers to his own baptism on the cross, the true baptism that gives meaning to the sacrament that goes by that name. Jesus hardly baptized others, as the Fourth Gospel assures us (John 4:2), but only allowed himself to be baptized by John the Baptist in the Jordan, and by the Father on the cross. Christian discipleship consists in "taking up the cross" (Matt. 10:38), and it is this self-transcending and altruistically joyful spirit of selfless love that decides who is a Christian and who is a "pagan."

Christian education consists in inculcating the value of the cross. Conversion means accepting these values. Such a baptism is more important than its ritual expression, which, for Christians, is a grace and an initiation to the way of the cross, the path to eradication of selfish desire *(taṇhā)*. The children of a mixed marriage must, in this sense, be "baptized" and be "converted," so that they may truly be "religious" in both the Buddhist and Christian understanding of the term. This is difficult, but certainly not impossible.

10

Christianity in a Core-to-Core Dialogue with Buddhism

Christian dialogue with Buddhism is said to be genuine only when it truly springs *"from* the core of Christianity." The theme of this chapter makes a further appeal that such dialogue must necessarily be *"with* the core of Buddhism." For nothing short of a core-to-core dialogue merits to be called dialogue.

However, we have no illusions about the psychological and even theological obstacles, not to mention problems of conscience, that pile up before a Christian who embarks on this ambitious project. This is why we adopt here what might seem to be a negative methodology—namely, that of discussing Buddhist-Christian dialogue in terms of that which prevents it from taking place. To bring clarity to an otherwise complex question, I have singled out three of the major impediments to dialogue: (1) the *language barrier,* which can be overcome with a certain amount of psychological adjustment; (2) the inevitability of a *communicatio in sacris* (communion in ritual) in a core-to-core dialogue, which implies a new theological understanding of religions; and finally (3) the most challenging difficulty that arises when Christology is confronted with the competing claims of Buddhology.

THE LANGUAGE BARRIER

Buddhist Gnosis and Christian Agape

The "core" of any religion is the *liberative experience* that gave birth to it and continues to be available to successive generations of humankind by developing its own peculiar medium of communication, as we shall see in the second part of this chapter. It is this primordial experience that functions as the

A paper given at the Fifth Workshop on Theology of Religions, which dealt with the general theme "Dialogue from the Core of Christian Theology," at St. Gabriel, Mödling, Austria, April 1987. Published in *Cross Currents,* 37 (1987) 47–75.

core of a religion at any time in any given place, in the sense that it continuously re-creates the *psycho-spiritual mood* proper to that particular religion, imparting at the same time its own peculiar character to the *socio-cultural manifestations* of that religion.

In Buddhism, this core experience lends itself to be classed as *gnosis* or "liberative knowledge," whereas the corresponding Christian experience falls under the category of *agape* or "redemptive love." Each is *salvific* in that each is a *self-transcending* event that radically transforms the human person affected by that experience. At the same time, there is an indefinable contrast between them that largely determines the major differences between the two religions, differences quite obvious even to a casual observer.

In fact, in a country such as Sri Lanka, where a strong Christian minority coexists with the Buddhist majority, the average pedestrian who sees the statues of the meditating Buddha and of the crucified Christ erected on our roadsides has learned to distinguish at least intuitively, if not articulately, between the "tree of knowledge" and the "tree of love"; the tree beneath which Gautama, the Indian *mystic* sits in a posture of contemplative calm, and the tree upon which Jesus the Hebrew *prophet* hangs in a gesture of painful protest; in short, between the tree that *bears* the *fruit of wisdom* and the tree that *bares* the *cost of love*.

What must be borne in mind is that both gnosis and agape are *necessary* precisely because each in itself is *inadequate* as a medium, not only for experiencing but also for expressing our intimate moments with the Ultimate Source of Liberation. They are, in other words, complementary idioms that need each other to mediate the self-transcending experience called "salvation." Any valid spirituality, Buddhist or Christian, as the history of each religion attests, does retain both poles of religious experience—namely, the gnostic and the agapeic. The movement of the spirit progresses through the dialectical interplay of wisdom and love, or, to put it in Buddhist terms, through the complementarity between *prajñā* and *karuṇā,* and in the Hindu tradition, the sapiential spirituality known as the *jñāna-mārga* and the affective-active paths called the *bhakti-* and *karma-mārga*.

Hence the first major obstacle to a core-to-core dialogue between Buddhism and Christianity is not certainly the idiomatic difference just alluded to, but the failure on the part of Buddhists and Christians to acknowledge the reciprocity of these two idioms; their refusal to admit that gnosis and agape are both legitimate languages of the *human* spirit or (as far as the Christian partner in dialogue is concerned) that they are languages that the same *divine* Spirit speaks alternately in each one of us. Hence the "language barrier" I speak of here is the prejudice that each party has toward the other's epistemology. More bluntly said, Christian thinkers are all too often antignostic and Buddhist intellectuals antiagapeic, in their "official" positions.

A breakthrough in this language barrier is a conditio sine qua non for a core-to-core dialogue because it is precisely these two languages that constitute the "core" of these two religions. To make this clear, I propose the following four considerations, mainly addressed to the Christian partner in dialogue.

1. In the first place, the aforementioned antignostic prejudice of Christians is to be viewed against the background of a series of gnostic aberrations in the history of Christianity: docetism, Manicheism, Catharism, Albigensianism, encretism, Jansenism, quietism, illuminism, and the rest. The memory of these heresies impedes the Christian from acknowledging the legitimacy of a *Christian gnosis* such as the one bequeathed to the church by the Alexandrian school. As Louis Bouyer pleads, the heretical gnoses were only the embroidery along this orthodox line of Christian gnosis.[1] The misuse of a good thing does not preclude its good use.

The same advice should be proferred to influential Buddhist intellectuals, especially in Southeast Asia, who exhibit an unreasonable aversion to the *bhakti* aspect of Buddhism.[2] Gnosis is contrasted with faith or reliance on a person loved or trusted.[3] Certain currents of pathological deviations and even erotic extremes to which affective spirituality was stretched in many an esoteric cult[4] have created in the Buddhist intelligentsia a unilaterally gnostic repudiation of the agapeic idiom. But the truth is that "erotic mysticisms" are often the bitter fruits of an extreme gnosticism not rooted in the agapeic ethics of self-sacrifice and social concern.

2. Secondly, there is a lamentable ignorance among both Buddhists and Christians about the positive historical influences of these two modalities of religiousness in the cultures they have shaped. Christians tend to project onto Buddhism an ahistorical, apolitical, and acosmic character that they rightly or wrongly associate with the hellenistic forms of gnosticism. They are not aware of the socio-political changes that a gnostic soteriology such as Buddhism has brought about in the cultures it has shaped for over two millennia. The Weberian sociologists' caricature of Buddhism as a "world-denying asceticism" is a sophisticated extension of this basic antignostic prejudice of Christians. One must acquire a better understanding of the social role of the gnostic religions of Asia, which, unlike their hellenistic counterpart, have survived for centuries precisely because they have been active agents of socio-political processes.[5]

Conversely, the Buddhist who sits on the other side of the dialogue table suffers from antiagapeic bias, and invariably reads into Christian agape his or her concept of "affective spirituality" derived from the theopathic religiosity of certain sects not only in Hinduism but also those found on the fringes of Buddhism itself.[6] Here again, such Buddhists must be helped by Christian partners to acquire an unbiased view of agape—namely, that it is a creative force in the history of Christianity—something that transforms rather than enfeebles persons; that it is a kind of love that blooms into justice, bringing peace through the conflict of the cross, raising us from the terra firma of infantile innocence to the insecure heights of spiritual maturity, as the lives of many Christian saints testify.[7]

3. My third observation rests on a widely accepted axiom in contemporary psychology that any given human instinct, if repressed, tends to reappear in a dangerously deviant form. This is eminently true of the gnostic instinct that has

not been allowed to develop freely within Christian spirituality. As a result, we have at least two "gnostic aberrations" in contemporary Western culture. Langdon Gilkey has detected one, and Fergus Kerr names the other. The first is the contemporary trend in "scientism" to locate humankind's *self-liberative power* in the *scientific knowledge* of nature's secrets—a species of neognosticism practiced and preached by certain circles of "white robed clerics" officiating in the Holy of Holies of scientific laboratories![8]

The other gnostic aberration is Carthesianism, which treats the noncorporeal part of our being as a subsistent "human ego," a thesis that Piet Schoonenberg, a post–Vatican II progressive theologian inadvertently but dangerously supports when he refers to the human body as part of the "non-I," or "the world which he [the human being] makes *his* world"[9]—a position that Thomas Aquinas with all his "gnostic Christianity" (which I discuss below) carefully avoided. As Kerr's alarming account suggests, this species of heretical gnosticism has so pervaded and even perverted so much of contemporary Western culture that not only avowed Thomists such as Garigou-Lagrange, and progressive theologians of our own times (see Kerr for names), but also secular philosophers and scientists of modern Europe (not to mention, of course, the Holy Office in its instruction of August 31, 1979, on eschatology) have all been soaked and drowned in it.[10]

I therefore share Kerr's concern that contemporary European and Christian culture be delivered from this cancer of Carthesian gnosticism, but I wish to reiterate that this cannot be achieved without allowing the gnostic instinct to express itself freely within Christian orthodoxy.

The converse is true of Buddhism. The practice of esoteric cults of a sexo-yogic nature on the fringes of orthodox Buddhism and the prevalence of exaggerated devotionalism even in Theravada cultures, far from warranting the condemnation of an affective spirituality, argue for a restoration of a healthy practice of *bhakti* and *śraddhā*,[11] and a reconfirmation of the Buddhist belief that it is "knowledge" fertilized by "love" that brings forth the final emancipation.[12]

4. My fourth and final observation recapitulates the implications of the other three just made, and also takes us just where the language barrier between gnosis and agape is broken through. For I believe that there is a *Christian gnosis* that is necessarily agapeic; and there is also a *Buddhist agape* that remains gnostic. In other words, deep within each one of us there is a Buddhist and a Christian engaged in a profound encounter that each tradition—Buddhist and Christian—has registered in the doctrinal articulation of each religion's core experience. What seems impossible—the interpenetration of the two irreducibly distinct idioms—has already taken place both within Christianity and within Buddhism. If this fact is readily accepted, then the first major obstacle to a core-to-core dialogue between Buddhism and Christianity is eliminated for good. Let us then dwell longer on this "idiomatic exchange" as it has taken place in Christianity through its "agapeic gnosis" and in Buddhism with its "gnostic agape".

The "Agapeic Gnosis" of Christians

The gnostic formula that "*knowing* the liberating *truth* is, or leads to, salvation" finds no direct equivalent in biblical soteriology. For the expression "knowing" receives a peculiar semantic coloration from the way one understands "truth." Neither the *aletheia/veritas* of the Greco-Roman stoics nor the *sat/satya* of Hindu/Buddhist saints can adequately translate the Hebrew word *emet*, which weighs more toward "truthfulness" rather than simply "truth." In the concrete context of the formal agreement to a mutual commitment between Yahweh and his people, it means fidelity or "*being true to*" each other. Inasmuch as this agapeic contract or covenant between God and the people is concretized in the law according to the Jews, but personified in Jesus according to Christians, it is not surprising that in both the Old and the New Testament, to *know* God amounts to a faithful adherence to the covenant obligation to *love*.

Thus, in the gnostic milieu in which Christianity was nurtured in its early formative centuries, a theological formula had to be found that would relate *ginōskein* with *agapan* without compromising the agapeic thrust of the covenant soteriology. Already in the New Testament we see John and Paul taking the first steps in this direction, allowing others to go further and further in the same path in later centuries.

From Bultmann's summary of John and Paul with regard to this question,[13] we can infer (without implicating Bultmann in our conclusions) that both these pioneers of "Christian gnosticism" could not have conceived the salvific experience of a Christian in terms of a direct awareness of God (the Father) as many theologians seem to have done later. According to the Johannine view, all that we *know* of God is the Son, and even this knowledge is not acquired by us but given to us by the Spirit. The mutual *knowing* between God and the Son and between the Son and his disciples coincides with the mutual *being* (living, abiding) in each other, and is, in turn, rooted in the mutual *loving* that defines ultimately the God-Son and Jesus-disciple relationships. More specifically, *loving one's neighbor is the Christian way of knowing God.* In other words, love is Christian gnosis, because one who does not love one's fellows does not know God (1 John 4:7f.). Our love for one another here in the world is the Christian *art* (but according to Bultmann, only the "criterion") of knowing God.

In the Pauline vision, too, "to love God" does not amount to direct "mystical relationship with God" (as it was in later mystical theology), but "finds expression in brotherly love" as Bultmann insists. Perhaps Paul admits the possibility of "knowing" divine things—but clearly regards such knowledge worthless without love (1 Cor. 13:2)! Probably a greater distance between *ginōskein* and *agapan,* as between two differing modes of human experience, is admitted in Paul than in John. But one can infer that for both these writers, the Sinai covenant of justice has received its final fulfillment in Jesus in whom mutual love among humans is the (path to) true gnosis or the knowledge of God through the Son in the Spirit.

With the evolution of what was known in medieval times as mystical theology, the gnostic idiom was more fully integrated into Christian spirituality. Three characteristic results of this tendency seem to be: (1) a demotion of neighborly love to the level of a mere prelude or a corollary to the love of God, and (2) overemphasis on the immediate (i.e., nonmediated) awareness of God as the constitutive element of Christian mysticism, so that, one fears, even Gregory the Great's concise formula *amor ipse notitia est* (love itself is knowledge), despite its Johannine ring, actually refers basically to one's direct relationship of love with God.

To this must be added (3) the fact that the distinction between *ginōskein* and *agapan* as different mental processes received greater philosophical clarity in the Middle Ages than in John and Paul. Hence, in evolving a Christian gnosis, the process of *cognitio* (as distinct from *amor*) was further analyzed into mere intellectual knowledge *(scientia)* and salvific knowledge *(sapientia)*.

With these three characteristics Christian gnosis is only a few steps away from "Buddhist agape," which reached almost the same place from the gnostic end of the spectrum. However, before I discuss this interesting question—the main point of my analysis in this section of my presentation—I must tarry a little longer on the two forms in which medieval writers conceived the mystical awareness of (or direct relationship with) God.

Some medieval definitions of *theologia mystica*[14] clearly uphold the almost exclusively agapeic character of the mystical experience: *motio analogica in Deum per amorem fervidum et purum.* This notion of an agapeic movement toward God is clearest in the Franciscan school of spirituality. St. Bonaventure saw it as the human heart stretching itself out toward God in loving desire: *animi extensio in Deum per amoris desiderium.* Parente suggests that this definition is based on Plotinus's *Ennead VI* where it is said that God is beyond intelligence but that we could stretch ourselves in prayer toward God.[15] Granted Plotinus's gnostic influence, the fact remains that for Bonaventure God is beyond human intelligence, beyond the faculty of human cognition, but within the horizon of love. One recalls again the pithy utterance of Gregory the Great: *amor ipse notitia est.*

But the most popular trend in medieval times was to define mysticism in terms of both *cognitio* and *amor,* with an alternating emphasis according to one or the other school of theology. According to the most frequent definition, mysticism was an experiential knowledge of God mediated through love: *experimentalis cognitio habita de Deo per amoris unitivi complexum.* The Franciscan school in particular advocated the primacy of love over knowledge, but the Thomistic school, by holding the opposite thesis, produced the most articulate form of Christian gnosticism.

The Greco-Roman idiom with its gnostic flavor is clearly in use in St. Thomas and its affinity with some Hindu-Buddhist philosophical formulations is little more than verbal. He clearly speaks of salvific experience as *cognitio veritatis* or "knowing the truth." For him, however, there are two ways of arriving at this knowledge: either by supernatural means *(per gratiam)* or by natural means *(per naturam)*. But supernatural knowledge (which is what concerns us here) is also of two kinds: purely "speculative" knowledge, a revelation of divine mysteries *(secreta divinorum)*, and "affective" knowledge that (is such that it) produces love *(producens amorem)*. St. Thomas concludes by equating this affective knowledge with wisdom proper or *sapientia*,[16] a medieval synonym for mystical theology.

The important phrase here is *producens amorem*. Thus we do not hear of "the love of neighbor leading to the knowledge of God" as in Paul and John, or of the "love of God mediating the knowledge of God" as in the other medieval theories, but of *knowledge of God producing love of God*. The primacy of *ginōskein* over *agapan* seems unambiguous here. St. Thomas's Christian orthodoxy lies precisely in that he maintains only that kind of "knowledge" to be salvific and sanctifying that tends toward love as to its end, for Love remains for him the end of all things.[17]

The distinction between speculative and affective knowledge is significant. Elsewhere, St. Thomas refers approvingly to Denis's description of Hierotheus as one who not only *studied* but also *experienced* the divine mysteries.[18] The two Latin words used by St. Thomas here *(discens* and *patiens* by which he seems to translate the Greek *mathōn* and *pathōn*, respectively) are illustrated by two examples: first by the case of one who judges on moral questions intellectually *(per modum cognitionis)* through the principles of *scientia moralis*, and the other by the example of a morally upright person who judges moral matters by a connatural bend toward virtue *(uper modum inclinationis)*. This latter he regards as *sapientia* and a gift of the Holy Spirit.

This sapiential or affective knowledge given as a grace by the Holy Spirit is also called experiential knowledge—*cognito experimentalis*—and is illustrated once more by a reference to Hierotheus who (according to Denis) *didicit divina ex compassione ad ipsa*[19]—that is (in a free paraphrase), "learned of the divine mysteries not just through the mind but through the heart attuned to such mysteries through praxis." It is gnosis consummated through agape.

This is as far as Christian gnosis or agapeic gnosis can go within Catholic orthodoxy, and this is orthodox because St. Thomas has been the *doctor communis*—that is, the only "magisterium" that the hierarchical Roman Church followed during the last four centuries! But there are others who have gone further; for there are "Christian Neoplatonists" who are on the fringe of Christian orthodoxy, living close to the border between Buddhism and Christianity and hence speaking a language that makes sense to Buddhists.

Here we must first go to the other side of the border and hear Buddhists speak in their own tongue and then come back to see how the Neoplatonists break through the language barrier.

The "Gnostic Agape" of Buddhists

The acid test of a successful breakthrough in the language barrier between the two religions is the notion of "God" and "soul." According to the gnostic experience of Buddhists, these words are sheer nonsense! It is here that the

Christian who refuses to learn the gnostic idiom fails the test. Traditionally Christians have learned to build their whole life around these two basic concepts or, rather, realities. In the Christian vocabulary, "person" is a pivotal word that in the concrete stands for the "Loved Lover"—the origin, center, and destiny of all love. Hence "person" is predicated of both the redeemer God and redeemed individuals. For redemption, like Redeemer, is agape. The Buddhist, on the contrary, can conceive neither the Ultimate Truth nor any being that is in search of It in personalist terms. Neither of them is a "person": no God, no soul.

The Buddhist uses only gnostic categories to express final liberation: *prajñā* (wisdom), *vipassanā* (intuitive vision), *jñāna* (higher knowledge), *bodhi* (enlightenment), *prativedha* (penetrative insight), and so on. But the human mind in its normal state cannot experience gnosis without making a "qualitative jump" from the level of ordinary perception *(saṃjñā)* or discriminative knowledge *(vijñāna)*. One recalls here the Christian mystics' distinction between *scientia* and *sapientia*.

To gnosis there corresponds a special supernoetic faculty called the *prajñā-cakshuh* (Pali: *paññā-cakkhu*), the sapiential eye that is hidden and hindered, so to say, by nonknowledge *(avidyā/avijjā)* and by subliminally compulsive tendencies *(saṃskārā/samkhārā)*. Hence the faculty of gnosis is developed to full maturity by a process of renunciation of inordinate desires and by self-purification. This process, in the final analysis, consists of removing the three roots of evil: (1) *rāga,* erotic, sensual, selfish, and acquisitive "love," which is the exact opposite of Christian agape; (2) *dvesa/dosa,* hatred and ill will, which again is the very negation of agape; (3) *moha,* delusion, slowness of mind and ignorance of an intoxicated consciousness incapable of awakening to the Saving Truth. Thus two out of three roots of evil from which liberation is desired by a Buddhist are the absence of what Christians call love; the third is the absence of gnosis.

The nirvanic experience or gnosis is consistently referred to as the nonexistence of these three roots of evil. Inasmuch as in the gnostic idiom the most positive notions are evoked by use of negative language (e.g., health as non-sickness—*ārogya*), so also nirvana, according to the most frequent "definition," is *arāga, adosa,* and *amoha*—that is, nonselfish love, forgiving love, and liberative knowledge, respectively. The Buddhist who is keen on dialoguing with the Christian would do well to acknowledge that nirvana, which cannot be "conceived," is yet affirmed in terms of "love" experienced within the context of perfect "knowing."

Yet the constitutive dimension of this experience is gnosis, which nevertheless cannot take place without love. This is why in practically all schools of Buddhism, the complementarity between *prajñā* and *karuṇā* has been affirmed as the defining essence of Buddhahood. The former is salvific knowledge implying disengagement from *saṃsāra* (world of sin and sorrow); the latter stands for "redeeming love," which engages the buddha in a program of restructuring the psycho-social life of human society in tune with the supreme goal of nirvanic freedom. By *gnosis* the buddha anticipates the Beyond Here and Now; but by *agape* (so to say) the buddha transfigures the here and now in terms of that Beyond. Thus, wisdom *(prajñā)* is thought to have provided the buddha with a vantage point to serve the world with compassionate involvement *(karuṇā)*. In fact, the buddha's posture toward the world is summed up in these two words: wisdom and love—that is, respectively, gnostic detachment and agapeic involvement.[20]

Nevertheless, *karuṇā* is not in itself salvific, just as its "object" is not Ultimate Reality. It is essentially oriented toward all "beings" (*sattva*, a term not applicable to the ultimate truth; for nirvana is *nissattva*). *Karuṇā,* moreover, is the prelude, the accompaniment, and the clear manifestation of gnosis. Love has no salvific value in itself, so to say, except in terms of knowledge, which alone liberates but always in and through love.

Though it is true that selfless, self-immolating love may make one a bodhisattva (a candidate to Buddhahood), the fact remains that it is gnosis that finally makes him a buddha. The Mahayana emphasis on the bodhisattva ideal may make its spirituality appear proximate to the Christian view of holy life, but only up to a point. For in most major schools of Buddhism, including those of Mahayana, the affective currents of mysticism must ultimately flow into the sapiential stream that alone reaches the ocean of nirvana. Hence even when speaking of love, the orthodox Buddhist would nuance the agapeic modes of expression by introducing the "impersonalist" language proper to the gnostic spirit.

It is here that "Christian gnosis," especially of the Neoplatonists, arrives from the opposite direction through a similar process. In the Neoplatonist's apophatic turn of language, as Professor Hilary Armstrong observes, "personalist" and "impersonalist" ways of speaking are both necessary because both are individually inadequate.[21] Vis-à-vis the Ultimate Reality, both *plerōma* and *kenosis,* fullness and nothingness (Abbot Chapman's "blank") are the "antipodes of the unimaginable"[22] and both defy personalist and impersonalist categories. Thus, the Neoplatonist's "contentless knowing" or "knowing as such"[23] is also what a Buddhist sees in impersonalist terms as the final purpose of all love. It is a knowing that does not admit a knower or a known. This means that to talk of the personhood of the (finite) knower and the (infinite) Known (or vice versa: the personhood of the infinite Knower and the finite known) is non-sense. There is no God; no soul!

The "no soul" theory is even more plausible if placed in the context of "knowing as such." The most liberating experience of God for a Christian gnostic is to experience one's own *creatureliness,* the "dust-ness" of one's origin and destiny (Gen. 3:19)—and to the Christian this is the practical fruit of the gnostic path of the Buddha. "When I am touched by who makes me what and who I am," then "I experience being created."[24] And in the Christian gnostic's experience of God, the total sweeping *change* that a person is experiencing is "God"—that is, knowing of God.[25] The gnostic agape of the Buddhist mystic revolves around the experience of this *change*—not toward a person who produces the change (no God), or toward a person who is being changed (no soul)!

To help understand this "acid test" of a successful breakthrough between gnosis and agape—in other words, to appreciate a possible Christian understanding of the Buddhist's denial of God and soul—one would do well to make one's own the distinction that Armstrong makes between an *icon* and an *idol:*

> When we are told that God is really Being, or a Mind, or a Monad, or a Person, or a Tripersonal unity within relations between the persons very precisely defined, and all these words are being asserted to be used in an intelligible sense as descriptions or definitions which we are bound by reason or authority to accept, we are being invited in my opinion to idolatry.[26]

But these same concepts and epithets he would regard as *icons.* For icons are neither God nor images of God but "a vehicle of his presence and power, a means by which He comes to us and acts on us." These icons (such as God, Person, Creator, Redeemer) do not offer us a true description of God but are signs by which we may reach God. The Christian gnostic is an idoloclast as well as an iconodule.[27] This is what the Buddhist in each one of us might be telling the Christian in each one of us by the phrase: no God, no soul!

It is not farfetched to conclude that the core experience of Christianity is not agape pure and simple but agape in dialogue with gnosis; conversely, the core experience of Buddhism is not mere gnosis, but a gnosis intrinsically in dialogue with agape. Hence, a true Buddhist-Christian encounter is possible only at the depths of our being where the core-to-core dialogue has already taken place!

COMMUNICATIO IN SACRIS

Three Levels of Dialogue

The core of any religion, as said at the beginning, is the liberative experience that brought that religion into being. It is the spiritual sap that continuously flows through the vein of tradition and vivifies the cultures that grow around that religion. This is what makes that core experience available to anyone at any time in history. It is precisely through recourse to that primordial experience that a religion resolves its recurrent crises and regenerates itself in the face of new challenges. In fact, the vitality of any given religion depends on its capacity to put each successive generation in touch with that core experience of liberation.

This means that a religion would die no sooner than it is born if it fails to evolve some *means of perpetuating* (the accessiblity of) *this experience.* Religious beliefs, practices, traditions, and institutions that grow out of a particular religion go to make up a "communication system" that links its adherents with the originating nucleus—that is, the liberative core of that religion. This is why a religion fades out of history even after centuries of existence when its symbols and institutions lose their capacity to evoke in followers the distinctive salvific experience that defines the essence of that religion. Did this not happen to the great religions of ancient Egypt, Rome, Greece, and Mesopotamia?

Buddhism and Christianity are both vibrant with vitality because each has developed its own religious system (of doctrines, rites, and institutions) that can make the original experience available to contemporary society. Hence the conclusion is irresistible: a Christian who wishes to enter into a core-to-core dialogue with Buddhism must have two qualifications: (1) a preliminary empathic apprehension of the real nature of the other religion's core experience as I have shown in the first part of this chapter; and (2) an uninhibited willingness to make use of the religious system that the Buddhist offers to the Christian as the only means of access to that core experience. In other words, a readiness to enter into a *communicatio in sacris* with Buddhists. This is what I wish to discuss in this part of this chapter.

I grant that, although the logical force of this conclusion can hardly be disputed, its theological validity and its pastoral feasibility is bound to be questioned. This is because the church has not yet evolved a normative tradition to guide us in this matter, due to certain historical limitations in the church's conscious relationship with other religions; limitations that I cannot analyze here without making an unwarranted deviation.[28] But the churches in Asia may soon evolve a new tradition through "basic *human* communities" where Buddhists and Christians share life and life's most articulate self-expression: religious experience. A case for *communicatio in sacris* therefore can be made only within a theology of religions different from the one we are traditionally taught.

When this problem cropped up in the Second Asian Monks' Congress in Bangalore in 1973, long and apparently inconclusive discussions were brought to a close when the assembly, thanks to a timely intervention by Raimundo Panikkar, came to realize that our discourse on interreligious dialogue could focus on the three specific levels in which each religion operates—the levels of:

a) the primordial *experience* that has originated a given religion;
b) the collective *memory* of that experience stored up in religious traditions, practices, beliefs, and so forth; and,
c) the *interpretation* of that experience in philosophical, theological, exegetical schools.

Most often—especially in discussions such as these—we remain only at the level of interpretation without ever touching the first level of experience, which is ineffable and incommunicable but realizable. Hence our intellectual discourse here is not a very good example of a core-to-core dialogue! Besides, one cannot penetrate into the first level of the core experience unless it is mediated by the collective memory of that experience. Yet one realizes too soon that even this second level is an "interpretive" level. When I remember an experience, I have already framed it in terms of my historical and cultural categories. Hence those who consult the collective memory (tradition) must be ready to transcend it at some moment or other if they wish to touch the core of the other religion. It is the entry into the second level that we usually designate as *communicatio in sacris!*

The core experience (the liberative nucleus) of a religion is preserved and protected not only by the basic beliefs and practices that perpetuate its memory, but also by means of "interpretations" that grow around that religion. Far from belittling the importance of interreligious dialogue at this third level, I should rather foster it as a remote preparation for a core-to-core dialogue (see the last part of this chapter).

Note, however, that there are three overlapping degrees of interpretation: the *philosophical,* the *ideological,* and the *cultural,* each of which seems, in most instances, enveloped by the successive one. Thus it is not always easy to pick up a purely philosophical interpretation that is not ideologically inspired to some extent or culturally incarnate in a given context. This is easy to grasp if we concede that hermeneusis is often a process by which a religion becomes relevant in a new social situation. Interpretation, in other words, is a survival technique that reveals the vitality of a religion in the midst of a crisis. More concretely, it is the religion's attempt to make its core experience meaningful, and therefore accessible to the human *mind* in a given *political* and *social* context; this is why the philosophical, ideological and cultural strands of interpretations are often intertwined. Some of the earliest instances of such interpretations have resulted in the traditional schools of Buddhism such as the Theravada (in the sense of the Theriya Nikaya of Sri Lanka), the Sarvastivada, the Sautrantike, the Madhyamika and the Gocaravada.[29] Some Sino-Japanese schools such as Ch'an/Zen and Ching-tu/Jodo are later historico-cultural reinterpretations and adaptations of some of these earlier ones.[30]

Tendai and Shingon—being Japanese versions (i.e., adaptations or interpretations) of Chinese originals, T'ien-t'ai and Chen-yen—had a clear ideological orientation from the first moments of their arrival in Japan in the early ninth century.[31] It is especially in Nichiren[32] that we see a convergence of (apocalyptic) philosophy, (nationalist) ideology, and (Shintoist) culture, so much so that this school or sect has succeeded in developing this triple hermeneusis into a modern politically dynamic socio-cultural movement: the Soka Gakkai.

Similar observations can be made of movements and schools of thought in other Buddhist countries. What becomes evident to us, then, is that what we confront are always concrete forms of Buddhism—that is, philosophically, ideologically, and culturally interpreted forms of Buddhism. It is, however, understandable that in the academic world, especially in the Euro-American universities, the philosophical approach to dialogue seems on the whole preferred. One representative example is the work of John Cobb, Jr., who advocates a mutually transforming encounter between Buddhism and Christianity,[33] and accordingly suggests that Christianity be reinterpreted in terms of Whitehead's process philosophy.[34] The ideal form of Buddhism that meets such a Christianity, of course, is the Madyamika system evolved by the great Buddhist dialectician Nagarjuna.[35] Another example would be Waldenfel's effort to relate one particular theological interpretation of European Christianity with a corresponding school of thought in Japanese Buddhism.[36] Most doctoral dissertations on comparative religions emanating from Western seats of learning continue to make significant contributions to the development of this model of dialogue.

In the East, where religions are practiced rather than merely studied, the locus of dialogue shifts from the library to the socio-political and religio-cultural contexts in which Buddhists and Christians live their daily lives. Hence the emphasis is ideological and cultural rather than merely philosophical. Some Sinhala Christians have found in the ideology of Sinhalese nationalism a cultural point of entry into a Buddhist society that is sharpening its identity against Tamil militancy. The opposite trend is seen in the Buddhists and Christians who have opted for the ideology of class struggle as the rallying point of their common efforts to bring ethnic harmony and ensure justice to all. There are others who move on to the cultural side of the spectrum rather than stay on the ideological. They are busy with ''inculturation''—that is, relating Christianity to the cultural experiences of Buddhism.

Very rare would be the case—for example, the Christian Workers' Fellowship—where the ideological and cultural wings of Buddhist-Christian dialogue help participants to soar higher into the threshold of a *communicatio in sacris:* Buddhists celebrating the Easter rites with Christians, and Christians joining Buddhists in the *Vesak* festival, each group perceiving the ''liberative core'' of the other religion in one another's idiom.

Communicatio in Sacris

The churches in the West, where Christianity was first fragmented, are busy discussing doctrinal and disciplinary questions regarding intercommunion, but we in Asia, who cannot present a dismembered Christ to a non-Christian world, are summoned to become a ''pentecostal'' event that allows us to speak in the tongue that other religionists understand, and therefore we are called to study their idiom as a language of the Spirit. Our problem, then, is not interecclesial ecumenism, which we take for granted,[37] but a transecclesial communion with non-Christians in their experience of redemption—even if the inquiry into the agent, mode, and recipient of redemption may sound redundant or even misleading to the one who attains it.

The new theology of religions that underlies this new praxis aims at focusing not only on the liberative experience of Buddhists but also on the ''naming of the experience'' in which consists its collective memory. As mentioned earlier, our effort at consulting this collective memory is actually a process of appropriating the basic beliefs and practices that perpetuate this memory, a *communicatio in sacris* that we perceive as an epiclesis ensuring a breakthrough in the language-barrier between us and Buddhists. As already demonstrated in part one, we are given an initial acquaintance with the Buddhist idiom through the agapeic gnosis of the Christian tradition and through the subliminal dialogue between agape and gnosis that sensitive and introspective Christians can fathom in their own heart. Hence a Christian's passage through the Buddhists' collective memory is, in some sense, a déjà vu experience. The Christian will recognize in the liberative nucleus of Buddhism the mirror image of Christianity's own core experience: a meeting of a gnostic agape with an agapeic gnosis.

To analyze the steps of this process, one must recall that the Buddha formulated the memory of his liberative experience in terms of a fourfold Truth *(satya/sacca)* and an Eightfold Path *(mārga/magga).* This formula is as dry and prosaic as any medical prescription can be to someone who is not conscious of having the disease for which it is prescribed. Hence, the first item in the formula is the naming of the disease: *dukkha*—that is, emptiness of all reality and the emptiness in us; and the pain, the frustration, the angst that such emptiness evokes. Then comes the diagnosis. The cause of this innate frustration in us is our obsessive thirst *(taṇhā)* for that which cannot quench that thirst—namely, an addiction to transient reality. The third item is the cure: the "surgical" removal of *taṇhā.* The fourth truth is the medical prescription proper: the (Eightfold) Path that leads to the total removal of obsessive thirst, the path to nirvanic freedom. This Eightfold Path is traditionally summed up under three heads: a life of moral uprightness *(sīla),* an ascesis of renunciation and purification climaxing in one-pointedness of mind *(samādhi)* and finally the mystical insight or liberative wisdom *(uprajñā/paññā)* that coincides with interior freedom from all self-love *(rāga),* from all vestiges of hatred *(dvesa/dosa),* and from all nonknowledge or delusion *(moha).*

The prescription or formula itself is not capable of bringing about liberation. It is the execution of the prescribed action that can lead to nirvana. The prescribed processes of "realizing the truth" *(vidyā)* and the prescribed process of "treading the path" *(carana)* are not obvious in the above formula; it is stored up in the collective memory of a rich tradition. Therefore, this traditional method can be acquired not from a study of written texts, but through humble discipleship under a competent monk. Like our Lord and Master who humbly let himself be initiated by a recognized Guru in Israel, John the Baptizer, so too should we plunge into the Jordan of Buddhist spirituality in the presence of an authoritative guide.[38] It is this self-effacing baptismal entry into the Buddhist tradition that I refer to as *communicatio in sacris.*

But this process of "gnosis and praxis" *(vidyā-carana)* communicated from master to pupil is to be undertaken in the context of a highly developed and extensively spelled out code of "doctrine and discipline" *(dhamma-vinaya),* these being a set of beliefs and practices that embody the truth and the path, respectively, and therefore serve as a medium for *Vidyā* (interiorization of the truth) and *carana* (treading of the path). It is the closest that one can come to the interpretive level and therefore it forms a stepping stone from the third to the second level of dialogue—from the level of interpretation to the level of collective memory.

May I conclude by stating that these three levels of dialogue correspond to the three levels at which the core experience of Buddhism is approached by Buddhists themselves? For they make a clear distinction between *paryapti,* the intellectual mastery of Buddhism, *pratipatti,* the practice of the means of attaining the final goal of Buddhism, and *prativedha,* gnosis, the core experience of Buddhism. Study must lead to practice, and practice culminates in insight.

THE BUDDHA AND THE CHRIST

The Christian encounter with the Buddhist's core experience (part one), which is possible only through recourse to the collective memory of that experience (part two), needs now to be tested at the third level of religious consciousness—namely, the level of interpretation (part three).

As far as Buddhism is concerned, the interpretive level has reached a high point in the doctrine of the Buddhahood, or "Buddhology" as I shall call it hence forth. But Christ being the very core of Christianity, it follows that Christology is both the axis and the acme of all Christian hermeneusis. Of course, my emphasis on the essentially hermeneutical character of both Buddhology and Christology is not intended to be a denial of either the theoretical validity or the historical basis of such interpretations. As suggested in part two, interpretations are a necessary means of communication, and as such they reveal the capacity of a given religion not only to *define* (limit) but also to *redefine* (expand) the boundaries of orthodoxy in the process of allowing its theoretical framework to accommodate the intellectual achievements and the historical challenges of a given era.

The focus of dialogue at this third level is the historical figure of the founders of these two religions, who are believed to play a soteriological role in the lives of their followers. This claim is not made by the adherents of other religions. This is what makes the Buddhist-Christian dialogue a dangerous exercise. Far from being a religious conversation about Jesus and Gautama, or a comparative study of their different historical and cultural backgrounds, it can easily explode into a kerygmatic confrontation between Jesus interpreted as *the Christ* and Gautama interpreted as *the Buddha.*

Gautama Interpreted as the Buddha

The Buddhist cultures of Asia project a composite picture of the Buddha. Prof. D. J. Kalupahana, himself a Buddhist, offers us a slow-motion replay of the process by which the scriptural portrait of an extraordinary human teacher grew, in the minds of his followers, into the Transcendent Being of the Mahayanists.[39] The figure of the human teacher *(satthā)* that Kalupahana draws out of the Pali scriptures was not omniscient; nor was his experience of nirvana thought to be different from that attained by his disciples. For quite unlike Jesus of the New Testament, Gautama of the Tripitaka did not seem to have clearly claimed that the saving truth or the liberating path was identical with his own person. He was only the path-finder and truth-discoverer.

But it would be a grave mistake to think of him as a Socrates or a Plato, a mere founder of a school of thought. The kind of Buddhism that Europe imported in the nineteenth century was a "religionless philosophy" and its founder seemed more a thinker than a holy man.[40] He came to be presented as an areligious person, beloved of rationalists and agnostics, and noted for the skepticism of his style.[41] This description disregards the fact that the Buddha had listed "logic, inference, and reasoning" among the means that cannot lead to the truth[42] and put down "skepticism" among the five hindrances on the path to nirvana[43] and as one of the three fetters to be freed from.[44]

Much more perceptive in this regard was Clement of Alexandria (third century, A.D.), who was one of the founding fathers of Christian gnosticism; he sensed that the Buddha was more than a mere teacher of a philosophy. According to Clement, those who observed the Buddha's *regula (monastica),* "regarded him as divine" *(hos theon tetimekasi)*—that is to say, more than human, on account of his superlative sanctity *(di'hyperbolen semnotetos).*[45] It was his sanctity that medieval Christians celebrated liturgically when they raised St. Joasaph (= bodhisattva) to the altars![46]

This is also the image that emerges clearly from the Buddhist cultures in Asia: a saint recognized as such by his followers and therefore revered as the noblest of beings that has ever set foot on earth, higher than the highest of gods, his sanctity alone being the root of his authority over all things in heaven and on earth.

The *locus classicus* that parallels the "Who do people say that I am" of Matthew 16:13 is found in the Anguttara Nikaya.[47] Could you be a god? asks a Brahmin, and the Buddha's answer is 'No!' A *gandhabba* (demi-god)? No! A *yakkah* (a ghost)? No! A human being? No! The questioner pursues: What then could you be?[48] The answer begins with a reference to the Buddha's perfect purity: like the lotus that sprouts and grows in water but remains unsullied by that water, so is the Buddha born and nurtured in this world but untouched by it, as one who has "overcome the world" *(lokam abhibhuyya).*[49] Then comes the long-awaited answer: "Bear in mind Brahmin that I am Buddha."[50] For what distinguishes him from all other beings is his spotless purity.

The legend that describes the Buddha's mother, Maya, as a virgin both *ante partum, in partu* and *post partum* is a symbolic variant of the simile of the lotus, and is iconographically expressed in the form of a white elephant,[51] just as in Christian art the dove represents the Holy Spirit hovering over Mary to make her the virgin mother of Jesus. In the first centuries of Buddhism, no artist dared to paint or build a human figure of the Buddha who could not be classed under any category of being, all of which he transcended by his infinite purity. Instead, they resorted to symbols: the riderless horse represented his great renunciation (i.e., his leaving home for the forest); a tree with no one seated beneath it represented the enlightenment; the wheel symbolized the first sermon; his death was signified by the stupa, the funeral mound. But when statues did begin to be made in later centuries, they were frequently of gigantic proportions suggestive of the superhuman stature of his personality. Even today in Theravada countries, to impersonate the Buddha on the stage or in a film is considered blasphemous.

As in the plastic arts, so also in the medium of the spoken and written word, there was a struggle to formulate this inexpressible dimension of Buddhahood, a dimension that in no way eclipsed Gautama's humanity but in some way transcended it. For, though "docetism" *(lokottaravāda)* was rejected as a heresy, especially in southern Buddhism, the Mahayanists did equate the Buddha with the Dharma—that is, with the eternal Truth that preexists Gautama,[52] similar to the way Jesus of Nazareth was recognized as the preexistent Logos in the fourth Gospel.

Hence there has been from very early times a desperate effort to create Buddhological titles from terms judiciously selected from the religious vocabulary of contemporary cultures. A random survey has come up with forty-six such titles used in the Pali scriptures,[53] among which some describe the Buddha's "person" as such *(mahāpurisa* = supreme person; *mahāvira* = great hero; *purisuttama* and *naruttama* = the most exalted of humans; *mahājuti* = the brilliant, etc.); others indicate his relationship with other humans *(vinayaka* = leader; *purisadamma-sārathī* = trainer of tameable humans; *sarathīnam varuttamo* = the most excellent of guides, etc.); still others point to his supremacy over the whole of creation *(lokanātha* = lord of the universe), and so on.

As one scholar has observed,[54] the long series of epithets cited in the Upali Sutta of the Pali canon[55] recalls the *stotra* (doxological) literature known as *sáta-nāma* ("hundred names") so characteristic of Hindu devotionalism. The first impression one gets is that here affective or devotional spirituality *(bhakti-mārga)* has replaced the gnostic spirituality *(jñāna-mārga)* proper to Buddhism. The fact, however, is that almost all these epithets refer to the Buddha's gnostic detachment and his internal purity.

Because Buddhahood is conceived as the pleroma of gnosis *(prajñā)* and "agape" *(karuṇā),* as shown in the first part of this presentation, one can easily understand why the Pali commentators linked up these two Buddhological qualities with the two most hallowed Buddhological titles—namely, *arahan* (the worthy one) and *bhagavan* (the blessed one), respectively; the former implying gnostic disengagement from the world, and the latter connoting his agapeic involvement with the liberation of all beings as well as his sovereignty over the whole of creation.[56] These two epithets occur in the most ancient doxology (used even today at the beginning of any liturgy): "Hail to Him, the Blessed One *(bhagavato),* the Worthy One *(arahato),* the supremely Enlightened One!" The exegetes claim that by gnosis (proper to the *arahan*), Gautama crosses the ocean of samsara and reaches the further shore of nirvana, but by agape (proper to the Bhagavan), he also gets the others across.[57]

The convergence and concentration of *prajñā* and *karuṇā* in the Buddha (which explains, respectively, his absolute purity and his soteriological impact on the final destiny of others), has also earned for him such titles as *lokavidū* (knower of the world) and *lokanātha* (lord of the universe), already in the canonical writings.[58] Also in the subsequent postcanonical literature, his transcendental status and his cosmic lordship began to be indicated through a long string of Buddhological epithets such as "King of kings," "Self-existent," "Self-luminous," "God above (all other) gods" *(devātideva).*[59]

Some modern Buddhist scholars (e.g., Kalupahana quoted above) seem to question the orthodoxy of this development. Could not, perhaps, its scriptural roots be traced back to what we might call the catechetical method or the pedagogy of the Buddha? The scriptures testify that he changed the god-infested cosmos of his contemporaries into an anthropocentric universe wherein the humans who fulfill their innate capacity to realize the metacosmic goal of nirvana were held to reach a state far above the level of gods. Thus he divested the gods of all salvific power; even their cosmic influence was restricted to helping or harming humans in their day-to-day temporal needs. The canonical writers make their point when they portray the highest deity of the Brahmanic religion crouching in reverence before the Buddha and his disciples.[60]

This catechetical procedure of the Buddha was continued as a missiological technique in later times in that missionaries did not uproot the cosmic religiosity of those whom they converted but gave it a metacosmic orientation not only through the doctrine of nirvana but also by installing the Buddha as the sovereign lord immediately *above* and yet wholly *beyond* the local deities of each culture.

This seems to be the origin of what I alluded to as ''the composite portrait'' of the Buddha emerging from Buddhist cultures. This certainly is what Gautama the Buddha means for millions of Asians today. He is as much the Great Being *(mahāsatta)* to be revered and praised, the Lord *(bhagavan)* to be loved and trusted, as he was a human teacher *(satthā)* to be followed and a saint *(arahan)* to be emulated.

This portrait was brought out in clearer focus during a Buddhological controversy that erupted some years ago in Sri Lanka. A renowned Buddhist layman and writer, a humanist and socialist, Dr. Martin Wickramasingha produced a Sinhalese novel based on the life of the Buddha, eliminating the mythical and the miraculous elements from the scriptural accounts and focusing on Siddhartha's *human* struggle not only for his own nirvanic freedom but also for *social* transformation. This novel provoked a massive public protest on the part of the monks and laity. The great monk-scholar, the Venerable Y. Paññārāma, who spearheaded this protest movement, compiled a two-volume refutation of the Buddhological and other inaccuracies said to be contained in that novel.[61]

In this critique of the novel, the venerable monk complains, among other things, that in portraying the character of Siddhartha as a human seeker, the novelist had overlooked the quality specific to Siddhartha's Buddhahood.[62] Yet, lest he should be accused of docetism *(lokottaravāda),* the monk insists that his criticism should not be construed as a plea for retaining the mythical and the miraculous elements at the expense of Gautama's true humanity. To prove his orthodoxy, he quotes extensively from one of his devotional poems addressed to the Buddha,[63] indeed a credo on the Buddha's historical humanity:

> Had I sensed thee not to be a human
> Never, never indeed would I find in me
> Any love, regard, or fear for thee! . . .

> My Lord is indeed a Man!
> Man in body and thought
> In virtue and action!
> Yet, going beyond common humanity
> He bore a Splendour Transcendent!

Then, presuming himself to be the Buddha's contemporary, he expresses his longing to nurse his aging Master, to touch and massage his limbs, kiss his feet and wash his ailing body.

It is very clear that for this defender of orthodoxy, Buddhahood implies a *truly transcendent* dimension of a *truly human* being. Both these aspects are proclaimed with as much firmness as the *verus Deus* and the *verus homo* are predicated of Jesus in traditional Christology.

There is also a third aspect implicit in this credo: the soteriological role of the Buddha. In the orthodox Theravada stream, the Buddha is never regarded as a Savior. His soteriological role is restricted to his discovering and preaching the dhamma (the eternal salvific truth that preexists him) and to the forming of the sangha (a community that, emulating him, realizes this truth and continues to preach and practice the path that leads to it). But once the dhamma was equated with the Buddha, and the sangha was devalued (as happened in certain Mahayanist schools, e.g., in Amidism), Buddha became the Savior who grants the grace of salvation to those who invoke him in faith. An agapeic religiosity using a personalist idiom has become a characteristic of such schools of Buddhism.

The more intricate element in the Buddha's soteriological influence is his *cosmic lordship*, at least as far as popular Buddhism is concerned. This should not, however, be confused with the cosmic function of gods and spirits. Yet, the cult of gods—this cosmic religiosity—includes as one of its manifestations the *socio-political* regulation of human life. This is at the root of the "divine right theory of kingship," which the Buddha categorically rejected in favor of a social contract theory.[64] Yet the feudal societies that hosted Buddhism in Asia continued to be dominated by the older theory. Hence, the socio-political order, even in Buddhist cultures, continued to be associated with cosmic religiosity to which Buddhism imparted a metacosmic orientation by placing the Buddha, the dhamma, and the sangha above and beyond the socio-political order.[65] The kingdom of Thailand continues this tradition.

Nevertheless, the social dimension of Buddhist ethics is reclaimed from oblivion and reexpressed as the Buddha's vision of a just political order for today,[66] so that social justice is regarded at least as an inevitable by-product of Buddhist soteriology.

Here, we can cite an extreme example from *Dalit Sahitya* ("literature of the oppressed") produced by schedule castes of Maharashtra in India. Many of them embraced Buddhism, which served them as a doorway to social emancipation. The following poem addressed to the Buddha, the liberator of the oppressed, is a sample of *Dalit Sahitya:*

Siddhartha
Never do I see you
In the Jetavana
Sitting in the Lotus position
With your eyes closed
Or in the caves of Ajanta and Wcrule
With your stony lips touching
Sleeping your final sleep.

I see you
Speaking and walking
Amongst the humble and the weak
Soothing away grief
In the life-threatening darkness
With torch in hand
Going from hovel to hovel.

Today you wrote a new page
of the Tripitaka.

You have revealed the
New Meaning of suffering
Which like an epidemic
Swallows life's blood.[67]

This indeed is a new interpretation of the Buddha's soteriological role. Belief in his cosmic lordship is hermeneutically extended to the socio-political structures whose radical transformation is believed to be possible under the Buddha's soteriological influence. Undoubtedly, this is "a new page in the Tripitaka" (Buddhist scriptures), as the poet declares.

Jesus the Christ in the Context of Buddhology

The "missionary Buddhology" that installed the Buddha as the cosmic lord in so many Asian cultures has anticipated by centuries the missiology of Paul, who did the same with Christ in the hellenistic cultures that he evangelized. He preached and confessed Jesus to be the Lord of all creation, whom all beings "in heaven, on earth, and in hell" adore in fear and trembling (Phil. 2:6–11). Far from suppressing hellenistic belief in "cosmic elements," Paul acknowledged their existence and their power to enslave human beings (Gal. 4:3) and cause disobedience (Eph. 2:2). Though they appear to be gigantic powers arrayed against humankind (Eph. 6:12), they have all been decisively domesticated by the risen Jesus (Col. 2:15). Thus by liberating us from this "dominion of darkness" (Col. 1:13), Christ has made himself "the head" of all such cosmic forces (Col. 2:10). In other words, he is at once the meta-cosmic power and the cosmic mediator because in him the whole of existence—in heaven and on earth, visible and invisible—is recapitulated and reconciled (Col. 1:15–16).[68]

Undoubtedly there is a striking parallelism, though not strictly a similarity, between the two confessional formulae, the Buddhological and the Christological. No wonder that in some Asian countries the first Christian encounter with Buddhism was to push the Buddha out and install Christ in his place. The Buddhists replied in kind!

In fact, in the polemical mood of the late nineteenth century, when the anticolonial movements, by historical necessity, had to be anti-Christian, the great Buddhist revivalist, Anagarika Dharmapala, took delight in making odious comparisons between the two founders.[69] The "Nazarene Carpenter," as he referred to Jesus with disdain, had no sublime teachings to offer, and understandably so, because his parables not only reveal a limited mind but they also impart immoral lessons and impractical ethics:[70]

> Jesus as a human personality was an utter failure. He made no impression on the public during the three years of his ministry. No thinker or philosopher took the least notice of his philosophy which helped to create imbeciles. The few illiterate fishermen of Galilee followed him as he promised to make them judges to rule over Israel.[71]

In Dharmapala's speeches and essays, Jesus is reduced to the stature of a spiritual dwarf before the gigantic personality of the Buddha. But let us humbly acknowledge that this species of Buddhist revivalism owes its anti-Christian thrust to an initial Christian offensive aimed not only against the doctrine but also against the *person* of the Buddha through the written as well as the spoken word.[72]

The peak of this revivalism, as one sociologist sees it,[73] manifested itself in the proliferation of Buddha statues in the major towns of Sri Lanka's western coast; it was an attempt to reaffirm Buddhism against Christianity as a sociopolitical force. May I add my own explanation: Was it not also an attempt to put the Buddha back where he belonged in the urban culture of the Westernized Buddhist elite, presumably because in that elitist culture the cosmic lordship of the Buddha taken for granted in rural areas was eclipsed by the colonial impact of Western Christianity?

There is also a less aggressive way of affirming the supremacy of the Buddha over Christ and vice versa. The Hindu theology of religions has pioneered this technique. Hinduism neutralizes the challenge of another religion by absorbing it into its own theological framework. Brought within the Hindu salvific umbrella, Jesus and Gautama become Hindu avatars (incarnations) whom Christians and Buddhists can hardly recognize as *the Christ* and *the Buddha*, respectively.

This ancient theology of religions prevails today in the frontiers of mainstream churches. The Buddha is accepted as a precursor of Christ, a "holy pagan" preparing the way for Christ, the only Savior, as Daniélou, following

Guardini, seems to have maintained.[74] Marco Polo's spontaneous observation about the Buddha ("Had he been a Christian, he would have been a great saint of Jesus Christ"), had already anticipated this theology of religion. In fact, it was as a saint of Jesus Christ that the medieval church accepted the Buddha in the Joasaph cult, as mentioned earlier. No Buddhist is going to be flattered by this condescension. Yet, this theory has deep roots in the New Testament approach to the patriarchs and prophets of Judaism, the same that Islam adopts toward Jesus!

Many a well-meaning Buddhist, too, condescends to give Jesus a niche in the Buddhist weltanschauung. At best, Jesus receives the welcome given to a Bodhisattva, being full of compassion but still on the way to Buddhahood! This is about the maximum that Buddhists can concede to the founder of Christianity. If they concede one bit more to Jesus, they would cease to be Buddhists.

We are, therefore, obliged to conclude that both the exclusivist and the inclusivist theories of religion end up in asserting the supremacy of Christ over the Buddha and vice versa. There seems to be no way out of this dilemma, for there cannot be two cosmic lords! This is the impasse that any "dialogical" theology of religion, even in its most progressive form, runs into. Is there no other way of *seeing* the problem? Or, another *starting point?*

I believe that the *false start* that leads theologians into blind alleys is their obsession with the "uniqueness" of Christ. At the risk of anticipating my conclusions, I would suggest that the real debate is about the "uniqueness" of *Jesus* in terms of the "absoluteness" that Christians indicate with titles like *Christ and Son of God,* and the Buddhists with similar terms: *dharma, tathāgata,* and the like. To put it more precisely, the crux of the problem is whether it is Jesus or Gautama who is *unique* in the sense of being the *exclusive medium of salvation for all.*

That Jesus is unique is obvious even to Buddhists, just as Christians would hardly question the uniqueness of Gautama. Is not each one of us unique? The issue is whether Jesus' uniqueness consists in his absoluteness as conveyed by certain Christological titles; and whether the uniqueness of Gautama should be understood in terms of the absoluteness that the word *dharma*—or in certain schools, *Buddha*—seems to convey.

Note that "the Absolute" has a soteriological connotation in our discourse here. Christians know it as the *mysterium salutis,* and have learned to distinguish three dimensions in this mystery:

1. *Source* of salvation
2. *Medium* of salvation
3. *Force* of salvation.

This is what the "economic trinity" is about. In the scriptures these three aspects are distinguished as *theos, logos,* and *pneuma,* respectively; or, more anthropomorphically, as the Father, the Son and the Consoler/Advocate, and conceptually clarified in Chalcedonian Christology as three distinct *persons* sharing one divine *nature;* and so on.

This tridimensionality of the mystery (and process) of salvation is implicitly acknowledged in the soteriology of practically all major religions as I have suggested elsewhere.[75]

In Buddhism, however, the first dimension is not seen as the source of salvation, but seems to be affirmed as the final metacosmic destiny of an individual's cosmic and human history: nirvana. Because there is no primordial source of salvation, there is no doctrine of creation (ex nihilo) either, and consequently no doctrine of eschatological consummation, nor a theory of grace. But Christianity sees the source not only as the Alpha but also as the Omega point of history. Hence, in its agapeic framework, this world and human life itself appear to be *consummated* (fulfilled, perfected) in the eschaton. This species of extrapolation characteristic of Christian theology contrasts neatly with the apophatic language of Buddhist gnosticism, which sees nirvana as the utter *cessation* rather than the consummation of all that constitutes reality as we now know and experience it. Furthermore, nirvana is the cessation of the human *individual's* history, whereas the *eschaton* is the consummation also of the *collective* history of humankind.

There is, however, a significant point of convergence. Both religions insist: (1) that a positive human endeavor (an *ascesis*) is a necessary condition for the arrival of final liberation, and yet (2) that this final liberation (the absolute future or the further shore) is never really the automatic end-product of human causation; for nirvana seems to defy the categories of *phala* and *aphala*—that is to say, it is beyond human manipulation; similarly, for the Christian, the *eschaton* is believed to "break in" from the other side of the human horizon.

Though these distinctions and qualifications are necessary when speaking of the source of salvation, there is greater agreement when we come to the medium of salvation. Salvation implies a paradox: the inaccessible "beyond" (source) becomes one's salvific "within" (force), and the incomprehensible comes within the grasp of human insight. This is possible only because the Absolute contains within its own bosom a *mediatory* and *revelatory self-expression,* an *accessible dimension:* the *dharma/logos.* The transhuman horizon stops receding only because there is a path *(mārga/hodos)* leading toward it. For in the beginning was the Word by which Absolute Silence came to be *heard;* and the Icon by which the Invisible was brought within our *sight!*

But how could we humans who have *dust* as our origin and destiny (Gen. 3:19) ever respond to this medium (*dharma/mārga/logos/hodos*/word/icon) unless we are equipped with a "response-apparatus" commensurate with that medium? No wonder all religions seem to postulate a certain *given* capacity within us to seek and find the transcendent truth, or (as in theistic religions) a certain innate *force* that pulls us toward the Absolute. This "given capacity" appears as the Spirit in the Christian's vocabulary.

The Buddhist postulates it in the context of the twofold doctrine: "no soul" and "no God." Because there is no primordial source of liberation admitted ("no God"), the human being who is merely a fluctuating series of psychophysical events without any permanent substratum ("no soul") has to rely on his/her own "self" or *citta* for liberation.[76] This *citta* is therefore that which is developed toward the full attainment of absolute freedom or nirvana. The idea of a *given* human potentiality for the transcendent is the most significant presupposition in Buddhist soteriology, though it is never explicitly analyzed.

Having thus clarified the three aspects of salvation in Buddhism and Christianity, we can now proceed to juxtapose Buddhology and Christology with the aid of a common vocabulary.

Let us note first that there is an "ascent Buddhology" and a "descent Buddhology," if we may borrow terms from Christian theology. The former defines Buddhahood in terms of a distinctive way of attaining nirvana not attributed to the *arahan*s. The term *arahan,* which used to be a Buddhological title, is now used as a synonym for those attaining nirvana in a manner different from the Buddha. The Buddha is therefore a human being who has reached a state that makes him a category of his own, as explained above. This Buddhology is prevalent in Southeast Asia. But northern Buddhism equates the Buddha with the eternal preexistent dharma. Gautama, then, would be the human manifestation or incarnation of this revelatory medium of salvation. All Buddhological titles are human efforts to express the transhuman dimension of the Buddha in the context of one or the other Buddhology. Belief in his cosmic lordship is an interpretive extension of these two basic affirmations.

Christology, too, consists in interpreting Jesus as the exclusive medium of salvation for all, the *logos,* the image, the word, the path, and so on. But as in Buddhology, so also in Christology, it is not the interpretation that saves! What saves is the *mediating reality* itself, in whatever way it may be recognized and named. Nor are the titles in themselves salvific. Such names as "Christ" are only a human categorization limited to a given culture. What saves is the mediating reality to which one culture as much as another can decide what name to give: Christ, Son of God, and the like, or *dhamma, tathāgata,* and the like.

Not even the acclamation "Jesus is the Lord" is in itself salvific. For it is not someone who says "Lord, Lord," but the one who "does the will of the Father" who is saved (Matt. 7:21). To say "Jesus is the Word" is not enough; the word must be heard and executed for one to be saved. To say "Jesus is the path" is not enough; one must walk the path to reach the end. Moreover, not all who obey the Word nor all who walk the path are obliged to know its proper name to be Jesus. For, what saves is not the "name" of Jesus in the hellenistic sense of the term "name," but the name of Jesus in the Hebrew sense of "the reality" that was seen to be operative in Jesus, independent of the name or designation we may attach to it. In fact, the knowledge of the name or title is not expected by the eschatological Judge, but knowledge of the path is expected (Matt. 15:37–39 and 44–46).

This holds good for Buddhology, too. Buddhists must agree with their Christian partners that liberation is possible only through what they both accept to be the "revelatory medium of salvation" and not the titles one gives to it. The real parting of ways begins when either Gautama or Jesus is identified with it by means of these titles. It is here that dialogue must once more change direction if it is to avoid a blind alley, as we are dealing here with kerygmatic affirmations.

A kerygma is always a metalogical proclamation that cannot be demonstrated rationally. The only convincing proof it adduces is *martyrion,* for we are dealing with soteriology, not philosophy or mathematics. That is to say, liberation is the only proof of liberation! To say Jesus is the medium of salvation is to show the fruits of such liberation in the person who says it. A Christology that remains a speculative hermeneusis fails to be a soteriological proclamation about Jesus. A Christology receives its authenticity from a transforming praxis proving that in the *story of Jesus that continues in his followers,* the medium of salvation is operative, though it is not the total mystery of salvation *(totus Deus, non totum Dei).* In our theological vocabulary, this medium is designated by titles like "Christ" and "Son of God," as applied to Jesus, for this liberation is believed to take place through Jesus the man (therefore through every man and woman *in* Jesus).

This is the inchoative Christology found in Paul and in need of refinement. But in the process of being refined, this Christology split up into at least two incomplete models: (1) the classical (Chalcedonian) model, which focused too narrowly on the theandric composition of the Incarnate Logos (Jesus) and on the philosophical problem of "one and many" with respect to the triune mystery of salvation, thus neglecting the whole process of salvation in its cosmic magnitude and in its eschatological dimension; and (2) a popular catechetical model that stressed the *divine* lordship of Jesus ("Christ the King" reigning in heaven) over and above a given, unchangeably created cosmos, without defining this lordship in terms of our co-mediation with him in the task of co-creating—that is, transforming this world psycho-spiritually and socio-politically into his kingdom of peace and justice.

This co-redemptive role of the corporate Christ, missing in both these partial Christologies, is being supplied by the emergent theologies of liberation, which are essentially kerygmatic and are critical of the Christology of domination—the theology of the colonial Christ, which could not be "good news" either for Buddhists or for Christians!

A liberation Christology sees the medium of salvation in the form of *Jesus on the Cross,* the symbol of the twofold ascesis that constitutes the salvific path—the *via crucis:* (1) Jesus' *renunciation* of biological, emotional, and physical ties that bound him to the "world" (Jesus' *struggle to be poor*), and (2) his open *denunciation* of mammon, which organizes itself into principalities and powers by dividing humankind into the class of Dives and the class of Lazarus (Jesus' *struggle for the poor*).[77]

The first form of Jesus' ascesis focuses on interior liberation, so well symbolized by the Buddha seated under the *tree of gnosis.* The second involves a ruthless demand for a structural change in human relationships in view of the new order of love or the kingdom of God, a demand that led Jesus to a type of death reserved for terrorists (zealots) on what turned out to be the *tree of agape.*

The uniqueness of Jesus (we are no more concerned with the uniqueness of Christ but with the absoluteness that titles such as "Christ" were meant to convey), lies in that his claim to be the absolute medium of salvation is demonstrated on the cross by his double ascesis, which nevertheless would not be a convincing proof of this claim but an empty boast of his followers unless this double ascesis continues in them as an ongoing salvific process completing in their bodies what is still unfinished in the ascesis of Jesus (Col. 1:24).

This double ascesis is the nucleus around which an Asian theology of liberation evolves into a Christology that does not compete with Buddhology but complements it by acknowledging the *one path* of liberation on which Christians join Buddhists in their *gnostic detachment* (or the practice of "voluntary poverty") and Buddhists join the Christian *agapeic involvement* in the struggle against "forced poverty" as it truly happens today in the basic *human* communities in Asia.[78] Here, co-pilgrims expound their respective scriptures, retelling the story of Jesus and Gautama in a core-to-core dialogue that makes their hearts burn (Luke 24:32) and it is only at the end of the path, as at Emmaus, that the path itself will be recognized by name (ibid.) if a "name" would then be necessary.

Notes

CHAPTER 2

1. Geoffrey Parrinder, *The Christian Debate: Light from the East* (London: Gollancz, 1964), p. 22.
2. Harvey Cox, *Turning East* (New York: Simon & Schuster, 1977).
3. Thomas Merton, "Marxism and Monastic Perspective," in *The Asian Journal of Thomas Merton*. Naomi Burton, Br. Patrick Hart, and James Laughlin (eds.) (New York: New Directions Books, 1975), pp. 326–43.
4. Ursula King, "Teilhard's Comparison of Western and Eastern Mysticism," *The Teilhard Review*, 11 (1975) 13.
5. Teilhard de Chardin, *How I Believe* (New York: Harper & Row, 1969); S. Radhakrishnan, *East and West in Religion* (London: Allen & Unwin, 1933), pp. 46–70; Carl Gustav Jung, *Psychology and Religion: East and West* (New York: Pantheon Books, 1958); R. C. Zaehner, *Foolishness to Greeks* (Oxford: Clarendon Press, 1953), p. 17.
6. *The History of Christian Spirituality, Part 1: The Spirituality of the New Testament and the Fathers*. Louis Bouyer (ed.) (London: Burns & Oates, 1963), pp. 15–16.
7. Langdon Gilkey, *Religion and the Scientific Future* (New York: Harper & Row, 1970), pp. 76–77.
8. Fergus Kerr, "The Need for Philosophy in Theology Today," *New Blackfriars* (June 1984) 248–60.
9. See Aloysius Pieris, *An Asian Theology of Liberation* (Maryknoll, N.Y.: Orbis, 1988), pp. 103–4.
10. Bonnie Thurston, "Thomas Merton on the Contemplative Life: An Analysis," *Contemplative Review*, 17 (1984) 2.
11. Ibid.
12. Ibid., pp. 5–6.
13. Quoted ibid., p. 4.

CHAPTER 3

1. These first three paragraphs are taken almost verbatim from my editorial, "Mutual Exposure of Religions," in *Dialogue* (Colombo) n.s., 2/2 (Aug. 1975) 45.
2. See, e.g., David W. McKain (ed.), *Christianity: Some Non-Christian Appraisals* (London: McGraw–Hill, 1964).
3. E.g., H. D. Lewis, *Philosophy of Religion* (London: English Universities Press, 1965/1973), p. 28.
4. R. Panikkar, "Philosophy of Religion in the Contemporary Encounter of Cultures" in R. Klibansky (ed.), *Contemporary Philosophy. A Survey* (Florence: La nuova Italia, 1971), p. 228.
5. E.g., A. J. Toynbee, *A Study of History* (3 vols., Oxford: Oxford University

138 Notes

Press, 1934); *A Historian's Approach to Religion* (London: Oxford University Press, 1956); *Christianity among the Religions of the World* (New York: Scribner, 1957); etc.

6. E. Durkheim, *Les formes élémentaires de la vie religieuse* (Paris: F. Alcan, 1912); M. Weber, *Gesammelte Aufsätze zur Religionssoziologie* (3 vols., Tübingen: Mohr, 1920–1921); E. Troeltsch, *Die Absolutheit des Christentums und die Religionsgeschichte* (Tübingen: Mohr, 1902).

7. W. James, *The Varieties of Religious Experience* (London/New York: Longmans, Green, 1922); C. G. Jung, *Psychology and Religion: East and West* (New York: Pantheon Books, 1958).

8. G. Van der Leeuw, *Phänomenologie der Religion* (Tübingen: Mohr, 1933).

9. H. de Lubac, "The Origins of Religion" (French original, 1937), in J. de Bivort de la Sandée (ed.), *God, Man, and the Universe. A Christian Answer to Modern Materialism* (London: Burns & Oates, 1954), pp. 195–315, as referred to in Dermot Archer, "Philosophical Theology and Anthropology," *The Irish Theological Quarterly,* 10/1 (Jan. 1973) 70.

10. G. Rabbeau, *Dieu, son existence et sa providence* (Paris: Bloud & Gray, 1933), p. 65; M. Chossat, s.v. *"Dieu," Dictionaire de Théologie Catholique,* 1939, vol. 4, col. 923. Both references are from Archer, "Philosophical Theology."

11. See E. E. Evans-Pritchard, *Theories of Primitive Religions* (Oxford: Clarendon Press, 1965), p. 104.

12. Van Steenbergen, *Hidden God* (Louvain: Publications Universitaires de Louvain, 1966), p. 47, and A. Vergote, *The Religious Man* (Dayton, OH: Pflaum Press, 1969), p. 40, referred to in Archer, "Philosophical Theology," p. 71.

13. See A. C. Bouquet, *Comparative Religion* (London/New York: Penguin, 1941), pp. 296ff.

14. E.g., M. Dhavamony, "Fenomenologia Storica delle Religioni" (manuscript, Rome, 1972/1973).

15. G. P. Malalasesekera, "Buddhism and Problems of the Modern Age," *Dialogue,* o.s., 26 (April 1973) 8ff.

16. Archer, "Philosophical Theology," p. 70.

17. See Robert Slater, "The Coming Great Dialogue," in McKain, *Christianity,* pp. 14–15; Panikkar, "Philosophy of Religion," p. 70.

18. T. V. Murti, *Central Philosophy of Buddhism* (London: Allen & Unwin, 1955), p. 30.

19. Panikkar, "Philosophy of Religion," p. 234.

20. On the significance of the appointment of Ven. Dr. Walpola Rahula, Buddhist monk and scholar, as the Charles Wesley Brashares Visiting Professor at Northwestern University, Evanston, Ill., see Edmund F. Perry, "Teaching Buddhism in a Western University," *World Buddhism* (Colombo), 22/10 (May 1974) 267–69.

21. R. A. Markus, "Faith and Philosophy," in A. H. Armstrong and R. A. Markus, *Christian Faith and Greek Philosophy* (London: Darton, Longman & Todd, 1960), pp. 139–47.

22. See John Nilson, "To Whom is Justin's *Dialogue with Trypho* Addressed?" *Theological Studies,* 38/3 (Sept. 1977) 538–46.

23. Aloysius Pieris, S.J., "The Church, the Kingdom, and the Other Religions," *Dialogue,* o.s., 22 (Oct. 1970) 3.

24. See chap. 1, pp. 3–6.

25. A. I. Chupungsco, O.S.B. (summarizing Jungmann and others), *Towards a Filipino Liturgy* (Manila, 1976), pp. 26–28.

26. W. Pannenberg, *Theology and the Philosophy of Science* (London: Darton, Longman & Todd, 1976), p. 10.

27. Chupungsco, *Filipino Liturgy,* pp. 3ff.

28. That is, with regard to the controversies about the Chinese rites and the Malabar rites: Jean Delmeau, "Les Reformes, la protestante et la catholique, ont imposé aux masse la religion de l'élite" (extracts of an address given at the Collège de France on Feb. 13, 1975, and reported in *Informations Catholiques Internationales,* 479 (1975), pp. 21ff.

29. See Walter Ullmann, "Boniface VIII and His Contemporary Scholarship," *Journal of Theological Studies* (Oxford), n.s., 27/1 (April 1976) 58–87.

30. José A. Izco, "Actitudes de los Cristianos ante otras religiones hasta el Vaticano II: Apuntes para una historia," *Misiones Extranjeras* (Madrid), 43 (Jan.–Feb. 1978) 47.

31. Greek descriptions of India existed before Alexander's invasion in the 4th century B.C., such as those of Hecataeus and Herodotus. Alexander is thought to have been accompanied by scholars whose reports came to the West only through secondary works written much later. See J. W. McCrindle, *Invasion of India by Alexander the Great as Described by Arrian, Q. Curtius, Diodorus, Plutarch, and Justin* (London: Westminster/A. Constable, 1893). Megasthenes, a Greek ambassador in India, and Patrocles, a military commander, and others (e.g., Deimachus, Dionysius, et al.) compiled information on their Indian experiences. For a critical evaluation of Greco-Indian relationships and also a very rich bibliography, see M. de Give, "Chandragupta le Maurya (324–300 avant J.-C.) et l'efflorescence de rapports entre l'Inde et l'occident" (manuscript, vols. 1 and 2, Louvain, 1967), pp. 15–306; bibliography, pp. 385ff.

32. I.e., the Pali text *Milinda Pañha* (Questions of Milinda), in which the Buddhist monk Nagasena dialogues with the Bactrian King Menander and convinces him of the truth of Buddhism. Even granted that the story is not factual, the literary genre points to a mutual exposure of Greek culture and Buddhist religion.

33. The Rock Edict XIII of Asoka mentions Buddhist missions to *Antiyoko* (Antiochus II of Syria), *Turameya* (Ptolemy of Egypt), *Antakini* (Antigonos of Macedonia), *Alikasundara* (Alexander of Epirus, northern Greece), and *Magas* of Cyrene (North Africa). Inasmuch as Eastern missions seem to have a historical basis, there is no compelling reason to doubt a priori the authenticity of Western missions.

34. Besides the evidence of Alexander Polistor (1st century B.C.), there is a clear reference to it in the *Stromata* of Clement of Alexandria.

35. *Stromata,* i, xv, 71, 6.

36. For a rigorous commentary on various theses regarding Greco-Buddhist relationships, see H. de Lubac, *La rencontre du bouddhisme et de l'occident* (Paris: Aubier, 1952), pp. 205 ff.

37. A. J. Edmunds, *I Vangeli di Budda e di Cristo* (Milan, after 1908).

38. J. E. Bruns, *The Christian Buddhism of St. John. New Insight into the Gospel* (New York: Paulist Press, 1971); A. J. Edmunds, *Buddhist Texts Quoted in St. John* (Philadelphia: Innes & Sons, 1911).

39. See de Lubac, *Rencontre,* p. 9. An Oriental origin of gnosticism (from Iran and from Manicheism) is, however, not ruled out.

40. Clement of Alexandria, *Stromata* (see n. 35, above).

41. Henri Baudet, *Paradise on Earth: Some Thoughts on European Images of the Non-European Man* (New Haven: Yale University Press, 1965), pp. 10–15.

42. Wilhelm Bousset, *Evagrius Studien* (Tübingen, 1923).

43. See Evagrius Ponticus, *The* Praktikos, *Chapters on Prayer.* Cistercian Studies, no. 4 (Spencer, Mass., 1970); translator's Introduction pp. xlviii–lviii, and also Dom Jean Leclerq's Preface, pp. vii–xxii.

44. Hans Urs von Balthasar, "Metaphysik und Mystik des Evagrius Ponticus," *Zeitschrift für Aszese und Mystik* (Munich), 14 (1939) 32.

45. Ibid.

46. David Griffin, O.S.B., "Evagrius Ponticus, Mystic Theologian," *Benedictine Confluence* (Latrobe, Pa., Winter 1973), p. 15.

47. S.v. "Joasaph" (Barlaam et Joasaph), November 27, in H. Delahaye et al. (eds.), *Prophyleum ad Acta Sanctorum, Decembris* (Brussels: Meester Fratres, 1940).

48. See I. V. Abaladze's Introduction, in D. M. Lang, *The Wisdom of Balahuar, A Christian Legend of the Buddha* (London: Allen & Unwin, 1957). For texts, see D. M. Lang, "Life of Blessed Iodasaph. A New Oriental Christian Version of the Barlaam and Joasaph Romance," *Bulletin of the School of Oriental and African Studies* (London), 20 (1957) 389ff.; also, by the same author, *The Balavariani (Barlaam and Joasaph): A Tale from the Christian East Translated from the Old Georgian* (Berkeley/Los Angeles: University of California Press, 1966).

49. Lang, *The Wisdom of Bilauhar* (see note 48, above), p. 9.

50. See "The Journey of William Rubruck" in C. Dawson (ed.) *Mission to Asia. Narratives and Letters of the Franciscan Missionaries in Mongolia and China in the Thirteenth and Fourteenth Centuries* (New York: Harper & Row, 1966), pp. 187ff.

51. Lang, *The Balavariani,* p. 46.

52. C. G. Jung, *Psychology and Religion: East and West* (New York: Pantheon Books, 1958), passim.

53. E.g., Teilhard de Chardin, *How I Believe* (New York: Harper & Row, 1969), passim; idem, "L'apport spirituel de l'extrême-orient: quelques réflexions personnelles," *Monumenta Nipponica* (Tokyo), 22 (1956) 1–11.

54. S. Radhakrishnan, *East and West in Religion* (London: Allen & Unwin, 1933), pp. 46–70.

55. Ursula King, "Teilhard's Comparison of Western and Eastern Mysticism," *The Teilhard Review*, 11 (Feb. 1975) 13.

56. Ç. Zaehner, *Foolishness to Greeks* (Oxford: Clarendon Press, 1953), p. 17.

57. To Thi Anh, *Eastern and Western Cultural Values: Conflict or Harmony?* (Manila: East Asian Pastoral Institute, 1975), p. 127.

58. Aloysius Pieris, S.J., "God-Talk and God-Experience in a Christian Perspective. A Response to Dr. Dharmasiri's Critique of Christian Mysticism and Christian Doctrinal Framework," *Dialogue,* n.s., 2/3 (Dec. 1975) 116–128.

59. Ibid., pp. 127–28. See also chap. 2 above.

60. Louis Bouyer (ed.), *The History of Christian Spirituality. Part 1: The Spirituality of the New Testament and the Fathers* (London: Burns & Oates, 1963), pp. 15–16.

61. L. Gilkey, *Religion and the Scientific Future* (London: S.C.M. Press, 1970), pp. 76–77.

62. Aloysius Pieris, S.J., "Monkhood: Some Elementary Facts about Its Origin and Its Place in a Buddhist-Christian Dialogue," *Dialogue,* n.s., 1/1 (April 1974) 9.

63. K. Malalgoda, *Buddhism in Sinhalese Society* (Berkeley: University of California Press, 1976), p. 192. For a sample of "Protestant Buddhist" literature, see A. Guruge, *Return to Righteousness: A Collection of Speeches, Essays, and Letters of the Anagarika Dhammapala* (Colombo: Anagarika Dhammapala Birth Centenary Committee, Ministry of Education and Cultural Affairs, Ceylon, 1965), pp. 439–67.

64. The limited scope of my discussion compels me to restrict my observations to interreligious conflicts between European Christianity and Asian religions. A much wider background of a socio-cultural and politico-economic nature must be taken into account to understand the question in depth. Such a background is not readily available in a comprehensive but readable form—except perhaps in Giorgio Borsaf's *La nascita del mondo moderno in Asia Orientale: La penetrazione europea e la crisi delle società tradizionali in India, Cina, e Giappone* (Milan: Rizzoli, 1977).

65. Aloysius Pieris, S. J., "The Church, The Kingdom," pp. 2–3.

66. G. R. Welbon, *The Buddhist Nirvana and Its Western Interpreters* (Chicago: University of Chicago Press, 1968), pp. 18–22. A later work (P. Mitter, *Much Maligned Monsters: History of European Reactions to Indian Art* [Oxford: Clarendon Press, 1977]) shows that the European bias against oriental cultures was not restricted to the religious sector and that Greco-Roman cultures served as the measuring rod in the European evaluation of non-European expressions of religious thought, even in art and sculpture.

67. For a brief description of the coming of contemporary Buddhism to various European countries, see René de Berval (ed.), "Présence du Bouddhisme," *France-Asie* (Saigon), 14 (Feb.–June 1959) 918–58.

68. Welbon, *Buddhist Nirvana,* pp. 154–71, 184ff.

69. Ibid., pp. 68–69, 76–77.

70. Malalgoda, *Buddhism,* pp. 192–255.

71. See Aloysius Pieris, S.J., "Buddhist-Christian Dialogue in Sri Lanka," *Impact* (Manila), 11/5 (May 1976) 158–61.

72. For a sample of this species of Buddhism, see S. Cromwell Crawford, "The American Youth and the Buddha," *World Buddhism,* 18/8 (March 1970) 199ff.

73. One prominent example was Harvard University's "Center for the Study of World Religions," functioning under the inspiring patronage of William Cantwell Smith.

74. P. Schebesta, *Origine della Religione* (Rome, 1966) lists about 150 definitions of religion!

75. Definitions vary according to the approach one adopts in the study of religion, such as functionalist, phenomenological, etc. This seems to hamper contemporary discussions on religion. For a concrete instance, see William Meacham, "Notes on the Thirteenth Congress of the International Association for the History of Religions," *Ching Feng* (Hong Kong), 19/1 (1976) 69.

76. See U. Bianchi, "The Definition of Religion," in U. Bianchi et al. (eds.), *Problems and Methods of the History of Religions* (Brill, 1972).

77. H. Cox, *Turning East. The Promise and the Peril of New Orientalism* (New York: Simon & Schuster, 1977).

78. Geoffrey Parrinder, *The Christian Debate: Light from the East* (London: Gollancz, 1964).

79. E.g., J. M. Déchanet in the hermitage of Valjouffrey in France (himself the author of a well-known book, *The Christian Yoga* [London: Burns & Oates, 1960/1976]); H. Slade of the Anglican "Anchorhold" monastery in Sussex, also author of *Exploration into Contemplative Prayer* (New York: Paulist Press, 1975).

80. E.g., Dom Bede Griffiths (author of numerous writings on Hindu-Christian dialogue) in Shantivanam, South India; the late Dom Le Saux (Swami Abhishiktananda), the wandering ascetic in the church in India and author of *Prayer* (Delhi, 1967); Francis Acharya in the Kurusimala ashram in Kerala.

81. For the papers of the Bangkok Conference (1968), see John Moffitt (ed.), *A New*

Charter for Monasticism (London/Notre Dame, IN: University of Notre Dame Press, 1970); for those of the Bangalore Conference, see *Les Moines Chrétiens face aux religions d'Asie: Bangalore, 1973* (Vanves, 1974).

82. See *Asian Monastic Conference, Kandy, Sri Lanka*, Aug. 1980, (Aide Inter-Monastères, rue d'lssy, 7, Vanves, France) 1981.

83. See Bernard de Give, "La rencontre monastique inter-religieuse de Bethanie," *Collectanea Cisterciensia*, 4 (1977) 310–21.

84. The following is a sampling of sources on which I base my observations: R. Guardini, *Religion und Offenbarung* (Würzburg: Werkbund Verlag, 1958); J. Cuttat, *Phänomenologie und Begegnung der Religionen* (Studia Philosophica, 18, Basel, 1958); W. Hocking, *The Coming World Civilization* (New York: Harper, 1956); K. Rahner, "Das Christentum und die nicht-christlichen Religionen," *Schriften zür Theologie*, vol. 5 (Einsiedeln: Benziger Verlag, 1962), pp. 132–58; R. C. Zaehner, *The Convergent Spirit: Towards a Dialectic of Religions* (London: Routledge & Kegan Paul, 1963); R. L. Slater, *Can a Christian Learn from Other Religions?* (New York: Seabury Press, 1963); Paul Tillich, *Christianity and the Encounter of World Religions* (New York: Columbia University Press, 1963); Gustav Thil, *Propos et problèmes de théologie des religions non-chrétiennes* (Tournai, 1966); J. Heislbetz, *Theologische Gründe der nicht-christlichen Religionen* (Freiburg: Herder, 1967); Heinz Robert Schlette, *Die Religionen als Thema der Theologie* (Freiburg, 1967); David Edwards, *Religion and Change* (London: Hodder & Stoughton, 1969). I was helped too by John Shirieda's list in *Bulletin* (Secretariatus pro non-Christianis, Vatican City) 12/1–2 (1977), nos. 34–35.

85. A. Pieris, S.J., "The Church, The Kingdom," p. 3.

86. A. Pieris, S.J., "Contemporary Ecumenism and Asia's Search for Christ," *Teach All Nations*, 13/1 (Jan. 1976) 25–26.

87. W. Kasper, "Are Non-Christian Religions Salvific?" in M. Dhavamony (ed.), *Evangelization, Dialogue, and Development (Documenta Missionalia, 5, Rome, 1972)*, p. 160.

88. J. Daniélou, *Message évangélique et culture hellénistique IIe and IIIe siècles* (Paris: Desclée Fayard, 1961), pp. 41–72.

89. See J. Daniélou, *L'oraison, problème politique* (Paris, 1965), p. 88.

90. Note, for instance, that in the *Holy Pagans of the Old Testament* (London: Longmans, Green, 1957), p. 22, Daniélou quotes approvingly Guardini's respect for the Buddha as the precursor of Christ but has not hesitated to warn Christians against being "contaminated" in the course of even merely studying Buddhism: see *The Salvation of the Nations* (New York: Sheed & Ward, 1950), p. 64. Naturally my suggestion that the church should be baptized in the waters, say, of Asian Buddhism, would seem preposterous in the framework of Daniélou's fulfillment theory!

91. Y. Congar, "Non-Christian Religions and Christianity," in Dhavamony, *Evangelization*, p. 140.

92. Quoted in W. Kasper, "Non-Christian Religions," p. 161.

93. Charles Davis, *Christ and the World Religions* (London, 1970), pp. 26–27.

94. Mark Schoof, O.P., *Breakthrough. The Beginnings of the New Catholic Theology* (Dublin: Gill & Macmillan, 1970), p. 17.

95. Ibid., pp. 23–30.

96. It is observed, ibid., p. 26, that the new theology began by making the "whole life of the church" the locus of a theological reflection, especially, "the world in which this community [of the church] lives especially, the *world of contemporary philosophy*"

(italics added). The way *the world in which the church lived* is filtered into "the world of philosophy" would not escape Latin American criticism.

97. For a lucid exposition of this Latin American breakthrough, see Jon Sobrino, "Theological Understanding in European and Latin American Theology" in *The True Church and the Poor* (Maryknoll, N.Y.: Orbis, 1984), pp. 7–38.

98. The first Asian meeting of EATWOT was held in Wennappuwa, Sri Lanka, January 1979. Conference papers are printed in Virginia Fabella (ed.), *Asia's Struggle for Full Humanity* (Maryknoll, N.Y.: Orbis, 1980). See my own contribution, "Towards an Asian Theology of Liberation," in *An Asian Theology of Liberation*, pp. 69–86.

99. For a North American reaction, see Alfred T. Hennelly, S.J., "Theological Method: the Southern Exposure," *Theological Studies*, 38/4 (Dec. 1977) 728–35, esp. part 4. See also the "Actes du Colloque Méthodologique" (Institute Catholique de Paris, Feb. 1976), published under the title *La déplacement de la théologie* (Paris, 1977). Fr. Geffré's concluding remarks (p. 175) about the *cercle herméneutique* adds the binomial *faire-croire* to the classic European doublet *croire-comprendre*.

100. Ibid., passim.

101. However, a relatively early example of a pioneering and perhaps premature but certainly praiseworthy attempt at a Christian assessment of the Marxist challenge can be found in R.B.Y. Scot and G. Vlastos (eds.), *Towards the Christian Revolution* (London: Gollancz, 1937).

102. According to the thesis put forward by Pannenberg (*Theology*, n. 26, above), the main task of theology is to establish rationally the truth of theological propositions.

103. For a self-understanding of Catholic theology as a "scientific pursuit," see Y. Congar, O.P., *A History of Theology* (Garden City, N.Y.: Doubleday, 1968), pp. 221ff.

104. Here, Sobrino quotes Moltmann: Sobrino, *True Church*, pp. 30–33; see Hennelly, "Theological Method," p. 721.

105. See Hennelly, "Theological Method," pp. 710–13.

106. For an accurate description of these events, see L. W. Moses, *The Political Role of Mongol Buddhism* (Bloomington, IN: Asian Studies Research Institute, Indiana University, 1977), esp. chap. 7 onward. For an official Marxist interpretation of these same events, see Dulamzhavyn Dashzhamts, "Non-Capitalist Development and Religion," *World Marxist Review* (Dec. 1973), pp. 27–29.

107. See Aloysius Pieris, S.J., "Buddhism and Marxism in Dialogue: An Historical Approach," a response paper read at the Marxist-Christian dialogue, Kandy (Lewella), May 1974, reprinted in *Dialogue*, n.s., 12 (1985) 1–3, p. 68–86.

108. This is substantially treated in H. Welch, *Buddhism Under Mao* (Cambridge, MA: Harvard University Press, 1972), pp. 1–41 and 340–63.

109. For a sociological analysis of how the development ideology has been in operation in these countries in the recent past, see F. Houtart, "Les sociétés non-socialistes du Sud et l'Est Asiatique après la guerre du Vietnam," *Civilizations* (Brussels), 1973, pp. 219–31, and 1976, pp. 36–54.

110. Pieris, "Contemporary Ecumenism," pp. 32–34.

111. A. Th. Van Leeuwen, *Christianity in World History: The Meeting of Faiths of East and West* (London: Edinburgh House Press, 1964).

112. As quoted by Davis, *Christ*, p. 21.

113. This means that, as Roy Preiswerk has perceptively observed ("La rupture avec les conceptions actuelles du développement," *Relations interculturelles et développement* [Geneva, 1975], pp. 71–96), besides the "dependency" model, which is the target

of Latin American criticism, there is also a "cultural" factor that, I presume, should be
a major Asian concern in the face of the imminent threat that technocracy poses to the
profound religious values of Asian peoples.

114. Pieris, "Contemporary Ecumenism," p. 33.

115. S. Sivaraksha, "Religion and Development," *Dialogue*, n.s., 3/2 (Aug. 1976)
52.

116. Pieris, "Contemporary Ecumenism," pp. 34–36.

117. Ibid.

118. See Merton's own observation in "Marxism and Monastic Perspectives," in
John Moffitt, *A New Charter for Monasticism* (London/Notre Dame, IN: Notre Dame
University Press, 1970), pp. 69–81. See also D. Q. Mclnery, *Thomas Merton: The
Man and His Work* (Spencer, MA: Cistercian Publishers, 1974), p. 60.

CHAPTER 4

1. T. V. Murti, *Central Philosophy of Buddhism* (London: Allen & Unwin, 1955),
p. 30.

2. For a justification of this term, see Nyanaponika, *Abhidhamma Studies* (Kandy:
BPS, 1965), pp. 18–20, and H. V. Guenther, *Philosophy and Psychology in the Abhid
harma* (Lucknow: Buddha Vihara, 1957), p. 145.

3. See MA, I, 37ff. and ItvA, I, 82ff.

4. The process off interdependent origination *(paticcasamuppāda)* is described by
the Buddha in S, II, 1–4, 27–29, and parallels.

5. M, III, 62; S, I, 134; *Therig*, vv. 43, 472; Ps. 1:17; II:230; Dhs 358, 552, etc.

6. A, II, 50.

7. *Abhidhammattha-Sangaha* with the *Purāna Sannaya*, Paññāmoli Tissa (ed.),
(Columbo, 1960), p. 6.

8. Ācariya Dhammapāla, *Paramattha-mañjusā*, M. Dhammananda (ed.), (3 vols.:
1928, 1930, 1949), 510. For a scriptural basis of this statement, see S. IV. 15.

9. See T. Stcherbatsky, *The Central Conception of Buddhism and the Meaning of
the Word Dharma* (Calcutta: S. Gupta, 1961), p. 35.

10. Ibid., p. 55.

11. D. J. Kalupahana, "Sarvastivāda and Its Theory of Sarvam Asti," *University of
Ceylon Review*, 29/1–2 (April, Oct., 1966) 104.

12. Nyanaponika, *Abhidhamma*, p. 19.

13. In its primary sense, *dukkha* denotes hollowness, emptiness. "Evil" or "suffering" is the secondary, developed sense.

14. Y. Karunadasa, *Buddhist Analysis of Matter* (Colombo: Department of Cultural
Affairs, 1967), p. 174.

15. Buddhaghosa (MA, I, 29) and Dhammapala (ItvA, I, 53) speak of them as *ñāta-
pariññā, tīrana-pariññā,* and *pahāna-pariññā,* respectively.

16. D. I, 89; II, 16; J. IV, 232; Sn p. 106, etc.

17. MA, V, 36–37. At the time of writing, my attention was drawn by Fr. E. Denis,
S.J., to p. 7 of a yet unedited manuscript of "Lokapannatti" (a manual of Buddhist
cosmology) where this same scale of values is indirectly referred to.

18. Richard Gombrich maintains in his *Precept and Practice* (Oxford University Press,
1971) that contemporary Sinhala Buddhism does not diverge much from what Buddhaghosa saw in his day.

19. I.e., the ex-monk, Kapilavaddho. See *Sangha*, vol. 3, no. 5, p. 6.

20. Aloysius Pieris, S.J., "Some Christian Reflexions on Buddhism and Secularization in Ceylon," *Dialogue,* 24 (June 1972) 4–6.

21. Edward Conze, *Buddhism* (Oxford University Press, 2nd ed., 1953), pp. 72–77.

22. See *In Search of South East Asia, A Modern History,* D. J. Steinberg, ed. (Oxford University Press, 1971), pp. 37–39.

23. See Donald K. Swearer, *Buddhism in Transition* (Philadelphia: Westminster, 1970), pp. 52 and 76. See also Earl N. Consternoble, "Buddhism Still Treads the Traditional Path," *World Buddhism* (Nov. 1969), p. 493.

24. "Religious Symbolism and Political Change in Ceylon" (cyclostyled, July 1966, later published in *Modern Ceylon Studies* (University of Ceylon), 1/1 (1970) 43.

25. Guido Auster, "Role of the Sangha in Modern Society," *World Buddhism* (Feb. 1969) pp. 181–82.

26. This is the nearly unanimous opinion of scholars. For the opposite view, see K. P. Mitra, "About Buddhist Nuns," *Journal of Bihar Orissa Research Society,* 3/2 (1921) 58.

27. *Vinaya,* vol. 2, chap. 10.

28. Richard Gombrich, "Some Feminine Elements in Sinhala Buddhism" (cyclostyled, London, 1971).

29. Lynn A. de Silva, "Popular Buddhism" (manuscript), chap. 6.

30. Commemoration of the enlightenment and death of the Buddha.

31. See report in *World Buddhism,* Feb. 1969, p. 197.

32. See articles of Michael Ames and Nur Yalman in *Religion in South Asia,* E. B. Harper (ed.), (Seattle: University of Washington Press, 1964), pp. 21–52 and 115–50, respectively.

33. Melford E. Spiro, *Burmese Supernaturalism* (Englewood Cliffs, N.J.: Prentice-Hall, 1967), pp. 247–80.

34. *The Buddhist Pantheon in Ceylon and Its Extensions in Anthropological Studies in Theravada Buddhism,* Manning Nash (ed.) (Yale University Press, 1966).

35. *Precept and Practice,* p. 9.

36. "Traditional and Doctrinal Interpretations of Buddhahood. An Outline for a 'Theology of Buddhahood' " (London: SOAS, Seminar on Aspects of Religion in South East Asia) (cyclostyled, 1971). Reprinted later in *Bulletin of the Secretariat for Non-Christians,* 5 (1970) 3–24.

37. ItvA, I, 55.

38. ItvA, I, 13.

39. Conze, p. 61; see also A. L. Basham, "The Rise of Buddhism in Its Historical Context," *Journal of Asian Studies,* 4/3 (Dec. 1966) 395–411.

40. *Vimuttimagga (Path of Freedom)* (Chinese version translated into English by Ehara, Soma, and Kheminda), chap. 6, deals with characterology. See also *Visuddhimagga,* chap. 3, verses 60ff.

41. See M, I, 23; III, 36; A, II, 211, etc.

42. A, I, 189; II, 167–70, 191 (also D, II, 123–26).

43. G.S.P. Misra, "A Buddhist Legend Re-written. Devadatta and His Character," *Bharatiya Vidya,* 28/1–4, p. 28. The *Vinaya* text referred to here is from *The Book of Discipline* (PTS tr.), vol. 4, pp. 96–97.

44. M. E. Spiro, *Buddhism and Society. A Great Tradition and Its Burmese Vicissitudes* (London: Allen & Unwin, 1971), p. 330.

45. Rashtrapal Bhikkhu, "Dhutanga or Ascetical Practices," *World Buddhism* (March 1969), p. 210.

CHAPTER 6

1. "Beliefs Underlying the Ancient Indian Conception of History," *Journal of Indian History* (Trivandrum), 57/1, i–ii.

2. See, for instance, Piyasena Dissanayaka, *Political Thoughts of the Buddha* (Colombo: Department of Cultural Affairs, 1977). This is an important summary of the Buddhist vision of politics and has been followed here in this chapter.

3. Ibid.

CHAPTER 7

1. For a brief outline of these events and relevant bibliographical references, see chap. 3, pp. 28–31.

2. See Kitsiri Malalgoda, *Buddhism in Sinhalese Society* (Berkeley: University of California Press, 1976), p. 192.

3. See Gottfried Rothermundt, *Buddhismus für die moderne Welt. Die Religionsphilosophie K. N. Jayatillekes* (Stuttgart: Calwer Verlag, 1979), pp. 31–33, 115–16, 125ff.

4. D. Snellgrove, "Traditional and Doctrinal Interpretation of Buddahood: An Outline for a Theology of Buddhahood," *Bulletin of the Vatican Secretariat for Non-Christians*, 5 (1970) 3–24.

5. See *Buddhist Christian Studies*, 3 (1983) 3–60.

6. Lynn A. de Silva, *Reincarnation in Buddhist and Christian Thought* (Colombo: Christian Literature Society of Ceylon, 1968), pp. 161–63; idem, "Reflections on Life in the Midst of Death," *Dialogue*, 10 (1985) 4–17.

7. Lynn A. de Silva, *The Problem of the Self in Buddhism and Christianity* (Colombo: Study Centre for Religion and Society, 1975).

8. Lynn A. de Silva, *"Anatta* and God," *Dialogue*, 2 (1975) 106–15.

9. Aloysius Pieris, "L'Asie non sémitique face aux modèles occidentaux d'inculturation," *Lumière et Vie*, 33 (1984) 50ff. See *An Asian Theology of Liberation*, chap. 5.

10. L. Bouyer, *La spiritualité du Nouveau Testament et des Pères* (Paris: Aubier-Montaigne, 1960), p. 34.

11. See David Knowles, *What is Mysticism?* (London: Burns & Oates, 1967), p. 86.

12. *Spiritual Exercises*, 23.

13. See M. M. Thomas, *The Acknowledged Christ of Indian Renaissance* (London: SCM Press, 1969).

14. See Ananda Guruge, *Return to Righteousness: A Collection of Speeches, Essays and Letters of Anagarika Dharmapala* (Colombo: Anagarika Dharmapala Birth Centenary Committee, Ministry of Education and Cultural Affairs, 1965), passim.

15. I developed this theme in my Theape Wescott Lectures delivered at Cambridge University (England) in October 1982.

16. Ibid.

17. See A. Pieris, *An Asian Theology of Liberation*, chap. 2.

CHAPTER 8

1. See chapter 7, "Toward an Asian Theology of Liberation," in Aloysius Pieris, *An Asian Theology of Liberation* (Maryknoll, N.Y.: Orbis Books, 1988).

2. Epist. XVIII, nos. 11–12; P.L. 16, 975.

3. *Samāgama Sutta* of the *Majihima Nikāya.*

4. See Nurul Islam, "Revolt in the Peripher," in *Towards a New Strategy of Development: A Rothko Chapel Colloquium,* Kim Q. Hill (ed.) (New York: 1975), pp. 177ff.

5. Oxford, 1978.

CHAPTER 9

1. Buddhist-Christian marriage comes under the category of *disparitas cultus,* whereas only the marriages of Catholics with validly baptized persons of other Christian denominations are categorized under *mixta religio.* This distinction seems to have settled down in the legal tradition somewhere in the eleventh century, but earlier in the Christian era marriages with Jews, "pagans," heretics, and catechumens were treated *en bloc.*

2. Matt. 19:3–11.

3. Mark 12:25. Conditions of the kingdom of God (in the parable of the feast, Luke 14:15–24) includes giving up one's wife (Luke 14:20).

4. For further elaboration on the *gnostic* and *agapeic* idioms in Buddhism and Christianity, see my "God-Talk and God-Experience in a Christian Perspective," *Dialogue,* n.s., 3/3 (1976) 116–28.

5. Eph. 5:21–30.

6. Acts 15:1–19.

7. Gal. 2:11–21.

8. 2 Cor. 6:14.

9. Cor. 7:12–16.

10. The so-called Pauline privilege, which allowed the Christian partner to remarry, seems to have arisen from the church's later interpretation of this teaching, though Paul gives no explicit instructions to that effect.

11. Quoted in Pierre-Marie Gy, "Le sacrament de marriage, exige-t-il foi?" *Revue des Sciences Philosophiques et Théologiques,* 61/3 (July 1977) 437.

12. Ibid., p. 439.

13. Ibid., p. 440.

14. Walter Ullmann, *A History of Political Thought: The Middle Ages* (Middlesex: Penguin, rev. ed., 1970), pp. 20–21.

15. Walter Ullmann, "Boniface VIII and His Contemporary Scholarship," *Journal of Theological Studies,* n.s., 28/1 (April 1976) 62, 77, etc.

16. Ibid., pp. 83ff.

17. For other facts and details, see Fr. Mervyn Fernando's position paper, "The Catholic Church and the Mixed Marriages," *Dialogue,* 5 (1978).

18. See M. B. Hooker, "The Indian Derived Law Texts of South East Asia," *Journal of Asian Studies,* 37/2 (Feb. 1978) 215.

19. Ullmann, *History,* p. 21.

20. Ullmann, "Boniface," p. 59.

21. See H. Rashdall in *The Universities of Europe in Middle Ages,* F. M. Powicke and A. B. Emden II (eds.), (Oxford: Clarendon Press, 1936), p. 38.

22. Lily de Silva, "Buddhist-Christian Mixed Marriages: A Buddhist View," *Dialogue,* 5 (1978).

23. See B. G. Gokhale, "Early Buddhist Kingship," *Journal of Asian Studies,* 26/1 (Nov. 1966) 22.

24. See A. P. de Zoysa, *Indian Culture in the Days of the Buddha* (Colombo: M. D. Gunasena, 1955), pp. 24–28.

25. See *Niti-Niganduwa,* T. Panabokke, (ed.), (Colombo: W. H. Herbert, 1880), pp. 18ff. For a comparison of it with the *Dharmasastras,* see H. W. Thambiah, *Sinhala*

Laws and Customs (Colombo: Lake House Investments, 1968), pp. 56ff. See Hooker, "Law Texts," p. 203, for points of contrast in the laws regarding adultery in *Manusmyti* and *Wagaru.*

26. See *World Buddhism,* 18/2 (July 1970) 321.

27. In the presidential address of the 53rd session of the All Ceylon Buddhist Congress, *World Buddhism,* 23/2 (Jan. 1972) 162.

28. B. Siri Sivali, *Bauddha Lokaya* (Colombo, 1975), p. 167, n. 1.

29. See *The Western Family and the Future of the Church,* Pro Mundi Vita no. 51 (Brussels, 1974) 16–17.

30. Ibid.

31. Ibid.

32. See Gy, "Sacrament," p. 437.

33. Swami Abhishiktananda, *Prayer* (Delhi, 1967/1975), p. 31.

CHAPTER 10

1. *The History of Christian Spirituality, Part 1: The Spirituality of the New Testament and the Fathers,* Louis Bouyer (ed.) (London: Burns & Oates, 1963), pp. 15–16.

2. E.g., Gunapala Dharmasiri, *A Buddhist Critique of the Christian Concept of God* (Colombo: Lake House Investments, 1974), pp. 212–13. The author regards Buddhism as nonbhaktic religion, and superior to Christianity on that very account.

3. Thus the late Prof. K. N. Jayatillekes. See F. Rothermundt, *Buddhismus für die moderne Welt. Die religiöse Philosophie K. N. Jayatillekes* (Stuttgart: Calver Theologischen Monographien, Band 4, 1979), 38–47.

4. See B. Bhattacharya, *An Introduction to Buddhist Esoterism* (Varnasi, Chowkhamba Sanskrit Series Office 1964), pp. 70, 96 and passim. See also M. Wickramasinghe, "Occultism Invades the Buddhist Temple," *Buddhism and Culture* (Dehiwela, Sri Lanka: Tisara Publishers), pp. 33–37.

5. I have illustrated this with concrete examples in "The Place of Non-Christian Religions and Cultures in the Evolution of Third World Theology," in *An Asian Theology of Liberation* (Maryknoll, N.Y.: Orbis, 1988), pp. 87–110.

6. This misunderstanding is clearly seen in Gunapalaia Dharmasiri's remarks (n. 2, above).

7. See my reply to Dharmasiri in *Dialogue,* 2 (1975) 116ff., esp. 117–18.

8. Langdon Gilkey, *Religion and the Scientific Future* (London: SCM Press, 1970), pp. 76–77.

9. *Sacramentum Mundi,* Karl Rahner et al. (eds.) (Basel/Montreal: Hermann-Herder Foundation) 19, vol. 3, s.v., *Sin.* no. 4, a.

10. Fergus Kerr, O.P., "The Need for Philosophy in Theology Today," *New Black Friars* (June 1984) 248–60.

11. See Ven. Ñānamoli Thera, "Buddhism: A Religion or Philosophy," in *Pathways of Buddhist Thought* (excerpt from *The Wheel,* edited by Ven. Ñānaponika Thera and selected by M.O'C. Walsh) (London: Allen and Unwin, 1971), pp. 13–48.

12. For an apologia for the gnostic purity of Buddhist Esoterism, as opposed to Shaktism in Hindu Tantra, and the Buddhist belief in the union of gnosis with the (male principle of) "active universal love and compassion," see Lama Anagarika, *Foundations of Tibetan Mysticism* (London: Rider & Co., 1960), pp. 94–99.

13. See G. Kittel, *Theological Dictionary of the New Testament* (Grand Rapids: Eerdmans, 7th printing, 1976), vol. 1, pp. 708–13.

14. For various definitions given here, see P. Parente, *The Mystical Life* (London: Herder, 1946), pp. 24ff.

15. Ibid.

16. *Summa Theologica,* Ia, q. 64, a.1.

17. Ibid., IIa-IIae, q. 184, a. 23, ad 4. See also Jerry Blacken, C.P., "Thomas Aquinas and Anselm's Satisfaction Theory," *Angelicum,* 62 (1985) 517.

18. *Summa Theologica,* Ia, q. 1, a.6, ad 3.

19. Ibid., IIa-IIae, q. 97, a.2, ad 2.

20. A clear exposition of the dialectics of wisdom and love in the person of the Buddha is set forth in great detail in (the sixth-century exegete) Dhammapala's commentaries, *Itivuttak'Aṭṭhakathā* (PTS edition), 1:15–16; *Cariyāpiṭak'Atthakathā* (PTS edition), 289–90; *Paramatthamañjusā (= Visuddhimaga-Ṭīka)* (Colombo: Sinhala edition by M. Dhammananda, 1928), 192–93. All Pali sources cited henceforward, unless otherwise specified, are from the editions of the Pali Text Society (PTS), London.

21. Hilary Armstrong, "Negative Theology," *The Downside Review* (July 1977) 176.

22. Sebastian Moor, "Some Principles for an Adequate Theism," *The Downside Review* (July 1977) 204.

23. Ibid., p. 203.

24. Ibid.

25. Ibid., p. 205, italics added.

26. Armstrong, "Negative," p. 188.

27. Ibid., p. 189.

28. I have singled out and illustrated these limitations in my "Western Christianity and Asian Buddhism," chapter 3 of this volume.

29. See D. J. Kalupahana, *Buddhist Philosophy. A Historical Analysis* (Honolulu: East-West Center, Hawaii University Press, 1976), chap. 8–12.

30. Ibid., pp. 163ff.

31. See Charles Eliot, *Japanese Buddhism* (London: Routledge, Kegan Paul, 1969), pp. 321ff and 336ff.

32. Ibid., pp. 416ff.

33. John Cobb, Jr., *Beyond Dialogue. Towards Mutual Transformation of Christianity and Buddhism* (Philadelphia: Fortress Press, 1982).

34. Ibid., p. 145; also, *A Christian Natural Theology* (Philadelphia: Westminster Press, 1965), p. 282.

35. See *Buddhist Christian Studies* (University of Hawaii, 1983), vol. 3, where this approach is given wide treatment.

36. Hans Waldenfels, *Absolute Nothingness. Foundations for Buddhist-Christian Dialogue* (New York: Paulist Press, 1980).

37. My argument, based on current Asian praxis, is set forth in "Contemporary Ecumenism and Asia's Search for Christ," *Teaching All Nations* (Manila) (Jan. 1976) 23–29.

38. For a theological excursus on the baptism of Jesus in the context of other religions, see my "Asia's Non-Semitic Religions and the Mission of Local Churches," in *An Asian Theology of Liberation,* pp. 45–48.

39. Kalupahana, *Buddhist Philosophy,* pp. 112–26.

40. I have briefly described these historical circumstances and given the relevant sources in chapter 3, above.

41. S. Cromwell Crawford, "American Youth and the Buddha," *World Buddhism,* 18 (1970) 199.

42. *Anguttara Nikaya,* vol. 1, p. 188, and passim.

43. Ibid., p. 161, and passim.

44. *Majjhima Nikaya,* vol. 1, p. 9.

45. *Stromata* XV.71.6.

46. For references to sources dealing with the Joasaph cult, see chapter 3, above.

47. *Anguttara Nikaya,* vol. 2, pp. 38–39.

48. In translating this passage, I. B. Horner (*Gradual Sayings,* PTS, 1952, vol. 2, p. 46) insists that the question, as the Pali original has it, is not about what Gautama *is* but what he *will become,* though the final answer is in the present tense—namely, that he *is* (already) the Buddha. See however, Kalupahana, *Buddhist Philosophy,* p. 112. See also n. 50, below.

49. Compare John 16:33.

50. Horner *(Gradual Sayings)* translates: "Take it that I am a Buddha." This answer is then summed up in the verse that follows: "Therefore, I *am* Buddha" *(tasmā Buddho' smi).*

51. Maya is believed to have conceived Gautama at the moment when a white elephant appeared to her in a dream.

52. The proof text adduced by the adherents of this theory is *Itvuttaka,* p. 91, where "seeing the Buddha" and "seeing the *dhamma"* are equated. As for the (eternal) preexistence of the *dhamma,* see *Samyutta Nikaya,* vol. 2, p. 25.

53. *Sic* B. G. Gokhale, *"Bhakti* in Early Buddhism," *Journal of Asian and African Studies,* 15 (1980), 18.

54. Ibid.

55. I.e., *Majjhima Nikāya* (PTS edition), vol. 1, p. 386.

56. E.g., *Itivuttak'aṭṭakathā,* vol. 1, pp. 13, 15–16.

57. Ibid.

58. E.g., *lokavidū* in *Digha Nikaya,* vol. 3, p. 76, and *lokanātha* in Sutta Nipata, vs. 995.

59. See Har Dayal, *The Bodhisattva Doctrine in Buddhist Sanscrit Literature* (Delhi: Motilal Banarsidas, 1931/1970), p. 24.

60. See *Samyutta Nikāya,* vol. 1, p. 235.

61. *Ghavatarana-maga ha Buddha-caritaya,* vol. 1 (1976) and vol. 2 (1978).

62. Ibid., vol. 1, p. 20, and passim.

63. Ibid., p. 25.

64. See *Aggañña Sutta,* which is summarized in chapter 6 of this volume.

65. See diagram with explanation of this worldview in A. Pieris, *An Asian Theology of Liberation,* pp. 71–74.

66. E.g., Piyasena Dissanayake, *Political Thought of the Buddha* (Colombo, 1977).

67. Dayar Powar, "Siddhartha," *Panchasheel* 17 (Oct. 1972) 7, translated into English and quoted in J. B. Gokhale-Turner, *"Bhakti* or *Vidroha.* Continuity and Change in *Dalit Sahitya," Journal of African and Asian Studies* 15 (1980), 38.

68. See Elias Mallon, "The Cosmic Powers and Reconciliation," *Centro Pro Unione* (Rome), 6 (1974) 18–22.

69. See *Return to Righteousness* (collection of speeches, essays, and letters of Anagarika Dharmapala), Ananda Guruge (ed.) (Colombo: Government Press, 1965), pp. 447ff.

70. Ibid., pp. 448–49.

71. Ibid., p. 475.

72. This thesis is documented in Kitsiri Malalgoda, *Buddhism in Sinhalese Society* (Berkeley: University of California Press, 1976), pp. 192–255.

73. G. Obeysekere, "Religious Symbolism and Political Change in Ceylon," *Modern Ceylon Studies* (University of Ceylon), 1 (1970) 43–63.

74. See Jean Daniélou, *Holy Pagans of the Old Testament* (London: Longmans, 1957), p. 22.

75. See A. Pieris, "Speaking of the Son of God in Non-Christian Cultures," *An Asian Theology of Liberation*, pp. 59–65.

76. For clarification regarding the "self" that is denied in Buddhism and the (empirical) "self" that is identified with *citta*, see A. Pieris, *"Citta, Attā and Attabhāva* in Pali Exegetical Writings," *Buddhist Studies in Honour of Walpola Rahula* (London: Gordon Fraser, 1980), pp. 212–22.

77. See the conclusions in chapter 7 of this volume, pp. 87–88; also, "To Be Poor as Jesus Was Poor?" in *An Asian Theology of Liberation*, pp. 15–23.

78. How this theology spells out what is *unique* in biblical/Christian revelation and liberation has been discussed already in my "A Theology of Liberation in Asian Churches?" in *An Asian Theology of Liberation*, pp. 111–26.

Glossary of Buddhist Terms

All terms are in Pali unless otherwise specified; Skt = Sanskrit; Snh = Sinhala.

Abhidhamma "higher doctrine," i.e., Buddhist phenomenology and ethico-psychology in a systematized and classified form

Abhidhamma-piṭaka the (third) part of the Buddhist scriptures *(tri-piṭaka),* containing the *Abhidhamma*

Abhidharma Skt for *Abhidhamma*

ābidhārmika (Skt/Snh) pertaining to the *Abhidhamma* or continuous with the method and content of the *Abhidhamma;* scholastic

adosa nonhate; absence of *dosa*

Aggañña-suttanta title of a discourse *(Suttanta)* in the second part *(Sutta-piṭaka)* of the Buddhist scriptures

ahiṃsā nonviolence

ājñā-cakra Skt for *āṇā-cakka*

amoha nondelusion; absence of *moha*

anāgārika "homeless" person, i.e., a celibate; originally, a synonym for a monk or a recluse; now, in Sri Lanka, extended to include a class of lay, celibate apostles observing the ten precepts *(dasa-sil)*

āṇā-cakka literally, "the wheel of government"; the secular or temporal power to be complemented by *dhamma-cakka*

anātma Skt for *anatta*

anatta without "self"; having no permanent substratum or soul

anicca impermanent, transient

aññā (salvific) knowledge; realization; gnosis; see *paññā*

arāga nonlust; absence of *rāga*

arahan(t)/arahā literally, the "Worthy One"; the saint; one who has attained *nibbāna/ nirvāna*

arahatta sainthood; state of one who has attained *nibbāna*

ārāma "(a place of) delight"; a technical term for a Buddhist monastery

āraññā forest

āranya Skt/Snh for *āraññā*

āraññā-vāsī (Skt/Snh) forest-dwelling (monks), contrasted with *grāma-vāsī*

ariya-magga (Skt *ārya-mārga*); Noble Path (see next entry)

ariyaṭṭhangika-magga Noble Eightfold Path; the path to nirvāna

ariya-puggala the "Noble Person"; anyone in one of the four higher stages of perfection: (1) one who enters the stream leading to nirvāna; (2) one who would return to *saṃsāra* only once; (3) one who would never return; (4) one who has reached *nibbāna*

ārya-pudgala Skt for *āriya-puggala*

ārogya (Skt/Snh) nonsickness, i.e., health

asubha repulsive aspect(s) of the human body; one of the forty meditation themes *(kam-maṭṭhānas)*

atta-kilamatha self-torture

aṭṭha-kathā commentary; exegetical literature

āvāsa cenobitic commune; dwelling place of a monastic community

avatāravāda (Skt) incarnational theory, namely, that God descends into human history from time to time

avidyā Skt for *avijjā*

avijjā ignorance

āyatana sphere of sensation, i.e., any of the six *senses* (eye, ear, nose, tongue, body, and mind) or any of the six *sensa* (form, sound, smell, taste, touch, and ideas)

bhagava(nt) the Lord; Blessed One; (an epithet of the Buddha)

bhakti (Skt/Snh) devotion to the Lord

bhakti-mārga (Skt) affective path; devotional spirituality

bhāvanā cultivation of the mind; mental development; "meditation"

bhikkhu mendicant; monk

bhikṣu Skt for *bhikkhu*

bhikkhunī nun (Skt bhikṣuṇī)

bhikkhunī-sangha order of nuns

bodhi awakening, enlightenment (the Buddha's attainment of nirvāna)

bodhi-tree tree of enlightenment, i.e., the tree under which the Buddha attained enlightenment

bo-tree Snh for *bodhi*-tree

bodhi-satta candidate to buddhahood; one who has vowed and therefore strives to be a Buddha

Budubhava (Snh) buddhahood

Buddha Enlightened One

Budurajānanvahansē (Snh) "Buddha, the king"

cakka wheel; symbol of "power" or "authority"

cakkavatti "wheel-turner," i.e., Universal King of Righteousness; here the "political wheel," *ānā-cakka,* is intended

Cakkavatti-sīhanāda-Suttanta a title of discourse *(suttanta)* in the second part *(Sutta-piṭaka)* of the Buddhist scriptures

cakkhu-viññāṇa visual sensation; seeing

Cakravartin Skt for *Cakkavatti*

Caraṇa treading the path to Nirvana; the practice of Buddhist doctrine; conduct (contrasted with *vijjā*)

carita temperament, character

cetasikā(ni) "belonging to the *Citta,*" i.e., functions of consciousness *(citta); chief* among them are *vedanā, saññā,* and *samkhārā*

citta consciousness; mind

dāna generosity; gift offered to monks

darśana (Skt) philosophy; view of reality; salvific intuition into existence

dasa-sil-mav(varu) (Snh) "mother(s) of the ten precepts"; female lay celibates who observe the ten precepts

dasa-sil (Snh) ten precepts, i.e., the usual five precepts (see *pañca-sīla*) plus five others: abstaining from (6) eating after midday; (7) from dancing, singing, music, and shows; (8) from garlands, scents, cosmetics etc.; (9) from luxurious beds; (10) from accepting gold and silver

deva God(s)

devātideva "God of Gods" (a Buddhalogical title)

dhamma (1) Salvific Truth; Buddha's preaching; Buddhist doctrine; (2) phenomenon, datum of experience, elements that constitute reality; units of existence (usually in the plural); (3) idea, concept

dhamma-cakka (1) "Wheel of Truth"; (2) spiritual authority (of a Buddha), contrasted with *āṇā-cakka*

dhamma-dhātu usually the same as *dhamma, 2*

dhamma-vinaya "doctrine and discipline"; the entire dispensation of the Buddha

dharma Skt for *dhamma*

dharma-vijaya (Skt/Snh) spiritual conquest; spread of doctrine; reign of righteousness

dharmaśāstra (Skt) Brahmamic "canon law" or jurisprudential code books of the Hindus

dhārmika (Skt) righteous; living according to the dharma

dhātu element (= *dhamma-dhātu*)

dhātu-kusalatā ability to see existence as consisting of disparate elements

dhutaṅga severe forms of ascetical practices

dosa ill-will, hate, aggressiveness

dukkha hollow, unsatisfying; meaninglessness or emptiness of all existence ending in death; pain and sorrow inherent in existence; existence itself as pain

dveṣa Skt for *dosa*

gantha-dhara "bearer of sacred texts," i.e., the expert in scriptures (contrasted with *vinaya-dhara*)

ghāṇa-viññāṇa olfactory sensation; smell

grāma-vāsī (Snh) "village-dwelling" (monks) contrasted with *āraṇya-vāsī* or *vaṇa-vāsī*

jivhā-viññāṇa gustatory consciousness; awareness of taste

jñāna (Skt) salvific knowledge, gnosis (see *ñāṇa*)

jñāna-mārga (Skt) gnostic spirituality; path of knowledge (see *bhakti-* and *karma-mārga*)

kammaṭṭhāna a meditation theme; object or focus of meditation

karma-mārga (Skt) path of action (see *jñāna-* and *bhakti-mārga*)

karuṇā compassion; compassionate involvement in the release of suffering beings

kāya-viññāṇa tactile sensation; awareness of touch

khandha aggregate, heap (see *pañcakkhandha*)

laukika (Skt/Snh) worldly, cosmic, secular

lobha greed

lokanātha Lord of the Universe (a Buddhalogical title)

lokavidū Knower of the Universe (a Buddhalogical title)

lokottara Skt/Snh for *lok'uttara*

lok'uttara transcendental; metacosmic; supramundane

lokuttara-vāda transcendentalism; docetism

majjhima-paṭipadā middle course (i.e., the Buddha's Eightfold Path)

manasikāra-kusalatā ability to reflect on the true nature of existence as transient *(anicca),* devoid of any permanent substance *(anatta),* and as a source of suffering *(dukkha)*

mano mind, the sixth sense that organizes the activities of the other five senses

mano-viññāṇa mind-consciousness

māra death personified as the Tempter

mārga Skt. for *magga*

mettā-bhāvanā meditation on the (infinite sphere of) altruistic love

moha delusion; slowness of mind; ignorance

nāma "literally name"; comprehensive term for the four groups of psychic components of the human personality; see *nāma-kkhandha*

nāma-kkhandha the (four) psychic aggregates: *vedanā, saññā, saṃkhāra,* and *viññāna*

ñaṇa gnosis, salvific knowledge

naruttama "most exalted of humans" (a Buddhalogical title)

nirodha-samāpatti "cessation trance," wherein sensation *(vedanā)* and intellection *(saññā)* are suspended

nibbāna final state of release and internal liberation (see *parinibbāna*); the summum bonum of Buddhism

nirvāna Skt/Snh for *nibbāna*

nihsattva (Skt) not a sentient being; nonpersonal

pabbajjā "going forth," i.e., renouncing the world; a technical term for entry into a novitiate

pañcakkhandha five aggregates that constitute the human person: *vedanā, saññā, saṃkhāra, viññāna,* and *rūpa*

pañca-sīla fivefold ethical practice; five precepts, i.e., abstaining from (1) harming life, (2) stealing, (3) misuse of senses, (4) lying and (5) intoxicants

paññā gnosis; wisdom; salvific insight; transempirical realization; (nontheistic) mystical knowledge

param'atthā four ultimate realities

param'atthato in the ultimate or absolute sense; from the point of view of ultimate concern

paribhoga use

pāribhogika-dhātu relics, i.e., objects used by the Buddha

parinibbāna nibbāna at the Buddha's death; his final release from samsaric existence

parinirvāna Skt for *parinibbāna*

pariyatti intellectual grasp of the *dhamma*

paryapti Skt for *pariyatti*

paṭiccasamuppanna originating interdependently

pātimokkha list of offenses (against the *Vinaya*) recited every Full Moon Day *(Poya)*

paṭipadā the path to nirvāna; the Buddha's way

paṭipatti practical living in accordance with the *dhamma;* the practice of the path leading to *nibbāna (paṭipadā)*

paṭivedha penetrative insight into the true nature of reality; gnosis

pirit chanting of *sutta*s for warding off evil and bringing the blessing of the gods

poruva (Snh) the platform on which the marriage ceremony takes place; hence "Poruva-Ceremony" = marriage ceremony

Poya (Snh) Full Moon Day; Buddhist "sabbath"

prajñā (Skt) salvific knowledge; gnostic wisdom

prajñā-cakshuh (Skt) special supernoetic faculty; sapiential eye

pratipadā (Skt) path of deliverance; way of life; religion (see *paṭipadā*)

pratipatti Skt for *paṭippati*

prativedha Skt for *paṭivedha*

purisa-damma-sārathi "guide of tameable humans"—a Buddhalogical title

purisuttama "most exalted of humans" (Buddhalogical title)

puthujjana "commoner"; one who has not even started on the way of perfection *rāga* erotic, sensual, selfish, and acquisitive "love"; passion, lust

ratana "gem" (see *ti-ratana*)

rūpa (1) material form, object of visual sensation; (2) physical body of a person

saddhā faith, confidence

samādhi mental one-pointedness; concentration; gathering of the mind; ascesis of mental discipline

samana recluse who renounced society and its religious institutions, in the time of the Buddha

sāmanera novice

saṃkhārā subliminally compulsive tendencies; karmic formations; conative functions of the *citta*

samatha calming of the mind; see *samādhi*

sammā-ājīva morally correct means of earning a living

sammā-diṭṭhi salvific vision of reality

sammā-kammanta morally correct activity

sammā-samādhi correct concentration or gathering of the mind

sammā-samkappa organization of thought in a manner conducive to liberation

sammā-sati correct mindfulness or introspection

Sammā-vācā morally correct use of speech

sammā-vāyāma ascetically conducive use of one's energy

sammuti human convention (see also *vohāra*)

saṃsāra this world of birth, death, and suffering

saṃnyāsin (Skt) world-renouncer

saṃsārika secular; worldly; connected with the unliberated state

saṃskārā Skt for *saṃkhārā*

sangha the community of those who follow the Buddha's path; especially, the monastic community

sānghika (Skt, Snh) belonging to the (monastic) community

saṃjñā Skt for *saññā*

saññā perceptions

sārathīnam varuttamo "Most excellent of guides" (a Buddhalogical title)

sāsana the institutional framework of Buddhism; Buddhist religion in its organized aspect; the Buddhist "church"

śata-nāma (Skt) "one hundred names"; devotional and doxological titles given to a god by devotees (in Hinduism)

Satta sentient being

satthā teacher

sattva Skt for *satta*

satya (Skt) truth

sāvaka "hearer"; a disciple of the Buddha (sometimes a synonym for *arahā*)

sīla morality; moral purity; moral precept

silabbata-parāmāsa addiction to rules and rituals; religious superstition

sīmā literally, "the boundary" (marking a chapter); the chapter

sota-viññāṇa auditory sensation; hearing

śraddhā Skt for *saddhā*

śramaṇa Skt for *samana*

stotra (Skt) literally "praise"; doxological literature in Hinduism

stūpa (Skt/Snh) massive stereometric structure containing the relics of the Buddha or of a saint; reliquary

sārīrika-dhātu bodily relics

sutta/suttanta ''string'' (of sayings); discourse of the Buddha

Sutta-piṭaka second part of the Buddhist ''Bible,'' containing the ''discourses'' *(sutta)* of the Buddha

taṇhā craving for samsaric existence; inordinate desire for things that cannot satisfy

ti-ratana ''triple gem'' (the Buddha, *dhamma,* sangha)

ti-sarana ''triple refuge'': taking refuge in the three gems

tri-piṭaka ''triple basket,'' term for the Buddhist canon or scriptures; so called because it consists of three parts; *Vinaya-piṭaka, Sutta-piṭaka,* and *Abhidhamma-piṭaka*

tri-ratna Skt for *ti-ratana*

tri-sarana Skt for *ti-sarana*

Uddesika-dhātu objects representing or indicating the Buddha, e.g., statues, images, pictures

upabhoga use, perusal

upādāna obsessive clinging to evanescent phenomena

upāsaka lay devotee (male)

upāsikā lay devotee (female)

upāsikārāma commune of women celibates who observe the ten vows *(dasa-sil mav)*

upekkhā equanimity that comes for non-addiction to anything or any person

vana-vāsa ''forest life'' (of ascetics)

vedanā affective function(s) of the consciousness; sensation, feelings, etc.

vidyā Skt for *vijjā*

vidyā-carana Skt for *vijjā-caraṇa*

vijjā-caraṇa knowledge and practice (of the *dharma*)

vijñāṇa Skt for *viññāṇa*

vinaya monastic discipline; monastic *regula*

vinaya-dhara ''bearer of monastic discipline''; expert in monastic law

vinayaka leader (a Buddhalogical title)

vinaya-karma capitular acts of a monastic community

vinaya-piṭaka first part of the Buddhist Bible that contains the monastic regula (see *tri-piṭaka*)

viññāṇa (1) consciousness (2) discriminative knowledge

vipassanā-bhāvanā ''insight meditation''

vohāra conventional use (of a word, etc.)

Index

Ontonomy, 20
Origenism, 24

Paganism, 21-22
Pai Chang, 92
Panikkar, Raimundo, 5, 18, 20, 21, 120
Paññā, 64, 66-67
Paññārāna, Y., 127
Pannenberg, W., 21
Parente, P., 115
Parrinder, Geoffrey, 8, 32
Pātimokkha, 66
Paul St., 15, 91, 99-100, 114, 129
Paul VI, Pope, 94
Person, 117
Peter Damian, 21
Philosophy of religion, 18-20
Pirit ceremony, 53, 54-55
Polo, Marco, 4, 25, 131
Poruva marriage rite, 108
Poverty, 78-79; Asian, 35-36, 38, 41; forced, 89; voluntary, 72, 87, 89-92, 94
Power, 21-22, 106
Prajñā, 12, 75, 85, 117, 126
Prevostin, 101

Rabbeau, G., 19
Radhakrishnan, S., 9, 12, 20, 26
Rahula, Walpola, 69, 138n20
Religion, 17, 119; Eastern and Western, 8-12, 16
Ricci, Matteo, 28
Rogers, Murray, 6
Rūpa, 46
Rupp, George, 84

Samādhi, 59-60, 66
Samana, 23, 61
Saṃsāra, 12, 74, 117
Sangha, 49, 51-53, 56, 62-63, 76
Schmidt, Wilhelm, 19
Schoof, Mark, 36
Schoonenberg, Piet, 113
Schopenhauer, Arthur, 29
Seevali Thera, B., 105
Senanayaka, Dudley, 76
Sīla, 59-60, 65-66
Sivaraksha, S., 40

Sinaraman, K., 5
Smart, Ninian, 39
Snellgrove, David, 55, 84
Sobrino, Jon, 37
Socialism, 38; "religious," 93-94
Society, "perfect," 102
Soteriology, Buddhist, 63
Spirituality, 37; Buddhist, 64-67; cosmic, 14-16
Spiro, Melford, E., 55
Sri Lanka, 52, 54, 67-69, 71, 75-76, 95, 104
Stcherbatsky, T., 48

Taṇhā, 49, 58, 77-79, 90
Technocracy, 13
Technology, 15-16
Teilhard de Chardin, Pierre, 9, 12, 15, 26
Temple, Buddhist, 53-54, 69
Tertullian, 20, 101
Theresa of Avila, 85
Thic Nhat Nanh, 6
Thomas Aquinas, 113, 115-16
Thurston, Bonnie, 13
To Thi Anh, 27
Toynbee, Arnold, 83
Trevoedjre, Albert, 94
Trinity, "economic," 131
Tripitaka, 66

Ulmann, Walter, 101, 103
Upādāna, 90
Urmonotheismus, 19
Urs von Balthasar, Hans, 24

Van Leeuwen, A. T., 39
Vinaya, 66, 76, 103-4
Violence, 57
Vipassanā-bhāvanā, 24

Waldenfel, Hans, 122
Wealth, 70, 79
Wheels of governance, 75, 78
Wickramasingha, Martin, 127
William of Rubruck, 26

Zaehner, R. C., 9, 12, 27